Library of Congress Cataloging-in-Publication Data

Strand, Bradford N., 1955-
    Assessing sport skills / Bradford N. Strand, Rolayne Wilson.
      p. cm.
    Includes bibliographical references and index.
    ISBN 0-87322-377-2
    1. Athletic ability--Testing.   I. Wilson, Rolayne.   II. Title.
GV436.5.S87   1993   92-22433
796'.07--dc20   CIP

ISBN: 0-87322-377-2

Acquisitions Editor: Rick Frey, PhD; **Developmental Editor**: Mary E. Fowler; **Assistant Editors:** Moyra Knight and John Wentworth; **Copyeditor**: Merv Hendricks; **Proofreader**: Kathy Bennett; **Indexer:** Barbara E. Cohen; **Production Director**: Ernie Noa; **Typesetters**: Ruby Zimmerman and Julie Overholt; **Text Design**: Keith Blomberg; **Text Layout**: Tara Welsch; **Cover Design**: Tim Offenstein; **Interior Art**: Gretchen Walters; **Printer**: Versa Press

Printed in the United States of America   10 9 8 7 6

Human Kinetics
Web site: http://www.humankinetics.com/

United States: Human Kinetics, P.O. Box 5076, Champaign, IL 61825-5076
1-800-747-4457
e-mail: humank@hkusa.com

Canada: Human Kinetics, 475 Devonshire Road, Unit 100, Windsor, ON N8Y 2L5
1-800-465-7301 (in Canada only)
e-mail: humank@hkcanada.com

Europe: Human Kinetics, P.O. Box IW14, Leeds LS16 6TR, United Kingdom
+44 (0)113-278 1708
e-mail: humank@hkeurope.com

Australia: Human Kinetics, 57A Price Avenue, Lower Mitcham, South Australia 5062
(08) 82771555
e-mail: humank@hkaustralia.com

New Zealand: Human Kinetics, P.O. Box 105-231, Auckland Central
09-523-3462
e-mail: humank@hknewz.com

ASSESSING SPORT SKILLS

Bradford N. Strand, PhD
Rolayne Wilson, EdD
Utah State University

Human Kinetics Publishers

Dedication

To my mother, Helen, whose encouragement, support, and love throughout my life have inspired me to accomplish goals that seemed unattainable. Your love for children and incessant reading have affected my life through my career choice. To my brothers, Jeff, Fred, Greg, Mark, and Rick, and my sister, Kimberly: May the enjoyment of sports and recreation and the thrill of competition stay with you throughout your lives.

BNS

To my parents, Wayne and Nikki, for your lifelong support and unconditional love. Thank you for believing in me and encouraging me to always aim high and believe in myself and others. To my family, Clyde, Ross, Shauna, Brent, their spouses, and children: Thank you for your friendship and love.

RW

Contents

Part II—Sport Skills Tests and Evaluations   37

Preface

Assessing Sport Skills is designed to help current and future middle school through college physical educators locate, select, and construct quality sport skills tests. We review reasons for giving skills tests, outline sound testing procedures, and describe numerous tests in detail. Tables and diagrams illustrate administration of the tests we've judged best for the most popular individual, dual, and team sports and activities.

Sport skills tests are not part of every physical education curriculum. Many teachers complain that they don't know where to find skills tests, that they are difficult to administer, that they take up valuable class time, and that so many skills tests are not gamelike.

In view of these complaints, several criteria guided our choices of tests: We looked for tests that are up to date, have high validity and reliability, are easy to prepare and administer, and simulate game conditions. Few tests meet every criterion, however, and compromises often were necessary. For example, a test might have high validity and reliability but take an entire class period to prepare and even longer to administer. In a case like this, we chose to highlight a test with lower validity and reliability that was realistic to use. In analyzing tests, we found that "new" did not always mean "better." We've eliminated tests with outdated or outmoded skills, but many of the skills tests developed in the 1950s and 1960s met our criteria and serve today's physical educators well.

In addition to the tests we describe in detail, we list others for most sports and activities. Many of those tests are very good, and in some instances could serve your needs as well as the tests which met our selection criteria. We made every effort to provide the most comprehensive list of published sport skills tests currently available. Such a massive undertaking is not always perfect. If you are aware of quality skills tests that do not appear here, we'd appreciate hearing from you.

As physical educators, you probably agree that our primary objective is to develop students' psychomotor skills. Appropriate evaluation is the only way to determine whether you're meeting that objective. By choosing good tests and administering them correctly, you can evaluate student skills as well as your own program. We hope that *Assessing Sport Skills* will encourage you in the task of sport skills testing.

Acknowledgments

This book would not have been possible without assistance from many people. We express our thanks to secretaries at Utah State University: Barbara Lutz, Gloria Harvey, Melisa Cragun, and Mary Kay Jones. Colleagues Richard Gordin, Peter Mathesius, and Hilda Fronske deserve thanks for listening to our complaints and generating new ideas. Thanks go to our department chairman, Robert Sorenson, for providing encouragement to complete this project. Thanks to the many individuals who developed skills tests included in this book. Without their efforts this book would never have been possible. Special thanks to the staff at Human Kinetics Publishing, especially Richard Frey and Mary Fowler. Finally, thanks to reviewers for their insight and comments.

Part I

Introduction to Sport Skills Testing

Chapter 1

Reasons for Skills Testing

At some point all physical education teachers will face the challenge of administrating sport skills tests to motivate, to grade, to diagnose, and to research. Information obtained through testing may be used for prediction, placement, and public relations.

To be of value, testing must be conducted with a specific purpose in mind. It makes little sense to administer sport skills tests simply because they have been ordered by a higher authority, but that is a common reason. This chapter discusses better reasons for administering sport skills tests and provides suggestions on how sport skills tests can be used to improve the educational process.

Psychomotor Learning

Many professionals believe the acquisition of psychomotor skills to be physical education's number one objective (Bucher & Wuest, 1987; Graham, 1987). If that is so, teachers need to demonstrate that students are developing psychomotor skills. Tests that relate to behavioral objectives and evaluate skill development are the means.

Many physical education students are haphazardly exposed to sport skills in ways that lack adequate development (Graham, 1987). Results of skills tests used for formative evaluation in a classroom or gymnasium can be useful in determining student strengths and weaknesses, and suggest where skill and drill work should be implemented.

Numerous psychomotor skills tests available in physical education and sport can evaluate skills. For example, the North Carolina State University (NCSU) Volleyball Skills Test Battery (Bartlett, Smith, Davis, & Peel, 1991) evaluates serving, passing, and setting skills. After a skill is introduced and developed, a teacher can easily administer one test item as a short formative evaluation. The one-item formative evaluation will not be as thorough as the full test, but it provides students a quick idea of how well they are developing.

Many teachers will use skill test items in teaching. In essence, using test items as drills for skill development increases the reliability and validity of a test because students have practiced test items.

At the end of a unit, you can use a complete skill test as summative evaluation. If you give students formative evaluation in each skill, if you use test items in drills, and if you help students improve their skills, their scores on a final skills test will be very good.

Motivation

Motivation is a force that leads individuals to ultimate achievement (Kirkendall, Gruber, & Johnson, 1987). Far too often, physical education teachers must motivate students who either do not enjoy physical education or who see no value in mastering certain physical skills. Through proper administration (such as following directions explicitly and making sure every student is tested under the same conditions) and careful handling (such as keeping results of skills tests confidential), you can motivate students to achieve greater physical education performance levels.

Properly administered, skills tests can provide students with very positive experiences; however, tests administered improperly can have devastatingly negative effects on children. Consider: Many children suffer public humiliation during physical education skills tests administered by uncaring or uninformed teachers who condescendingly ask, "You can only make one basket?" Unfortunately for the physical education profession, some of those humiliated children later in life become school superintendents, principals, and school board members who ultimately control funding and curriculum decisions. Is it any wonder many individuals question the continuance of physical education programs in public education?

Appropriately administered, skills tests may ignite the competitive spirit in many students (Miller, 1988), but physical education teachers must constantly guard against competition becoming an end rather than a means to an end. When an entire testing procedure is based on competition, some students will fail because they do not care to compete against others (Hastad & Lacy, 1989). When this is the case, self-competition in the form of skills test improvement is recommended.

The greatest motivator is success. For students to stay motivated, they must see that they are progressing in their skill development (Miller, 1988). Skills tests provide students both with self-competition and a way to gauge their progress.

Students must learn to set realistic, attainable goals that are specific to their individual situations. Once goals are set, skills testing can assist students as they evaluate their progress, establish new goals, develop competitive spirit within, and ultimately lead to physical improvement and self-actualization (Jenson & Hirst, 1980).

Teachers must constantly encourage students to attain their individual best whether in a test, practice, or game. Knowing they are improving is a great motivator for students who are developing new skills (Hastad & Lacy, 1989). Most students want to improve in skill development, social maturity, or cognitive knowledge. Continual improvement will inspire students and motivate them to attend class, to take an active role in developmental lessons, and to look forward enthusiastically to the next physical education class.

Many students enjoy comparing their performance with others'. Third-grader Derrick said to his friend Brock, "I jumped 10 feet! How far did you jump?" Comparing performance motivates some students, but it hinders a great many more, especially self-conscious individuals who are just learning new skills. Use comparison of student test results with extreme caution.

A teacher needs to inform students of their present skill level in relation to unit objectives. Once they know what is expected of them and realize their present level of skill, many students will develop enough interest and enthusiasm to raise their skill levels to accomplish unit objectives (Johnson & Nelson, 1986). When students can compare their individual performances with objectives or standards, they are much more likely to reach those levels.

All students hope for and many even seek out feedback from either peers, or teachers, or both. With this in mind, teachers must use skills tests that allow them to give objective feedback in a positive, nonthreatening environment. Such feedback can motivate students to improve their skills, not to please a teacher but for self-realization (Phillips & Hornak, 1979).

Grading

Because assigning grades may be the only link between parents and schools, this time-consuming administrative function must be taken seriously. Grading has many purposes. Mainly, grading tells students how they are progressing toward objectives and their standing within a group. The grade may influence their attitude toward physical education. Grading informs parents of their children's progress and achievement; it informs teachers of student progress and where additional assistance is needed; it informs administrators of program success and provides information used in administrative decisions; and it informs the public of the status of their schools in relation to other schools (Barrow, McGee, & Tritschler, 1989; Phillips & Hornak, 1979).

Too many physical education teachers assign grades based on proper dress, shower taking, attitude, and participation. These factors are important to the administration of an activity unit, but they have little to do with how much students have learned or accomplished. Properly used, skills tests help teachers make objective rather than subjective evaluations of students. Grades then are more indicative of student accomplishment in relation to course objectives and goals (Johnson & Nelson, 1986).

Students' grades are permanent records and can be used by colleges, universities, and future employers in awarding scholarships, promotions in job rank, determination of honors awards, and admittance to graduate schools (Hastad & Lacy, 1989; Miller, 1988). As a result, grades must accurately reflect students' accomplishments.

Parents, having experienced reward and denial at work, often place greater value on grades than children do. When children receive good grades they often earn money rewards. Conversely, when grades are poor, sanctions such as no television, no telephone, and no dating are imposed. Teachers who assign grades determined subjectively punish students twice, once by being graded in a manner that does not reflect true accomplishment and, second, through sanctions and putdowns at home.

All factors considered, grading must be executed objectively; it must relate to course objectives; and it must reflect progress, achievement, and improvement (Johnson & Nelson, 1986; Kirkendall et al., 1987). When students know they will be evaluated objectively on the accomplishment of stated course objectives, they will work harder and will more willingly accept their grades, knowing they were responsible for what they achieved. However, if objectives are never stated and students are never tested, final grades are meaningless. Rather than means to an end, grades become the end (Barrow et al., 1989).

Diagnosis

Diagnosis is an assessment based on observed facts. It is a teacher's function to continually and objectively search for weaknesses, strengths, and students' progress (Kirkendall et al., 1987).

Information obtained from skills testing helps teachers and students isolate deficiencies (Hastad & Lacy, 1989). It is difficult to see if students can properly handle a basketball if they get only one or two opportunities to handle the ball during a game. However, a basketball skills test can identify specific deficiencies, leading a teacher to prescribe specific developmental exercises for students needing help (Jenson & Hirst, 1980). As additional basketball skills tests are given, student progress can be reevaluated.

Teachers also can use skills test results to reevaluate old objectives and formulate new objectives and methods. If skills tests results reveal that students are not meeting objectives, teachers must either change the objectives so they are more in line with what students can accomplish or alter teaching approaches so more time is devoted to skill development and, ultimately, so better student performance on skills tests is achieved (Miller, 1988).

Prediction

Prediction is the act of foretelling an estimation of future performance based on present facts (Kirkendall et al., 1987). Students may be unsure of their abilities, especially if they are late bloomers. From skills tests and observations teachers can advise and encourage students to pursue certain activities or sports (Hastad & Lacy, 1989). A fumbling, bumbling 7th grader with few athletic skills may become an all-conference athlete as an 11th grader if he or she elects to stay with a particular sport. Too often, the fumbling 7th grader who does not realize his or her own potential gets discouraged and quits.

Informed, attentive teachers often can predict students' potential for future success in certain activities. However, for development to occur, students must realize their own potential for success. Skills tests provide interested students with the objective information they need to believe they have potential in a certain activity (Phillips & Hornak, 1979). Knowledge gained from a test also may provide students with the confidence to move from participation in physical education to interscholastic competition.

Skills tests also can be used to predict success in other sports or activities (Baumgartner & Jackson, 1982). For example, if students do well on a skills test that requires them to throw a ball while running, a teacher can recommend sports and activities that require a similar skill. This encourages students to pursue new avenues as they develop new skills.

Finally, skills tests can help coaches select varsity team members. Reliable tests are the most objective methods of choosing team members from the many individuals who try out (Johnson & Nelson, 1986).

Placement

In an attempt to improve learning, teachers may classify students into certain groups (Baumgartner & Jackson, 1982). Although mainstreaming has its pros and cons, it is believed that at times student classification is helpful (LaVay & DePaepe, 1987). Students with superior abilities should not be forced to hold back because of less-skilled classmates, and likewise students with lesser abilities should be able to enjoy success. Skills testing provides a quick, effective, and objective method of classifying physical education students into ability groups (Phillips & Hornak, 1979). As skills improve, students can easily be shifted from one skill level to another.

When students are placed into skill level groups, teachers can individualize instruction (Phillips & Hornak, 1979). For example, in a football activity unit, varsity team members could play a game that includes specialized offensive and defensive plays, while beginners play two-on-two keep-away to develop passing and catching skills while they run and dodge.

In many ways the objective placement of students into like groups can improve the educational setting (Hastad & Lacy, 1989). When students with equal skills are placed into groups for instruction, practice, or games, they are less intimidated, less inhibited, more comfortable, more active, learn more, and get greater enjoyment from the experience (Miller, 1988). Additionally, when students with similar skills are grouped, objectives can be tailored to specific needs.

Classification and placement of students are based on program philosophy, the type of unit being taught, unit objectives, and the type of students in a class (Hastad & Lacy, 1989). Many high schools offer advanced placement courses for college-bound students. The equivalent in physical education would be a course titled "Advanced Skills and Techniques." Most often an advanced skills course is open only to varsity athletes during their sport's season. Although allowing varsity athletes to practice during the academic day may be a questionable educational practice, in theory it has merit. The selection of class members, however, should be more than just students who are fortunate enough to play on a varsity team. A skills test is one way of determining if other highly skilled students should be in the class. If students have mastered skills, they should be allowed to enroll in the advanced course.

Although skills tests are generally not used in the classification of students—mainly because of inconvenience of setting up and administering the tests—the benefits to students (both skilled and unskilled), teachers, and the physical education pro-

gram are worth the time and effort (Barrow et al., 1989).

Program Evaluation

Program evaluation must be an ongoing part of every school system, for without evaluation it is difficult to know if, when, where, and how changes should be made (Johnson & Nelson, 1986). A program should be evaluated on how well it meets its stated objectives and goals. Additionally, various publics—students, teachers, administrators, school board members, parents, and other concerned citizens—should be allowed to offer ideas.

Without ongoing evaluation, many programs quickly become stagnant and outdated (Hastad & Lacy, 1989). For example, before the fitness boom in America, many schools taught only basketball, football, softball, and volleyball in their physical education programs. In retrospect, were those activities appropriate, especially when scope, sequence, and progression very seldom changed? With education dollars shrinking, the need for accountability growing, and reform measures highlighting the news, it is essential to a school district's success to identify strengths and weaknesses, to determine where changes can be made, and to improve programs (Barrow et al., 1989).

Skills testing assists with program evaluation in several ways. First, if tests reveal that students have greatly improved in certain skills, you might want to raise the goal by adding similar activities or to find activities to develop new skills. Second, if student skills show no improvement or marked decrease, you may need additional activities to develop the skill, or may decide to drop the activity from the curriculum. Third, skills tests provide comparisons of program outcomes to local, state, and national norms. Results can be used to modify units; justify faculty, equipment, and facilities; conduct pilot projects; and develop new techniques. Finally, skills test results can be used in adopting appropriate standards for program evaluation (Jenson & Hirst, 1980).

Instructor Evaluation

Instructors should be evaluated on variables they can control, such as student performance and achievement in relation to stated objectives (Barrow et al., 1989).

Skills tests can assist in teacher evaluation by providing information on whether objectives have been achieved (Baumgartner & Jackson, 1982). If certain objectives are not being met, as determined by skills tests, changes in teaching technique and methodology may be suggested. Skills tests also can identify teacher strengths and weaknesses (Johnson & Nelson, 1986).

Evaluation also can show equipment problems. When there is only one basketball for a class of 35 students, it is very difficult for a teacher to have a high percentage of time-on-task. Much of the problem in this scenario results from school administration decisions. Because there is a limited amount of money, an adequate number of balls cannot be purchased, and students are placed into overcrowded classrooms.

Public Relations

For many years questionable leadership and poor quality programs have led to misunderstanding and false beliefs concerning physical education. Too many people making decisions regarding physical education still believe it is simply playing basketball or volleyball. The lack of appropriate public relations is a consistent weakness of physical education programs (Barrow et al., 1989).

Concerned citizens believe that if local athletic teams win, the physical education program must be good. They also believe that schools could operate effectively without a physical education program. In most people's minds physical education is tied so closely with athletics that they think physical education *is* athletics, and that the only thing happening in physical education classes is the playing of games. Unfortunately, they are often correct.

As programs are being reduced and eliminated nationwide, physical education, as it is presently known, is in great danger of extinction. For physical education to maintain its rightful place in the educational system, we need ammunition that emphasizes benefits derived from physical education.

Skills testing that reveals that objectives are being mastered can be that ammunition. It can show that physical education deserves its long-standing place in the curriculum. In fact, two popular youth competitions in America—The Ford Punt, Pass, and Kick competition and the Pepsi Hot Shot competition—have a direct relationship to sport skills testing in physical education. Results from skills

tests can be used to develop interest in an activity, foster pride in a department, and applaud students who meet the highest standards (Johnson & Nelson, 1986).

Research

Research is a systematic investigation toward increasing knowledge. The quality of data collected through research depends on, among other things, the precision and accuracy of the measuring instruments, measurement techniques, and the appropriateness of tests (Barrow et al., 1989). The qualities of good tests are discussed in chapter 2.

Using skills tests in physical education research helps administrators select activities to be included in the curriculum (Johnson & Nelson, 1986). For example, if skills tests reveal that students are below average in throwing skills, throwing activities can be emphasized. Based on test results, teachers may see a need for changes in instruction methods. Low scores on test items may indicate that teachers are not spending enough time on skill development, not explaining techniques as clearly as they should, or not providing enough time-on-task.

Research using skills tests may discover solutions to classroom problems (Miller, 1988). For example, a teacher notices that seventh-grade students can't consistently put the volleyball into play using the overhand serve. This difficulty causes students to stand around, bored. The teacher decides to administer a skills test that compares the overhead serve with the underhand serve. Results reveal that students have a 10% success rate for the overhead serve but an 80% success rate with the underhand serve. Based on test results, this teacher decides to let seventh-grade students serve underhand.

Curricular changes and program evaluations also can be made intelligently after skills test research (Miller, 1988). Consider this scenario: Administrators at West Side High School have decided that students must master certain skills before they can receive credit in physical education. The present curriculum requires students to engage in basketball activity units from grades 7 through 11. However, the progression of skills in each grade level has not been revised for at least 10 years. A basketball skills test administered at the end of the eighth-grade activity unit reveals that all students have mastered the required skills. If this is the case, what changes should be made in the physical education curriculum? Should additional basketball skills be required in grades 9 through 11? Should the basketball activity unit be removed from grades 9 through 11? Should the required skills for students in grades 7 and 8 be increased?

Summary

Measurement and evaluation serve many purposes in physical education. In this chapter you have learned why sport skills tests are conducted and how sport skills testing can be used to enhance the quality of your physical education program and your effectiveness as a physical education teacher. You were shown how testing can motivate students; how testing can detect student strengths and weaknesses; how testing helps in the assignment of grades; and how test results can be used as a public relations tool for you, your program, your school, and your community.

Chapter 2

Selecting and Constructing Tests

Many physical education teachers do not use preconstructed skills tests because they often find that no published test meets their specific needs. Teachers also complain that the available tests are inappropriate because they do not measure skill achievement during game conditions. So these teachers either fail to administer tests or they hastily construct last-minute ones that fail to meet stated criteria.

This chapter provides guidelines to help you select and construct appropriate motor performance tests. The flow chart in Figure 2.1 illustrates 10 steps to complete the process. We will follow Ms. Erickson, a junior high school physical education teacher, as she proceeds through the steps to construct a pickle-ball skills test.

Step 1: Review Criteria of Good Tests

What constitutes an appropriate skills test? Several factors need to be considered. As a preliminary step Ms. Erickson should review the purposes and criteria of skills tests. The following are considered important properties of good tests.

Validity

Validity, probably the most important factor in test evaluation, is the degree to which a test actually measures what it has been designed to measure (Johnson & Nelson, 1986). For example, a test designed to measure placement accuracy for the tennis serve should not measure speed or power of serve. Take Mark, a seventh-grade student who beats all of his classmates in tennis but does poorly on one of the tennis skill tests. If the tennis skill test given to Mark has a validity correlation coefficient of .40, it is questionable whether the test actually measures what it is designed to measure. His tester should look for a test with higher validity.

Correlation refers to the agreement between two variables (Hastad & Lacy, 1989). The degree of agreement between the two variables (something that a score may be assigned to, i.e., weight, test score, speed) is reported as the correlation coefficient. A perfect agreement between two variables yields a coefficient of 1.00. Correlation coefficients are reported in hundredths from +1.0 to −1.0, e.g., .96, .80, −.45 (Mathews, 1968).

Although no test, scale, or inventory can be judged 100% valid (Barrow et al., 1989), you should look for tests with validity as close to 1.00

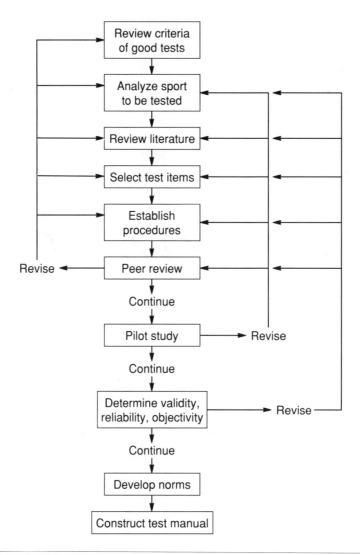

Figure 2.1 Ten-step flow chart for test construction.

as possible. Although authors have reported various acceptable coefficient levels (Barrow et al.,
1989; Mathews, 1968; Safrit, 1990), the acceptability of a coefficient depends on the appropriateness
of the criterion, the test purpose, and the intended
use of the test. Safrit (1990) also states that the
acceptability of coefficients depends on the type
of validity being determined. For example, construct validity (defined on page 20) should have
coefficients of at least .80, while predictive validity
(defined on page 19) coefficients are acceptable as
low as .50. Barrow and McGee (1979) suggested
the standards shown in Table 2.1 for evaluating
validity correlation coefficients.

When determining the validity of a test, you are
evaluating its fairness and appropriateness for a
particular purpose and a particular group. We'll
examine types of validity and methods for deter-

mining validity as we follow Ms. Erickson through
the test construction flow chart.

Reliability

Reliability is the consistency with which a test measures what it has been designed to measure (Bosco
& Gustafson, 1983). A reliable test should yield
similar results every time it is given. High reliability
requires minimizing measurement error. Measurement techniques, testing conditions, test administration, participant preparation, and environmental
conditions are among variables that should be
standardized as much as possible.

Reliability and validity are directly related (Johnson & Nelson, 1986). When reliability is high, test
scores do not differ markedly on repeated administrations of the same test; if test scores do vary, re-

Table 2.1   Standards for interpreting validity correlation coefficients

Coefficient	Validity
.85 - .99	Excellent
.80 - .84	Very good
.70 - .79	Acceptable
.60 - .69	Questionable

Note. From *A Practical Approach to Measurement in Physical Education* (p. 42) by H.M. Barrow and R. McGee, 1979, Malvern, PA: Lea & Febiger. Copyright 1979 by Lea & Febiger. Reprinted by permission.

liability is low. For example, if Jeff scores 40 points on a tennis wall-volley skills test on Monday and 41 on the same test a week later, the test can be considered to have a high degree of reliability. On the contrary, if Jeff scores 40 on Monday and 20 a week later, reliability can be considered low.

Although high reliability does not guarantee high validity, low reliability does guarantee low validity. When Jeff scores 40 and 41, reliability is shown to be high by the similar scores on repeated measures of the same test. However, even though a test item has a high reliability coefficient, one must ensure that a test item is appropriate for the skill being tested. If this same student scores well on a wall-volley test but does poorly in a tournament, validity is in question. Barrow and McGee (1979) suggested the standards shown in Table 2.2 for evaluating reliability correlation coefficients.

When determining a test's reliability, you are evaluating its consistency over repeated measures. We'll also examine types of reliability and methods

Table 2.2   Standards for interpreting reliability correlation coefficients

Coefficient	Reliability
.95 - .99	Excellent
.90 - .94	Very good
.80 - .89	Acceptable
.70 - .79	Poor
.60 - .69	Questionable

Note. From *A Practical Approach to Measurement in Physical Education* (p. 42) by H.M. Barrow and R. McGee, 1979, Malvern, PA: Lea & Febiger. Copyright 1979 by Lea & Febiger. Reprinted by permission.

for determining reliability as we study Ms. Erickson's situation.

Objectivity

Objectivity, a form of reliability known as rater reliability, occurs when two or more people administer the same test to the same people and obtain about the same results (Johnson & Nelson, 1986). The coefficient obtained when comparing results defines the degree of agreement between judges about the value of a measurement. Objectivity depends largely on how clearly and completely test instructions are given and how thoroughly test procedures are followed.

When judges obtain markedly different scores while evaluating the same subject, objectivity is absent and none of the scores can be considered reliable or valid. Differences in results occur when judges use different scoring or judging techniques and when test procedures are not followed. For example, teachers Rick and Teresa time Christopher as he runs around a series of cones. Rick adds 1 second to the final score each time Christopher makes a mistake such as knocking over a cone. Teresa records the time without considering mistakes. Obviously, final scores will differ greatly. To ensure objectivity, judges must evaluate subjects similarly and follow test procedures as closely as possible.

Norms

Norms—usually based on height, weight, age, grade, or combinations of those variables—are derived values determined from raw scores obtained from a particular population on a specific test (Johnson & Nelson, 1986). Generally teachers and students use norms to compare students' scores. An important consideration is that norm tables should be applied only to the specific group from which the norms were compiled. For example, a bowling score of 130 would not be spectacular for a college student, but would be for a ninth grader.

The American Alliance for Health, Physical Education, Recreation and Dance (AAHPERD) sport skills tests use national norms as their comparative measure. If a teacher wants to show that students are achieving above the national level, AAHPERD is the standard. Or, if a comparison to national norms revealed low achievement, the information could be used to negotiate for increased class time, teachers, or equipment.

Comparisons to national norms may not be practical because many local programs operate with limited class time, teachers, space, and equipment. In this case norms established for a specific school or region are the most meaningful.

Before using norms, evaluate their adequacy by considering the following questions (Hastad & Lacy, 1989; Johnson & Nelson, 1986).

1. How big was the normative database? The larger the sample, the more likely it is to represent the total population. If a norm table is established with fewer than several hundred scores for each age and sex, use it with caution.

2. From which group were norms obtained? Test administrators should not evaluate their students through norms obtained from and designed for a different population. For example, norms obtained from college athletes should not be used to evaluate high school physical education students.

3. From which geographic location were norms obtained? Variation in student performance is often found in geographic locations because of climate, socio-economic level, cultural influences, program emphasis, and other environmental conditions. Local norms are often more helpful than national norms.

4. Are directions for test administration and scoring clear enough to be followed explicitly? If not, the norms are worthless and should not be used for comparison purposes.

5. When were the norms obtained? Old norms must be used with caution because traits, characteristics, and abilities of today's students differ in many ways from yesterday's students. View norms as temporary and revise or update them regularly.

Equipment

Tests that require extensive equipment are often impractical. They can take too long to set up and the equipment can be too expensive. Quality tests provide directions that identify the type and amount of equipment and supplies necessary for test administration.

Personnel

You can test more students efficiently if support help is available. Student aides, the school nurse, other staff members who have a preparation hour during the testing period, and/or parents are excellent helpers. It is imperative that helpers be trained to ensure successful test administration. Tests that require many helpers may overextend your supply.

Space Requirements

Arranging testing stations requires careful planning to match space available with size of the classes. Energy expenditure at each station, availability of equipment, and facilities are factors that must be considered as stations are planned. Space required by a particular test may cause you to test on different days. Figure 2.2 provides an example of an overcrowded gymnasium designed for a basketball skills tests.

Preparation Time

Keep preparation time for test administration minimal although thorough. Set up and organize before administration because time and discipline are lost if preparation occurs during class time. Use support personnel to prepare tests.

Administration Time

Regardless how objective, valid, and reliable a test is, it is useless if it is not feasible in terms of time, money, and personnel to administer. A test that requires several class periods to administer may be unfeasible.

Ease of Administration

Teachers, who work under time constraints, often do not use skills tests simply because they are too difficult to set up, because directions are unclear, or because only a few students can be tested at one time. For example, the McKee Golf Test requires the tester to time to the nearest 1/10 second how long each ball is airborne, the distance the ball travels along the intended line of flight, and the distance the ball deviates from the intended line of flight. With this information, the tester is supposed to use trigonometric functions to determine the angle of deviation and the distance the ball actually travels. Obviously, this test is not feasible for a teacher with 40 students and a small testing area.

When selecting a skills test, several questions concerning ease of administration need to be asked. Although the answers may not be favorable, compromises can be made in test administration without affecting reliability or validity. Consider these questions when evaluating the ease of test administration:

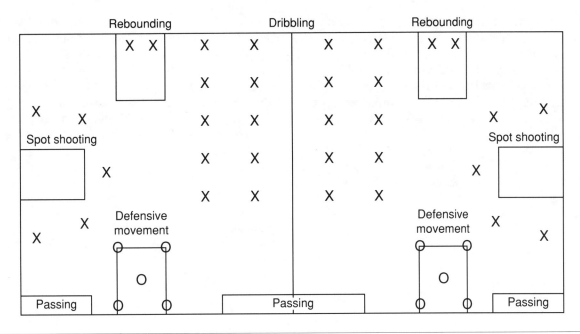

Figure 2.2 Crowded layout for a skills test.

1. Can the test accommodate large numbers of students?
2. Are directions standardized?
3. Are directions clear and simple?
4. How much space is needed?
5. Is the test reasonable in terms of physical demands required of students? (Students should not be exhausted or unduly sore after a test.)
6. How much preparation time is required?
7. Are equipment needs for the test reasonable?
8. Is assistance needed to administer the test?
9. Does the test require minimal practice?
10. Are skills being tested approximate to skills that students use in game situations?

Age and Sex Appropriateness

Skills tests must be specific to the age, sex, skill level, strength, and other variables of your students. Tests should account for differences between males and females and not be biased toward one or the other. It cannot be assumed that a test that works well for middle school students will work for high school students.

Bowling Norms for College Men and Women, developed by Martin in 1960, set norms for evaluating and classifying college men and women of different bowling skills. No bowling norms presently exist for high school or junior high school students, but it would be unjust for high school and junior high school students to have their scores compared with college norms. Similarly, Hooks (1959) used college males as the test group for his Baseball Ability Test, which measures strength and structure in hitting and throwing. To use this test unaltered to measure softball skills in a female physical education class would be unfair.

Educational Value

Testing for the sake of testing should be avoided. Tests should be relevant to the units taught, student/teacher goals, and the learning experiences planned to meet those goals (Johnson & Nelson, 1986). Tests should require students to use correct form and technique, follow the rules of the activity, and perform skills associated with the activity. Through testing, students should learn something about themselves and the variables being tested.

Affective attributes to be gained from participation in physical education and sport include the development of honesty, sportsmanship, self-esteem, integrity, and fairness. Some testing situations require students to test themselves or to count for a partner. During these special testing situations, teachers must emphasize and develop positive affective attitudes in their students. What better time to develop honesty than when reporting results from a self-administered test? Although cheating is easy and detection is difficult, a teacher's emphasis on honesty and integrity may reduce or even eliminate cheating.

Obviously, results from skills tests reveal how skilled an individual is. Sammy, like many junior high school students, dreams of playing college basketball. His parents tell him how good he is, and he always beats Benjamin, his younger cousin. Sammy's teacher sees room for improvement and tries to work with him on his skills. But Sammy doesn't heed his teacher's advice, saying, ''I am already good enough; I always beat my cousin.'' A skills test in this situation will help Sammy realize how he really compares to his classmates. If Sammy scores far below his peers, he may see he needs to improve and take his teacher's suggestions. Sammy's chances of being a college basketball player will improve.

Discrimination

Discrimination in testing is the ability of a test to differentiate the ability range of students. Teachers may choose tests difficult enough that no student receives a perfect score, but easy enough that no one receives a zero (Hastad & Lacy, 1989).

Ideally, scores should fall along a continuum from high to low so that separation of students' skill levels is obvious. One way to ensure that skill evaluation is fair is through point values on targets. One archery target (Figure 2.3) provides scoring areas with point values ranging from 0 to 9 points. Another archery target could simply provide two scoring areas: 0 points awarded if the arrow does not hit the target, and 9 points if it does. Using the described targets, Fred shoots 10

arrows at the first target and scores 90 points, while Greg shoots 10 arrows at the second target and also scores 90 points. Should these students receive the same evaluation in skill achievement? Had Greg shot at the first target he might have scored only 50 points. Obviously in this case, a second set of point values helps determine skill; however, finding tests that totally discriminate among student performance is difficult.

Safety

The threat of lawsuits makes it imperative that skills testing not endanger students. Before using any test, examine it to determine if students might overexert themselves or chance injury. Before beginning any physical testing, students must be allowed an adequate warm-up period, which includes stretching, exercise, and skills test item practice.

Obviously, young children cannot be expected to perform at the same intensity as older students. Even within age groups, consider students' height and weight situations.

Before testing, check equipment and facilities for damage and danger. Equipment that is frayed, broken, or damaged must not be used. If the piece of equipment cannot be repaired, dispose of it. Marking devices should be soft, unbreakable, highly visible, and appropriate for the test. Do not, for example, use chairs in place of cones as obstacles to be maneuvered around in a basketball dribble test.

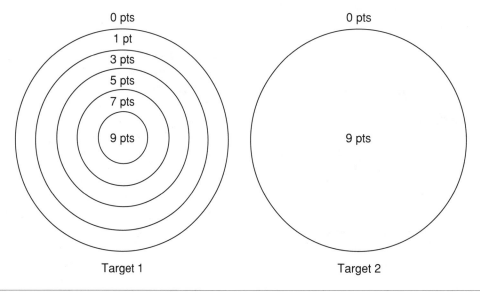

Figure 2.3 Examples for scoring discrimination.

Types of Tests

Psychomotor skill achievement can be measured in three fashions: simulated game conditions, game performance, and rating scales. Many physical education teachers prefer to use rating scales, but they are the least objective of the three measures and are open to greater validity questions (Baumgartner & Jackson, 1982). Using rating scales for sport skills evaluation is further examined in chapter 7.

A major purpose of testing is to determine whether educational objectives are being met. But to gauge that situation, tests must parallel instructional objectives. Because it is common for teachers to develop instructional objectives specific to their needs, teachers also often must develop their own means to evaluate whether objectives are being met.

Many teachers complain that sport skills tests represent simulated game conditions rather than actual game performance. This is often true; however, a test does not always have to recreate the exact playing environment as long as the activity is similar to the actual sport (Baumgartner & Jackson, 1982). For example, the serve test in the AAHPERD Tennis Skills Test (chapter 5) requires students to place 16 serves over the net into the proper service court. The test is not under game conditions, but the performance of the test item is similar to game requirements.

Simulated game condition tests require students to perform each skill as if they were playing a game (Phillips & Hornak, 1979). When simulated game conditions are used during testing, you must be sure students are executing the skill as they would in a game.

Phillips and Hornak (1979) described three advantages of using simulated game conditions. First, such tests usually can be administered in one class period. Second, scoring is simplified as students earn points based on performance. Third, you can use students as assistants and to record their classmates' efforts. On the negative side, setup for simulated game testing often takes time as teachers have to mark lines, set up ropes, etc. It also is possible that the simulated test does not accurately reflect an actual game.

Many teachers prefer game performance tests in their evaluation of student achievement. Yes, these measurements may be more valid than simulations, but they are not always feasible. To evaluate all students fairly in game situations, teachers must observe each student performing a skill several times before reaching a decision on performance. This process could take several days. Team equality also may affect competition and make it difficult to isolate individual performances. Activities such as archery and bowling are easy to evaluate during game performance. For example, a student's average score after 5 days of archery can easily be used as an achievement measure.

Sport skills tests used to evaluate achievement fall into six categories: timed tests, distance tests, accuracy tests, power tests, body movement tests, and form tests.

Timed Tests. Timed tests use a timing device to evaluate the duration of a skill (100-meter dash) or the repetition of the same skill for a specified period (wall-volley). Safrit (1990) believes, however, that when an object is hit into the air (such as in wall-volley), time as an achievement measure is questionable, but that timed measurement is appropriate for ground or floor sports.

Some question the validity of tests requiring repeated executions of the same skill (Phillips and Hornak, 1979). In many timed tests, students sacrifice accuracy for speed so they can complete as many attempts as possible during their allotted time. A second concern is that subjects have to retrieve their own miscues. For example, if Rene has difficulty catching she may not score well on a test that requires her to pass a ball against a wall, catch it, and pass it again to the wall. Obviously, poor catching skills would lower Rene's score. A final concern is that few sports require participants to retrieve or receive their own throw, hit, or shot, and that asking this of subjects during testing decreases test similarity to game conditions.

Distance Tests. Distance tests use a tape measure to measure how far one throws (softball throw), kicks (football punt), strikes (softball hit), or propels (long jump) an object or the body. These types of tests are normally reliable because the distance an object travels can be accurately measured (Baumgartner & Jackson, 1982). However, Safrit (1990) warned that throwing requires both force and accuracy and that tests of throwing ability should measure both velocity and accuracy.

Accuracy Tests. Accuracy tests use targets to evaluate how accurately one throws (basketball free throw), strikes (tennis serve), or kicks (soccer penalty kick) an object. Many accuracy test scoring systems fail to discriminate among skill levels. To solve this problem and increase the reliability of test accuracy, you should provide targets with a range of scores (for example, a target with a scoring range of 1 to 5 will better discriminate skill achievement than one with a scoring range of 0 to 2) and an adequate number of attempts (Baumgartner & Jackson, 1982).

Power or Velocity Tests. Power or velocity tests measure the speed, angle of projection, and distance components of an object. Velocity tests are used to measure skills used to project an object into the air and reflect force applied. A velocity test can use ropes to measure the height of a trajectory, can rate the vertical angle of projection to categorize the height of trajectory, can use a stopwatch and a wall target to measure force, or can use high-tech electronic equipment such as a velocimeter or radar gun (Safrit, 1990).

Body Movement Tests. Body movement tests, similar to timed tests, require subjects to complete a standardized test course as quickly as possible using movements characteristic to the sport. For example, the AAHPERD Basketball Dribble Test (chapter 6) measures the speed with which a player can dribble a ball around a predetermined course (Baumgartner & Jackson, 1982).

Form Tests. Form tests, usually rating scales or checklists, measure how a skill is executed. These tests often help gauge beginners and help in activities that are subjectively scored (dance, swimming, gymnastics, and aerobics). Once athletes advance beyond the beginner level, form evaluation should be deemphasized; by this time many individuals have developed their own patterns of execution (Safrit, 1990).

Step 2: Analyze the Sport

The second step in test selection or construction is to analyze the sport or activity to be tested. To begin, one needs to list and describe the skills necessary to play the sport proficiently (Phillips & Hornak, 1979; Safrit, 1990). For example, basketball involves dribbling; shooting jump shots, free throws, and lay-ups; rebounding; chest, bounce, and baseball passes; and defense. A teacher should emphasize skills to match students' ages. Many fourth-grade students can make lay-ups, but most cannot make free throws. For some the basketball is too large to handle, while others do not possess enough strength to shoot from 15 feet away from

the basket. After age-appropriate skills have been identified, review course objectives to determine which carry the most weight. It is both unfair and unethical to spend part of only one class period teaching a skill and then expect students to test well on that skill.

Remember our Ms. Erickson? She organizes a new unit in pickle-ball. The first thing she does when preparing her unit plan is to list all skills necessary to play pickle-ball. The list includes: forehand and backhand strokes, lob shot, overhead slam, clear shot, drive shot, net volley, drop shot, deep serve, and short serve. She quickly realizes that not only would seventh-grade students have difficulty with some of the skills but also that she has only 2 weeks to teach pickle-ball. From experience with racquet sports, she decides to teach forehand and backhand strokes, clear shot, drive shot, and long serve. She further refines the plan by deciding to spend most class time perfecting long serve and clear shot skills.

Note Ms. Erickson's process. She begins by reviewing all pickle-ball skills, next determines which skills would be appropriate for seventh-grade students, and then selects skills to emphasize. She thoroughly analyzes pickle-ball in preparing to teach and test.

Step 3: Review the Literature

After a teacher selects appropriate skills and writes course objectives, he or she should review literature on skills tests that measure the same or a related performance as the activity being administered (Miller, 1988; Safrit, 1990). If a valid, reliable, easy-to-administer skills test that measures what one is teaching can be found, the teacher should use it. If no such test can be located, the teacher needs to develop one.

For most common activities taught in junior high and senior high school physical education classes, many skills tests are available. For example, this book lists more than 40 skills tests for tennis (chapter 5). A review of the tests reveals that almost every tennis skill is covered in the tests. In addition, some tests appear to be more game-like than others, some require many persons to administer, and some are designed for indoors. Decisions on which tests to use must be made in relation to what a teacher is trying to accomplish.

Many teachers complain that they do not know where to find skills tests. Commonly the first source is a measurement and evaluation textbook.

Many excellent textbooks are on the market, and most college bookstores and libraries carry a ready supply. This book's reference section lists many current, popular measurement and evaluation texts.

A problem with most measurement and evaluation texts is that they present only a few tests for only a few activities. When an appropriate test cannot be located in a textbook, search out journals and periodicals. Skills tests are frequently published in *Research Quarterly for Exercise and Sport*; *The Physical Educator*; *Journal of Physical Education, Recreation and Dance*; state journals; and dissertation abstracts. AAHPERD offers test manuals in volleyball, basketball, tennis, softball, football, and archery. Skills tests also can be found in skills books (Curtis, 1989; DeGroot, 1980a, DeGroot, 1980b; Reznik & Byrd, 1987; Whiddon & Reynolds, 1983), physical education handbooks (Edgley & Oberle, 1986; Mood, Musker, & Rink, 1987; Seaton, Schmottlach, Clayton, Leibee, & Messersmith, 1983), and skills testing books (Collins & Hodges, 1978).

Because pickle-ball is a relatively new game, Ms. Erickson is not too surprised when she cannot find a pickle-ball skills test with proven reliability and validity. Realizing that pickle-ball has some characteristics of tennis, badminton, and racquetball she also searches those tests. As you remember, Ms. Erickson wants to concentrate on developing two skills, the long serve and the clear shot. After reviewing tennis, badminton, and racquetball skills tests, she eliminates all tests except those with long serve or clear shot components.

Step 4: Select or Construct Test Items

Ms. Erickson analyzes the remaining tennis and badminton tests and decides that none of the components will work for her test. Borrowing from badminton tests, she devises a serving test and a clear shot test. As she proceeds, she considers these guidelines of test construction:

1. Test items should be representative of the actual game skill (Kirkendall et al., 1987). For instance, serving is a closed skill, one performed in an unchanging environment with performers doing relatively the same movements every time. Clear shots, on the other hand, are open skills, ones performed in a changing environment with performers ad-

justing as dictated by situation. So, the serve test should be conducted from a stationary position and the clear shot test from a moving position.

2. Test items should be simple to understand and relatively easy to perform (Miller, 1988). If performing test items requires intricate detail, chances are most students will forget some aspect and unnecessarily delay the tests. Furthermore, if students don't perform the test exactly as described, reliability and validity are affected.

3. For practicality, test items should be inexpensive, easy to administer, easy to prepare, and make the best use of testing stations (Miller, 1988). Time is of the essence for most physical education teachers, and tests that require many measurements and markings will never be practical. Too many lines, markers, and scoring zones on the court, floor, or field also confuse administrators, testers, scorers, and recorders.

Step 5: Establish Procedures

Once test items have been selected, establish the test layout, scoring zones, performance directions, and administration procedures (Miller, 1988). Simplicity in each aspect reduces preparation time, administration time, training time, and lets students better understand the test. At this point in test construction, trial and error occurs as one attempts to determine the best procedures. Revision and adaptation are inevitable and in fact help clarify and improve a test.

Ms. Erickson needs to establish procedures for the long serve and the clear shot and determines that the serve test would be performed in a closed environment and the clear test in an open environment.

For simplicity, she decides the long serve will be performed exactly as in an actual game. That means the student must keep one foot behind the back line when serving and must use an underhand serving motion. The paddle must pass below the student's waist, and the ball must be hit in the air before it can bounce. The serve is made diagonally cross court and must clear the nonvolley zone. The cross court receiving zone is divided into three equal-sized scoring zones as shown in Figure 2.4. The deepest zone has a 5-point value, the middle zone a 3-point value, and the zone closet to the net a 1-point value. Areas

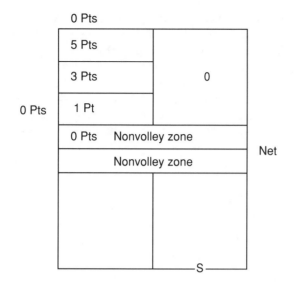

Figure 2.4 Layout for the Erickson long-serve test.

outside the receiving zone are marked as zero points. Each student is allowed 10 serves to each side of the court. Trial attempts (balls that bounce before being hit or are struck without having the paddle pass below the server's waist or are missed or hit the net) do not count. The final score is the number of points earned from 20 serves.

Ms. Erickson decides that she can test two students simultaneously on the clear shot. Partners positioned on both sides of the net volley a ball as many times as possible in 1 minute. To begin, one partner volleys a ball over the net by dropping the ball and striking it on the rebound from the floor or striking it before it contacts the floor. The second partner, using either a forehand or backhand stroke, performs a return volley. The score for the two partners is the number of times the ball goes over the net in the minute. Both students must stay behind the nonvolley zone during the test. If a player returns a ball while in that zone, it does not count. Balls that do not make it over the net must be re-served from behind the nonvolley zone.

Step 6: Arrange Peer Review

Step 6 involves having the new test reviewed by peers, college instructors, skills experts, or students (Miller, 1988). The review is designed to elicit objective constructive criticism to help fine-tune the test. As one develops something new, personal subjectivity often interferes with logic. It is easy to get caught up in technical procedures and become oblivious to simple things—or visa versa.

Reviewers' advice need not be explicitly followed. Some suggestions may be unfeasible and others may increase time required to give a test. Other suggestions, however, may point out important procedures you have overlooked. Listen to all suggestions openly, review them critically, and then decide if and how they should be included. This review may lead you back to any of the previous five steps as test refinement occurs. Whichever step you go back to, make changes (based on review recommendations), then proceed through the remaining steps a second time and have the test peer reviewed again at step 6.

Ms. Erickson approaches her colleagues—Mr. Walswick, an elementary physical education specialist; Ms. Domier, a high school physical educator and volleyball coach; and Mr. Knudson, a junior high school physical education teacher and racquet sport expert—to ask them to review her new pickle-ball skills test. All three commend her for developing a new skills test, one greatly needed, as Ms. Erickson found in her review of literature.

Ms. Erickson asks the reviewers to be as critical as possible and to look for every mistake she may have made. The three reviewers raise numerous questions and suggestions. Mr. Walswick asks, ''Where should the partners stand when beginning the clear test? Are they allowed to be anywhere behind the nonvolley zone or should they be positioned in one of the service courts?'' Ms. Domier asks, ''Are students allowed to have practice trials? If so, how many or how long of a time period?'' Mr. Knudson, the racquet sports expert familiar with skills tests for badminton and tennis, suggests, ''Balls landing on lines in the serve test should be counted as good and awarded the higher point value. In addition, the clear test exhibits partner dependency.''

Ms. Erickson heeds the suggestions, backtracks to step 5, and changes the testing procedures. Changes include using Mr. Knudson's scoring suggestions, clarifying starting positions for the clear test, limiting practice trials to 30 seconds for each test, and redesigning the clear test to test one student at a time. With changes, Ms. Erickson returns the test to her colleagues for further review. All three reviewers agree that the test appears to be satisfactory and encourage Ms. Erickson next to complete a skills test pilot study.

Step 7: Conduct Pilot Study

At this point Ms. Erickson is ready for a pilot study to see whether her pickle-ball test has any administration, preparation, scoring, and/or direction problems. If a pilot study reveals testing problems, she must return to the appropriate step, make additional revisions, and proceed again through the remaining steps. A pilot study may find, for instance, that scoring is too difficult or too easy, or that directions are too complicated or too general. Without a pilot study deficiencies may not appear until the test has been administered to a large group of students with only one instructor and limited testing space (Miller, 1988; Safrit, 1990).

Ms. Erickson wants this test to apply to both junior high and senior high school students, so she decides to do pilot studies with both age groups. She administers the test to her fourth-period 7th-grade class and Ms. Domier to her fifth-period 10th-grade class. After pilot studies both teachers find the tests to be straightforward and decide they should remain as designed.

Step 8: Determine Validity, Reliability, and Objectivity

Ms. Erickson must next determine the validity, reliability, and objectivity of her pickle-ball skills test (Miller, 1988; Safrit, 1990). As discussed previously in this chapter, it is important to remember that a test with high validity is always reliable, but a reliable test is not always valid. This is so because reliability indicates the degree to which an instrument consistently measures what it purports to measure. Even though an instrument is considered reliable, it may not be measuring what it is supposed to measure.

Validity

Because testing has different purposes and because validity is evaluated in terms of purpose, there are several types of validity. Generally, validity is categorized as content validity, face validity, criterion validity, and construct validity (see Figure 2.5). Each type of validity is used to provide data to show that the test is measuring what it is supposed to measure. Basically, a test's degree of validity should indicate to the user the degree to which that test is capable of achieving certain aims (Baumgartner & Jackson, 1982).

Content Validity. Content validity indicates how accurately a test measures the skills and subject material taught to a physical education class (Baumgartner & Jackson, 1982). Test items must represent the unit objectives and reflect the demands of the particular sport.

Because Ms. Erickson decides to concentrate on developing long serve and clear shot skills, to ensure content validity she must use tests that include the long serve, the clear shot, or both. If she uses a short serve skills test, content validity would be lacking because that test would not measure class content. Content validity is necessary if tests are to measure what students have learned in a class (Johnson & Nelson, 1986).

Face Validity. A test has face validity (also known as logical validity) if it appears to measure the skill under evaluation (Johnson & Nelson, 1986). It is called face validity because a cursory examination of the testing instrument reveals that it is logical to assume the testing instrument is appropriate. Although face validity is the weakest procedure for determining validity, at times it is the obvious procedure. For example, the obvious way to test students' ability to shoot arrows is to let them shoot a predetermined number of arrows and count their points.

Criterion Validity. Criterion validity shows that test scores are related to one or more external variable(s) (expert judge evaluation, tournament results, a validated test) that are considered direct measures of the characteristic or behavior in question (Barrow et al., 1989; Safrit, 1990). Criterion validity may be either concurrent or predictive.

Predictive Validity. Predictive validity shows how dependably a test can predict how a student will perform in a future situation (Safrit, 1990). For example, suppose 100 girls tried out for the junior varsity basketball team. Coach Knodle could use a basketball skills test that has a high correlation with a thorough subjective rating of basketball playing ability. For practical purposes, it would be advantageous to keep on the team girls who scored high on the skills test that has high predictive validity.

Concurrent Validity. Concurrent validity indicates how well an individual currently performs a skill. Test results are correlated with a current criterion measurement. Concurrent criterion measurements include expert judge evaluation, tournament results, or an already validated test that measures the same criteria as the new test (Baumgartner & Jackson, 1982).

In expert judge evaluation, two or more judges subjectively evaluate the skill ability of the subjects and rate them. The ratings are then compared with the results of a skill test, and the correlation between expert ratings and skill test results is the validity coefficient. It is vital that judges be experts

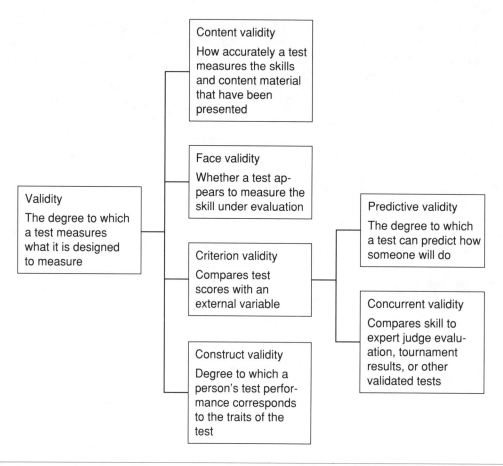

Figure 2.5 Summary chart for validity.

and that interrater reliability be high with a correlation of at least .80 (Safrit, 1990). Interrater reliability is defined as the consistency between two or more independent judgments of the same performance. Interrater reliability is essential when judging gymnastics, diving, or figure skating.

To determine validity through tournament results, compare final tournament standings with the skills test results. The correlation between final tournament standings and skills test results indicates the validity of the proposed test. Although this is an effective method for determining validity in individual and dual sports it is not recommended for team sports (Kirkendall et al., 1987).

A third method for establishing validity is by comparing test results from an already validated test with the results from a new test. The correlation between the two test results indicates the validity. This means of determining correlation must be used with caution because although the two tests may have a high validity correlation coefficient, the original test—the standard—may not have a high validity coefficient. The correlation between the two tests may be because of the new

test's relationship to an invalid part of the original test (Kirkendall et al., 1987).

Concurrent validity is important if the new test requires less equipment, less time, and less money to administer than other tests. For example, the 12-minute run has shown high concurrent validity to treadmill testing for cardiorespiratory endurance. The 12-minute run is easily administered to large numbers of people and requires little equipment in comparison to testing one person at a time on a treadmill (Hastad & Lacy, 1989).

Ms. Erickson uses tournament results as her criteria for determining validity. She has her students compete in a round-robin tournament before she gives the two skill test items. By comparing final tournament results to skill achievement, Ms. Erickson determines her pickle-ball test's validity. Correlation coefficients for the long serve and the clear shot are found to be .85 and .80, respectively. Validity coefficients of that magnitude are very good to excellent.

Construct Validity. Construct validity is the degree to which an individual's test performance corresponds to the abilities or traits that the test purports to measure (Safrit, 1990). A construct is a trait or quality that explains some aspect of behavior. For example, advanced tennis players should have high scores on a tennis serve skills test, while beginning tennis players will probably have low scores on a tennis serve skills test. If there is no significant difference, the test does not possess construct validity.

Reliability

Similar to validity, reliability can be determined several different ways. Typically, reliability is categorized as test-retest reliability, parallel forms reliability, or split-half or odd-even reliability (see Figure 2.6). Because reliability is easier to achieve than validity, reliability coefficients are expected to be higher than validity coefficients for the same skills test.

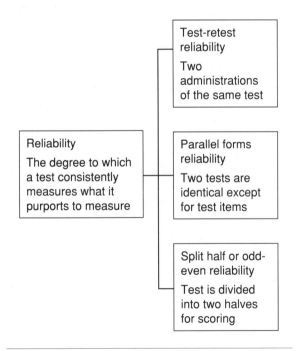

Figure 2.6 Summary chart for reliability.

Test-Retest Reliability. The test-retest procedure requires the same test to be given to the same group of students twice in as near the same conditions as possible for each test (Miller, 1988). The two sets of data are then correlated to determine the reliability coefficient. Maturational factors may influence the results of the retest if a long interval elapses between the two tests, but the appropriate time interval may be hard to determine. If the test-retest method is used, report the test-retest co-

efficient and the interval of time between test and retest.

Ms. Erickson elects to repeat the pickle-ball skills test 2 days after the first test. Because reliability is easier to prove than validity, one would expect correlation coefficients to be higher. Ms. Erickson finds reliability coefficients of .95 and .90 for the long serve test and the clear shot test, respectively.

Parallel Forms Reliability. Parallel or equivalent forms are designed to be identical except for test items. The two tests will have the same number of items, content, length, test directions, test conditions, and will be administered to the same group (Miller, 1988). Parallel forms are particularly difficult to generate for skills tests and therefore are impractical.

Split-Half or Odd-Even Reliability. Split-half reliability implies internal consistency. A group takes a test and then the test is divided into two equal halves for scoring. The correlation between the two scores from the two halves is determined. The longer the test, the more likely is the test's reliability (Miller, 1988). Generally, an odd-even method is preferred because it ensures that both halves of the test will be representative of the total test. For example, a skills test with an even number of trials would be divided into two halves, with the even-numbered trials being one half and the odd-numbered trials the other half. Split-halves, on the other hand, each could cover different material, or one half of the test could be easier than the other. Split-halves or odd-even eliminates the need for two test administrations (test-retest) and saves time and materials.

Objectivity

Determining objectivity is often conducted at the same time reliability is being determined. Objectivity is obtained by having two or more testers administer the test to the same group of students (Miller, 1988). The objectivity coefficient will be determined by the amount of agreement between test administrators.

Step 9: Develop Norms

When a test achieves validity and reliability, it is common to establish norms or standards that can be used locally, regionally, or nationally. Norms should be constructed for both boys and girls and for different age levels (Safrit, 1990).

Because Ms. Erickson's pickle-ball test achieves acceptable validity and reliability, she decides to develop local pickle-ball norms. She asks 20 junior and senior high school physical education teachers from her school district to administer the pickle-ball skills test. The test is administered to every class taught by the 20 teachers for 2 years. After 2 years of tabulating data, information is analyzed and norms are established. T scores, percentiles, and a recommended grading scale are computed.

Step 10: Construct Test Manual

As a final step in test construction, prepare a testing manual. Include information such as an overview of the sport; a history of testing in the sport; instructions for using the manual; a description of the tests with directions, diagrams, and scoring procedures; drills to develop proper techniques; norms; recording forms; and references.

Summary

This chapter seeks to help you select appropriate sport skills tests and to construct your own sport skills tests if no test to meet your specific needs is available.

Selecting appropriate sport skills tests is difficult and must be based on the program and its objectives. Variables such as equipment and space requirements, preparation and administration time, age and sex appropriateness, and safety require careful deliberation before a sport skills test can be accepted as a viable component of an activity unit. The most important variables to be considered, however, are validity, reliability, and objectivity. Techniques for determining validity and reliability are presented in the latter part of the chapter.

Chapter 3

Sound Testing Procedures

It is of little value to select or construct appropriate tests if they do not adhere to sound testing procedures. Careful attention must be given to duties before, during, and after the administration of a skills test. How will students warm up? What type of recording sheet works best? What should be done with nontesting students? How will results be presented? Answering these questions eases test administration and conserves class time.

Pretesting Duties

Pretest planning, essential to administering a sound test, ensures that everything will flow smoothly. Several pretest duties are mandatory.

Practicing Test Items

A frequently asked question regarding skills tests is, Should students be allowed to practice test items? The answer is a resounding YES! Students must be familiar with and be given opportunities to practice test items. Teachers should prepare handouts that state the purpose of a test, explain testing procedures, and define what performance is expected. Give test handouts (see Table 3.1) to students early in an activity unit so they can practice when they have free time—such as before class or while waiting on the sidelines for their turn.

When students are familiar with test items they can prepare better and need less explanation on test day (Clarke & Clarke, 1987). Anything teachers

Table 3.1 Instructions for the Benson Golf Test

Date of test—Friday, Oct. 21

Purpose of test—To evaluate five-iron ability in golf.

Test items—Hitting the five iron for distance and accuracy.

Test trials—5 practice shots are allowed followed by 20 test shots.

Dress—Dress in appropriate golfing attire. No street shoes or dresses.

Grouping—Students will be organized in groups of four. One will hit, one will call out the distance score, one will call out the deviation score, and one will write down the scores.

Scoring—Two scores will be recorded. One is how far the ball traveled in flight, and the other is how far the ball deviates from the intended line of flight. Final scores are the averages for the 20 shots.

do to lessen testing time is greatly appreciated by students, who often must wait for their skill attempts.

Inform students well in advance of a skills test so they can begin preparing (Hastad & Lacy, 1989). In math and English, students get weeks to read study guides or practice test questions. Physical education students are sometimes told the day they arrive in the gymnasium that "today is the skills testing day." Not only is this expecting a lot from students, but makes results less indicative of student achievement.

For tests to be valid they must test individuals on what they practice. As students become more familiar with test skill items, which depends largely on how much they practice, validity and reliability will increase. As a result, students must be allowed and encouraged to practice test items.

Should teachers provide students with a preclass warm-up (Siedentop, 1991)? Too often teachers unknowingly penalize students who arrive early by making them wait until all other students arrive. A planned preclass warm-up lets early-bird students practice new skills or refine previously learned ones. Preclass warm-up also is an opportune time for students to practice skills test items.

Equipment Preparation

Efficient and organized teachers determine at the beginning of a school year which skills tests they will administer. Once you select tests, develop a detailed checklist of all required testing equipment (Table 3.2). Typical equipment: floor and wall markings, cones, tape measures, stop watches, pencils, clipboards, and string or rope (Johnson & Nelson, 1986). Each skill test also will require specific equipment—footballs, basketballs, hurdles, high jump standards, or goals.

You'll also need to determine space needs (Kirkendall et al., 1987). For example, what is the minimum amount of space needed to conduct a punting test in football? Is that amount of space available? If not, it makes little sense to conduct that test.

Proper selection, use, and amount of equipment, space, and supplies will reduce testing time and ensure a quality test.

You need to check equipment and space for safety, availability, and working condition (Miller, 1988). If a weight lifting test requiring students to bench press a certain weight is being administered, the teacher must be sure the correct weights, bars, and collars are selected. If the test is being administered on a weight machine with cables, all cables and pulleys must be in perfect working condition. Likewise, unseen holes or obstructions that may cause injury on a running course must be filled, covered, or marked so all students are aware of them. A sample safety checklist appears in Figure 3.1.

Next, determine field and floor markings to allow for easy and rapid scoring. Most tests have predetermined markings that should be followed closely to maintain test validity. A teacher may, however, modify markings when it will not affect scoring (Barrow et al., 1989).

Finally, all testing stations should be identified and equipment should be properly placed before testing begins (Hastad & Lacy, 1989). When students must wait on the test administrator they both lose interest in the test and question the professionalism of the tester. Skills tests at their best are time consuming, and testers cannot afford to waste time searching for and preparing equipment.

A last item in equipment preparation, one often overlooked, is simply informing students the test's date and location, what they should wear, and what materials they should bring (Phillips & Hor-

Table 3.2 Activity Units and Testing Equipment Needs

Activity unit	Activity test	Equipment
Badminton	French Short Serve Test	Badminton racquet, shuttlecocks, nets and standards, rope, tape
Soccer	Yeagley Soccer Test	Soccer balls, wall surface, tape measure, cones, stopwatch
Speedball	Smith Speedball Test	Speedballs, tape measure, stopwatch
Archery	Farrow Archery Test	Targets, bows, arrows, arm guards, finger tabs, whistle, tape measure, stakes, chalk
Softball	AAHPERD Softball Test	Softballs, batting tees, gloves, cones, chalk, tape measure, stakes, bases, stopwatches
Tennis	Jones Tennis Test	Racquets, balls, tape measure, chalk, baskets, stopwatch
Golf	Vanderhoof Golf Test	Woods, five-irons, plastic balls, tape measure, hitting mats, cones, rope, standards
Volleyball	Kautz Volleyball Test	Volleyballs, tape measure, stopwatch
Swimming	Fronske Swimming Test	Lane dividers, stopwatches

Safety Checklist for Weight Training Equipment

Date inspected _____

Inspected by _____

Free weights	Okay	Needs repair	Comments
Plates			
Collars			
Bars			
Dumbbells			
Benches			
Universal machine			
Pulleys			
Cables			
Handles			
Pins			
Benches			

Figure 3.1 Sample checklist for equipment safety.

nak, 1979). Teachers must prepare to administer a test, and students must come prepared to participate on the assigned test date. If either does not fulfill their duty, everyone involved in the testing process suffers.

Order and Arrangement of Test Items

The order and arrangement of test items and stations is important. If test instructions state a specific order, follow that order explicitly. Deviation from the specifically stated order lessens test reliability (Barrow et al., 1989). If a test does not have a specific test item order, the test administrator must determine how best to order the items and arrange the stations.

The order of test items must ease the flow of students from station to station (Kirkendall et al., 1987). When students must wait they lose interest in the test, harass other students who are taking the test, and can become discipline problems.

When students move to the next station, do not allow them to interfere with students still testing. Before the test, tell students how and when they will move after completing a test component and where they should report for a particular test. In addition to giving students oral directions, draw diagrams of the test field or court and explain test item order and station sequence. Identifying stations by name or number expedites the moving of students from station to station and helps them understand what they should do when they get to a particular station (Phillips & Hornak, 1979). A sample of an order and arrangement of test items appears in Figure 3.2, page 26.

Consider safety when placing test items. When items overlap in physical space, a serious injury may occur (Barrow et al., 1989). For example, a teacher may assign some students to a basketball speed dribble test while other students perform a speed shooting test. A ball from the speed shooting test may rebound into the path of a student performing the speed dribble. The chance of injury greatly increased simply by how the teacher ordered the test items.

When test items involve different sets of muscles, stations and test items must be arranged to neutralize fatigue (Phillips & Hornak, 1979). Students should move from less strenuous to more strenuous or move so alternate sets of muscles will be tested.

Arrange stations in light of available equipment and the length of testing procedures. If testing equipment is sparse, one station may have to

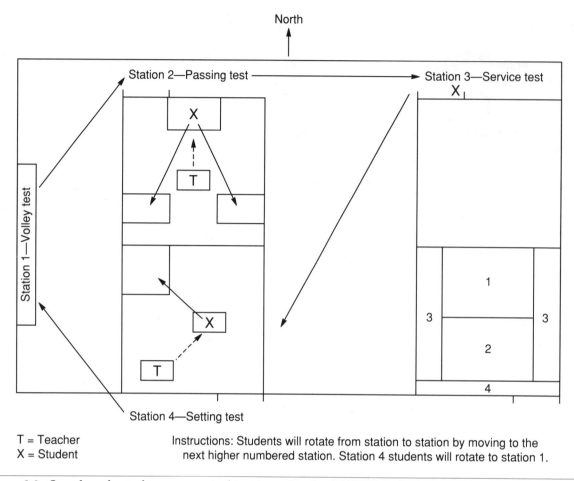

North

Station 2—Passing test ⟶ Station 3—Service test

Station 1—Volley test

Station 4—Setting test

T = Teacher
X = Student

Instructions: Students will rotate from station to station by moving to the next higher numbered station. Station 4 students will rotate to station 1.

Figure 3.2 Sample order and arrangement of test items for the AAHPER Volleyball Test.

suffice. But if both students and equipment are plentiful and time is of the essence, two or more stations may be set up to test the same item.

Recording Sheets

How teachers record student scores during skills testing affects test administration efficiency. Occasionally tests have preprinted score cards or score sheets (see Figure 3.3) that make it easy to record student results (Hastad & Lacy, 1989). If preprinted recording materials are available, use them, but teachers usually will have to devise their own.

The ways teachers devise recording materials also can lead to either efficient or inefficient test administration. Recording materials should be easy to read and understand and should facilitate accuracy and neatness in keeping scores (Miller, 1988). The arrangement of items on a recording

sheet should reflect logical sequence; in fact, the items should be in the same order as they are to be administered. Leave space between recordings where the administrator can record anecdotal observations. To save time during test administration enter student names on the recording materials before testing begins.

Three types of recording materials are generally available: grade book or class roll sheet, squad score card or score sheet, and individual score card or score sheet. Your specific testing situation will dictate which is most appropriate.

When teachers administer skills tests alone, the grade book or class roll sheet (Figure 3.4, page 28) is probably the best recording method (Hastad & Lacy, 1989). In this situation, each test item is administered individually. After a student finishes a test item, the examiner records the score next to that student's name in the grade book. Because the examiner will not have to transfer scores from a

I. Tumbling

  1. Rolls   2. Cartwheels   3. Kips

    <u>F</u> <u>B</u> <u>Ext.</u>   <u>R</u> <u>L</u>

    <u>3</u> + <u>3</u> + <u>5</u> +   <u>3</u> + <u>3</u>   +   <u>4</u> = <u>21</u>

II. Uneven bars

  1. Bar snap   2. Kip   3. Backward hip pullover

    <u>10</u>   +   <u>8</u>   +   <u>4</u> = <u>22</u>

III. Balance beam

  1. Locomotor   2. Arm support   3. Rolling

    <u>4</u> + <u>4</u> + <u>4</u> + <u>4</u> = <u>16</u> +   <u>4</u>   +   <u>7</u> = <u>27</u>

IV. Vaulting

  A. Straddle   B. Stoop   2. Approach Test

                         Board   + Wall Score − Height score

    <u>12</u> + <u>12</u> + <u>4</u> + (<u>5</u>) = <u>33</u>

V. Free standing floor exercise

  1. Tumbling total   2. Continuity

    <u>21</u>   +   <u>10</u> = <u>31</u>

Figure 3.3 Sample preprinted score sheet (Bowers Gymnastic Test).
Note. From ''Gymnastics skill test for beginning to low intermediate girls and women,'' by C.O. Bowers, 1965, unpublished master's thesis, Ohio State University, Columbus, OH. Reprinted by permission of the author.

score card or score sheet, this method saves time; but because most teachers do not allow students access to their grade books, this method does not allow students to see prior test performances and make comparisons between present and past achievements.

When students move as squads from station to station, squad score sheets (Figure 3.5, page 29) are most appropriate (Phillips & Hornak, 1979). A squad leader may be responsible for the score sheet and makes sure it is carried from station to station. When they arrive at a testing station, the squad leader or test examiner should arrange students as they are listed on the score sheet for ease and speed.

Besides being efficient in scoring, using squad sheets reduces the possibility of losing a score sheet and of students altering scores, which can occur with individual score sheets.

Individual score sheets (Figure 3.6, page 29) or cards, however, are more flexible because they al-low students to move from station to station without affecting other students (Barrow et al., 1989). For instance, students who finish quickly can move to the next station rather than stand around. When students assume responsibility for recording scores and maintaining score cards, they feel more involved in the testing process.

Using individual score cards lets students see and chart their own scores, providing a better sense of achievement status (Hastad & Lacy, 1989). Too often students take skills tests without understanding how they performed in relation to objectives or standards. With individual score cards, students can establish test profiles and from those can devise plans for improving individual skills.

Standardization of Instructions

Because consistent test administration increases reliability and objectivity of measurements, it is important for all testing aspects to be standardized

7th Grade						Class:		Third period									
Class roll	M	T	W	T	F	M	T	W	T	F	M	T	W	T	F
Anthony	50		5.1		5										
Maria	40		4.5		2										
Mark	51		4.1		6										
Susan	30		6.0		2										
Betty	55		5.6		2										
John	38		5.2		1										
Lou	20		6.0		0										
Mario	60		4.0		1										
Hector	65		4.0		0										
Chen	48		5.7		4										
LaRon	32		6.3		1										
Rod	20		7.0		2										
	Sit-ups		Dash		Pull-ups										

Figure 3.4 Sample grade book scoring.

(Phillips & Hornak, 1979). It is standard operating policy to practice giving test instructions and determining successful skill attempts from unsuccessful ones before actually administering a test.

Most tests have two sets of instructions, one for the administrator and one for the students. Instructions for test administrators relate to explaining, demonstrating, administering, and scoring the test, whereas student instructions relate to performance of the test, hints on techniques, and suggestions for improving scores (Hastad & Lacy, 1989). Each set of instructions should be standardized and in writing so everyone involved knows exactly how test instructions are to be given.

Keep instructions brief, concise, and focused on correct performance rather than on variance of correctness. Students should not be given additional or different information on how to perform, unless the additional information is given to every

Basketball skills test

Squad number ___4___

Squad leader ___Derrick___

Student	Passing			Shooting			Dribbling		
	Trial 1	Trial 2	Ave	Trial 1	Trial 2	Ave	Trial 1	Trial 2	Ave
Derrick									
Helen									
Michael									
Karen									
Donalee									
Samuel									
Ben									
Bobby									
Kathy									

Figure 3.5 Sample squad scoring sheet.

Football skills test

Student _____

Test item	Trial 1	Trial 2	Trial 3	Average
Punt for distance				
Punt for accuracy				
40-Yard dash				
Pass for distance				
Pass for accuracy				
Catching				
Kick for distance				

Figure 3.6 Sample individual scoring sheet.

student in exactly the same manner (Johnson & Nelson, 1986).

Additionally, every test item must be administered in exactly the same manner. For instance, Anthony can't be allowed two steps when Michael is allowed one. To answer questions on incorrect performance, it is helpful to write a policy on at-

tempt accuracy. For example, "The student is allowed to take one step before throwing the ball. If additional steps are taken, the throw does not count but the student is allowed to repeat the throw."

Test administrators often fail when they attempt to motivate students by using false norms. Statements such as "Last year, the boys threw the ball 100 feet" when in reality they threw it 50 feet can have adverse effects. The statements may initially motivate students to try harder, but when they realize they cannot throw the ball even 50 feet, disappointment and despair may appear. Let students perform the skill attempts without making any statements that relate to individual goals or past performance either of the students being tested or students previously tested (Johnson & Nelson, 1986).

Testing Duties

Testing duties are items addressed when students arrive in the gymnasium. With proper preparation the actual skills testing should proceed without incident, but if you have not planned how students will warm up or what will be done with nontesting students, many preventable problems will occur.

Testers

More than one person often is necessary to effectively and efficiently administer a skills test. Factors that determine the number of testers are the length of the test, the number of test items, the number of students to be tested, the number of stations available, or the amount of time available to complete the test (Phillips & Hornak, 1979).

No matter how many testers are being employed, all must follow the same test administration procedures. Not all persons who read the test instructions understand them. All testers must attend a practice session with sample subjects (Johnson & Nelson, 1986). Testers must be prepared to deal not only with typical testing procedures but with unplanned developments during tests. Practice sessions can clarify instructions and procedures, develop technical skills, familiarize testers with responsibilities, and emphasize safety precautions.

Students often act as throwers, setters, and opponents during their classmates' skill attempts. A performer's score on a test item often may result from how a classmate threw or set a ball (Johnson & Nelson, 1986). Safrit (1990) discourages using students as throwers and setters, but teachers who still decide to use students in these roles should conduct pretest meetings to explain how bad throws or sets should be handled.

Generally, four different groups of individuals can act as testers. The most common is a single physical education teacher who gives all instructions, does all setting and throwing, and records all scores. This is the most time-consuming method, but it is the most accurate because every student gets similar chances.

When tests are given on a massed basis, students commonly work with partners. While the examiner administers the test, scores are judged and recorded by a partner who is not performing the test item (Barrow et al., 1989). For example, each student is given an individual score card and finds a partner for a basketball quick pass test. One partner, basketball in hand, faces a wall and on the examiner's whistle begins to pass the ball against the wall as many times as possible in a 30-second time limit. The other partner, standing behind the student being tested, counts the number of passes. At the sound of the "stop" whistle, the counting partner records the score on a score card.

Although using partners reduces testing time, opportunities for inaccurate scoring greatly increase as compared with having a physical education teacher score and record all results. Obviously, if partners are used in a testing situation they must be taught correct scoring techniques and what constitutes a correct skill attempt (Barrow et al., 1989). If you doubt student accuracy, don't use the partner method.

When students are organized in squads that move from station to station, squad leaders commonly act as testers. It is important that squad leaders be trained in test administration techniques (Barrow et al., 1989). Even though the squad leader method of test administration saves time, it has a problem similar to that of partner testing. It is sometimes difficult for a squad leader to set personal feelings aside when judging a classmate, especially if that classmate is a friend or star athlete. Again, if squad leaders have been trained to judge attempts and have practiced giving standardized instructions, problems with friends will be lessened.

A fourth group of testers consists of trained testers—students, faculty, students from a local college, paraprofessionals, or nonschool personnel such as parents. Ideally, this would be the best way to test, but is seldom possible.

Group Organization

The grouping style a test administrator chooses depends upon variables such as how many students are to be tested, how many testers are available, and how much equipment and space are available. When tests specifically describe how to organize students, follow that organizational pattern (Phillips & Hornak, 1979).

Test administrators always should have backup plans. Student absences can affect grouping methods, so testers have to adjust quickly and appropriately (Miller, 1988). Some teachers, especially student teachers, prepare elaborate plans for grouping and rotating students only to have students absent on test day. In utter frustration, the teacher quickly tries to regroup the students, only to have them running everywhere trying to organize into new groups. The teacher with a back-up plan can quickly implement it without the students even being aware of it.

No one group organizational method is appropriate for all testing situations. If assistants are available and equipment and space are plentiful, many groups can be formed. Conversely, a teacher with limited help, equipment, and space may be forced to use only one group. Five grouping patterns are generally followed: mass, partner, squad, station-to-station, and combination.

Mass grouping is most effective and efficient in terms of time and facility utilization (Barrow et al., 1989). When students are grouped in mass, they generally score themselves and report the score to the tester. Mass testing is commonly used during fitness testing such as the mile run or push-ups. If students might cheat on their scores, find an alternative grouping pattern.

When partner grouping is used, one-half the class acts as performers, while the second half serves as helpers, scorers, and recorders (Barrow et al., 1989). For instance, during sit-up tests one student holds his or her partner's feet.

With squad grouping, assign an equal number of members in each squad and schedule tests at each station so all squads rotate at the same time. Don't use this method if the order of test items will handicap certain students.

With a large group and when the order of events is not important, station-to-station grouping is appropriate (Phillips & Hornak, 1979). With station-to-station grouping, students do not stay with any particular squad or group but instead complete the tests at one station and then move to the next station.

Combination grouping is appropriate when tests require alternative grouping formations for different skills or when equipment or space for certain parts of the test are insufficient. For example, students may complete the first part of a skills test in mass, but move to squads for the rest.

Warming Up

It is essential that students warm up before participating in any testing situation. Warming up prevents muscle and joint soreness and injuries and results in better test performance scores. It also gives students time to mentally prepare (Hastad & Lacy, 1989).

Warm ups need not be long and drawn out, but should be long enough and intense enough to prepare students both physiologically and psychologically. The warm-up period should last 5 to 10 minutes, be supervised, be specific to the skill being tested, and be skill practice rather than calisthenics. It does students little good to stretch leg muscles and do sit-ups before a badminton serving test. Rather, they should stretch their arms, shoulders, and backs as they practice volleying, rallying, and serving a shuttlecock.

Demonstration and Explanation

It is important that a test administrator properly demonstrate and explain the skills being tested and how they are to be executed. Such demonstration and explanation increases the chance for optimal performance by making certain that directions are understood (Phillips & Hornak, 1979).

When demonstrating or explaining, face the students, speak clearly and loudly so everyone can understand, and show or explain the correct fundamentals. It often helps to have a student demonstrate the test items while an administrator describes them (Miller, 1988).

Although most test administrators provide only one demonstration and explanation to students before testing begins, it is better to provide demonstrations and explanations as each group moves to a new station (Kirkendall et al., 1987). Skills being tested at the various stations usually consist of different test items. When demonstrations and explanations for every skill at every station are given only at the beginning of a test, many students will have forgotten the instructions by the time they move to a specific station. Giving demonstrations and explanations to small groups as they arrive at a station also increases the opportunity for questions (Phillips & Hornak, 1979). Students are more likely to ask questions, to understand the skill being tested, and to understand the procedures they need to have clarified when in a small group.

Test Trials

All students should practice test trials before they are expected to execute the skill being tested. But how many trials are appropriate? This depends on the number of students to be tested and the amount of time allowed for testing. Whatever the number of test trials allowed, maintain test equitability by giving each student the same number.

Nontesting Students

What should you do with nontesting students, students who finish their test early, students who aren't participating in the test for whatever reason, or students who are awaiting their turns? First, nontesting students can be judges, scorers, recorders, opponents, throwers, servers, setters, receivers, or retrievers. Second, have them practice their skill attempts away from the testing area where they don't distract students who are testing. Third, nontesting students can be engaged in an alternate activity. As students finish their tests, they change places with one of the nontesters in the activity. Finally, skills tests can be administered at the same time as a culminating tournament or league play. As a team finishes testing, it changes places with a team participating in the culminating activity.

Safety

The current threat of lawsuits in sport and physical education makes safety the number one priority at all times during testing procedures. The risk of operating without regard for safety is just too great; not only could it mean getting sued, but worse it could result in catastrophic injury (Phillips & Hornak, 1979).

Testing situations create excitement, enthusiasm, and competition. All of those may increase the chance of injury if students attempt skills unsafely. To protect themselves, teachers must review safety precautions and warn students of risks involved in the testing. Students must not be expected nor required to perform skills on a test that they have not practiced (Miller, 1988).

It is important that test sites be properly prepared (Hastad & Lacy, 1989). Running surfaces should be smooth, adequate deceleration space should be provided at the end of a race course, spotters must be properly positioned, fielders and catchers should be looking away from the sun, and extra equipment should be stowed so students do not trip. Also use soft, unbreakable, and visible marking devices.

Motivation

Unfortunately, all students are not ready for action when they arrive at a testing site. This being the case, teachers have a responsibility to conscientiously motivate and encourage students when necessary (Phillips & Hornak, 1979). Teachers can do this in a number of ways.

First, teachers must provide a clear explanation of the test's purpose. Too often, tests are given simply because they are supposed to be, with results never used for any specific purpose. Second, students should know previous levels of achievement, either their own or the achievement level of a different class (Phillips & Hornak, 1979). A word of caution: Don't attempt to motivate students by exaggerating how well a class did. Not only will many students give up because they know they can't achieve those standards, but a teacher who is found stretching the truth loses credibility.

Give all students the same degree of motivation and encouragement and give either all or no students a comment after their performance (Baumgartner & Jackson, 1982). It is common to hear teachers vocally praise students who do well, while silently acknowledging those whose best attempts fall far short of average. Although vocal praise and silent acknowledgment are thought by some to be in the students' best interests, many students are actually embarrassed by this and some take it as criticism. The best procedure is to merely announce a student's score after an attempt. It may be best to tell the score only to the student who completed the attempt. If individuals wish to share it with other students, that is their choice.

Performance

If all students are not required to perform test items in the exact same manner, the results' validity and reliability are affected (Miller, 1988). For example, a vertical jump-and-reach test states that students must place both feet on the floor before they jump. That is, they cannot take steps but merely are to jump straight up. If you let students take one step before they jump, results are meaningless in relation to the norms. Teachers must insist that all students perform the test items as stated in the instructions (Miller, 1988).

Posttesting Duties

We give skills tests to gauge students' psychomotor development and to help them improve. Unfortunately, students often are not told how they scored or how they can improve their skills. The sharing of posttest analysis is imperative.

Analyzing Scoring

Why should test results be recorded and scored? In the case of skills testing, the results can be used to compare against norms, classmates, and previous class and individual results. When comparisons are made against norms, it is important that norms be up to date (Johnson & Nelson, 1986). Many skills tests in use today were developed in the 1950s and '60s with norms established based on the performance of students at that time. In the years since those tests were normed, children have undergone many physical changes. That means many norms are inappropriate for today's children.

A second concern with norms is: Are they appropriate for the students, based on the length of unit activities? For example, students in a 3-week basketball unit will not score as well on skills tests as students in a 6-week unit. For this reason it helps to base norms on unit lengths. For most activities, this would require each teacher or school district to develop their own norms (Miller, 1988).

After scores are compared with norms, teachers also should calculate measures of central tendency and variability for the test. This information allows for comparisons of students, classes, and schools and is useful in reporting results to students, parents, school administrators, and the public.

Measures of central tendency describe the average or common score of a group of scores. Examples include batting averages and scoring averages. Common measures of central tendency include the mean, mode, and median.

Measures of variability describe the extent of similarity or difference in a group of scores. One measure of variability, standard deviation, determines how scores cluster about a mean.

Mean. The mean, or average, is the one best score that is representative of a group (Mathews, 1968). It is calculated by adding the values of all scores and dividing by the number of scores. In most cases, the mean is the score that best represents how well a group performed.

Table 3.3 illustrates how the mean is used with results from an archery test. The total score for the 20 archery students was 1,543 points. The 1,543 total was divided by the number of scores (20). The mean, or average, score for this archery class was 77.15 points.

Mode. The mode is the most commonly occurring value in a set (Barrow et al., 1989). It is calculated by inspecting the data set of raw scores and identifying which score or scores occur most frequently.

Table 3.4 illustrates how the mode is used with results from the archery test in Table 3.3. The most frequently occurring score in this archery test was 80, attained by four students.

Median. The median is the single value that is higher than half the scores and lower than half the

Table 3.3 Sample Calculation for Determining a Mean

Formula for determining a mean: $\bar{X} = \dfrac{\Sigma X}{N}$

$\bar{X}$ = Mean
ΣX = Sum of all scores
 N = Total number of scores

Student	Score	Student	Score
1	90	11	83
2	80	12	90
3	83	13	80
4	70	14	71
5	71	15	74
6	75	16	71
7	90	17	75
8	80	18	80
9	70	19	69
10	60	20	81

N = 1543

$\bar{X} = \dfrac{1543}{20}$

Mean = 77.15

Table 3.4 Sample Calculation for Determining a Mode

Scores	Frequency
90	3
83	2
81	1
80	4
75	2
74	1
71	3
70	2
69	1
60	1

Mode (most frequently occurring score) = 80.

scores (Barrow et al., 1989). It is used when extreme scores may affect the mean. A median is calculated by ordering scores from best to worst and then determining the middle point. With an odd number of scores the median is the number at the 50th percentile. For example, with scores of 45, 50, 55, 60, and 65, the median is 55. With an even number of scores the median is the midpoint between lower half and upper half. For example, with scores of 20, 30, 40, 50, 60, and 70, the median would fall half-way between 40 and 50 at 45.

Table 3.5 shows how the median is used with results from the archery test. Because there is an even number of scores, the median will be between the lower half and upper half. Because the midpoint is half-way between 75 and 80, the median is 77.5.

Table 3.5 Sample Calculation for Determining a Median

Scores	
90	75
90	75
90	74
83	71
83	71
81	71
80	70
80	70
80	69
80	60
Median = 77.5	

Standard Deviation. Standard deviation is a measure that indicates the scatter or spread of the middle 68.26% of the scores about a mean (Mathews, 1968). For example, a mean of 60 with a standard deviation of 3 would mean that about 68% of the subjects scored 60, plus or minus 3, or from 57 to 63. To determine the standard deviation, first calculate the deviation scores by subtracting the mean from every score. Next square each deviation score, sum those squares, divide by the number of scores, and take the square root of the obtained value.

Table 3.6 shows how standard deviation is used with results from the archery test. The result is a standard deviation of 7.76. This means that with a mean score of 77.15 and a standard deviation of 7.76 that about 68% of the subjects scored 77.15, plus or minus 7.76, or from 69.39 to 84.91.

When mean and standard deviation are calculated, it is easy to determine the distribution. If a distribution is normal, or bell-shaped, more than 99% of all scores will fall within three standard deviations above and below the mean. About 95% of the scores will be within two standard deviations above and below the mean, and about 68% of all the scores will be within one standard deviation above and below the mean. Relationships for the archery test are shown in Figure 3.7. In this

Table 3.6 Sample Calculation for Determining Standard Deviation

Subject scores	$(X - \bar{X})$	$(X - \bar{X})^2$
90	12.85	165.1225
80	2.85	8.1225
83	5.85	34.2225
70	−7.15	51.1225
71	−6.15	37.8225
75	−2.15	4.6225
90	12.85	165.1225
80	2.85	8.1225
70	−7.15	51.1225
60	−17.15	294.1225
83	5.85	34.2225
90	12.85	165.1225
80	2.85	8.1225
71	−6.15	37.8225
74	−3.15	9.9225
71	−6.15	37.8225
75	2.15	4.6225
80	2.85	8.1225
69	−8.15	66.4225
81	3.85	14.8225
$\Sigma = 1543$		$\Sigma = 1206.55$

Mean = 77.15
Mode = 80
Median = 77.5

Formula for determining standard deviation:

$$SD = \sqrt{\frac{\Sigma (X - \bar{X})^2}{N}}$$

X = Individual scores
$\bar{X}$ = Mean of distribution
N = Total number of scores

$$SD = \sqrt{\frac{1206.55}{20}} \quad SD = \sqrt{60.3275} \quad SD = 7.76$$

test, the mean minus three standard deviations is equal to 53.87, and the mean plus three standard deviations is equal to 100.43. One must understand that each distribution will have a mean and a standard deviation based on the actual scores for that particular distribution.

Presenting Results

As with written tests, results of skills tests should be made available to students as quickly as pos-

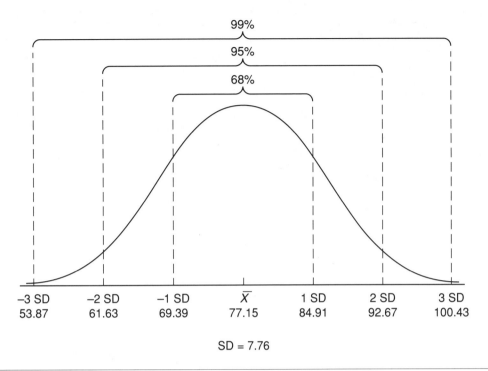

Figure 3.7 Distribution curve.

sible (Miller, 1988; Phillips & Hornak, 1979). Many teachers widely endorse immediate feedback for maximizing learning and increasing motivation. Presenting results should involve more than just reporting student grades. Results should allow students to see how they did compared with a pretest, norms, or fellow classmates.

Results should be expressed simply, clearly, and concisely without omitting important information. When effective teachers provide test results to students, they discuss why some students did not perform well and suggest to those students how they can improve for the next test (Kirkendall et al., 1987).

Confidentiality

Many physical educators were good athletes during their school days and so developing skills was relatively easy for them. They scored well on skills tests and their teachers recognized them, either verbally or with material rewards. Because of this, many physical education teachers often believe all students like to be recognized. Not so. Few students attain scores worthy of outstanding recognition, and those who do attain noteworthy scores are, more than likely, athletes. When the only stu-

dents rewarded are the high achievers, we perpetuate the myth that to be successful one has to be a winning athlete. So, present results confidentially (Corbin, 1987). A teacher should not announce nor display every individual's score but instead post norms, means, and medians. In this way, students can make individual comparisons and share their own results with others if they wish.

Summary

This chapter describes steps important to test administration. Before administering sport skills tests teachers must prepare score cards, determine group organization, determine space allocation, and prepare students.

As tests are being conducted, teachers must plan ways for keeping nontesting students active, ways to motivate students to do their best, and ways to ensure safety.

To understand test results, you must conduct correct analysis and comparisons. Three measures of central tendency (mean, mode, and median) and one measure of variability (standard deviation) were discussed in the last part of the chapter.

Part II

Sport Skills Tests and Evaluations

Chapter 4

Tests for Individual Sports

A popular movement in high school physical education is to include lifetime recreational activities such as weight lifting, golf, bowling, and archery. Many such activities are classified as individual sports and commonly receive their greatest emphasis in the 10th, 11th, and 12th grades, although sports such as swimming and track and field are better received in middle school (Annarino, Cowell, & Hazelton, 1980).

For some individual sport activities, skills tests are not necessary. For example, skill achievement in bowling, track and field, and weight training can be determined by a bowling score, a jumping distance, or a weight lifted. Other individual activities, such as figure skating and gymnastics, are commonly scored through judges' ratings.

This chapter includes skills tests for archery, diving, figure skating, golf, gymnastics, snow skiing, and swimming and ratings tests for aerobic dance and gymnastics. Instructors should develop their own tests for dance, bowling, cycling, track and field, and wrestling.

Aerobic Dance

One of the newest and most popular exercises, especially for females, is rhythmic aerobic dance. Although rhythmic aerobic exercise started in America's fitness clubs, most public schools now offer aerobic dance instruction.

A typical rhythmic aerobic dance rating test evaluates quality of movement, body alignment, effectiveness of warm-up, stretching exercises, cardiovascular conditioning, and cool down.

Jeffreys Rhythmic Aerobics Rating Scale (Jeffreys, 1987)

Purpose. To measure ability in rhythmic aerobics.

Validity and Reliability. Validity and reliability were not determined, but agreement between two judges was reported to be high.

Age Level and Sex. Originally conducted with college students. Appropriate for junior high school and senior high school students.

Personnel. Two judges.

Equipment. Tape player and prerecorded music. Score cards or recording sheets and pencils.

Space. Dance room or gymnasium.

Test Items. Movement and body alignment cues, warm-up and/or stretches, cardiovascular phase, and cool down phase. The four items together have 14 components.

Preparation. Prerecording and cueing the music.

Directions. Students divide into groups of three to five and design an exercise routine that combines all components of the rating scale. The exercise routine will be performed before evaluators. Test items and components follow.

I. Movement and Body Alignment Cues
  1. Move with the music; proper tempo and rhythm.
  2. Correct body positions to reduce compromising positions and injuries.
  3. Transitions and progressions noted by adding and combining several arm works to the same leg movement. Blending of movements smooth, permitting participants to follow with little difficulty.
  4. Eye contact along with verbal, body, and directional cues, singly or in combination.
II. Warm-up and Stretches
  5. Static stretches held 10 to 30 seconds. Stretch several muscle groups without compromising body alignment.
  6. Standing and floor stretches appropriate (correct sequencing).
  7. Duration adequate; includes most major muscle groups.
III. Cardiovascular Phase
  8. Interval training combining low, non-impact aerobics with recovery periods.
  9. Duration and intensity sufficient to reach medium and submaximal rates, gradually increasing, intensifying, and decreasing. Follows the aerobic curve.
  10. Heart rate monitored two to three times with the last count being after a 3-minute recovery period.
  11. Bout dense enough to allow most to reach and sustain their targeted heart rate for 15 to 20 minutes without overtaxing and causing strain.
IV. Cool Down Phase
  12. Static stretching of the legs and Achilles tendons sufficient.
  13. Relaxation, stretching, walking movements included. Supportive, encouraging, and informative.
  14. Time for questions and answers and sharing before departure.

Scoring. Group member receives one grade based on judges' ratings. Each of the 14 components has the same value and is scored from 1 to 3. A perfect score is 42.

1—*Poor*   Group shows lack of organization and preference for this activity. Group is not at ease.

2—*Average*   Group is at ease, working together, and sharing the experience by con-

tributing and communicating. All members contribute to the performance.

3—*Good*   Group is enthusiastic. Bouts are unique, innovative, and creative.

Norms. Not established.

Archery

The bow and arrow is one of the oldest weapons known to humankind. First used as a hunting tool by primitive people, it was later used for self-defense by American Indians. Since the advent of guns, the bow and arrow has been used primarily for sport.

Archery's popularity in high schools and colleges has increased as equipment improved and new shooting methods developed. In the 1972 Olympic Games in Munich, archery debuted as an Olympic event. Since that time, several Americans have captured gold, silver, and bronze medals.

Archery is ideal for physical education programs. It is easy to learn, can be performed by both sexes, has few technical skills, can be performed year-round both inside and outside, and can be learned quickly.

Archery challenges include target shooting, clout shooting, roving shooting, field shooting, novelty shooting, and small and large game hunting. Archery skills testing generally involves shooting accurately at a target.

Farrow Archery Test (Farrow, 1970)

Purpose. To evaluate arrow shooting ability in archery.

Validity and Reliability. Face validity was assumed because the item is the same as the skill tested. Reliability was estimated at .88 as computed by the split-halves procedure followed by the Spearman-Brown Prophecy Formula.

Age Level and Sex. Originally conducted with college women. Appropriate for junior high school and senior high school students.

Personnel. Single tester. Nonshooting students can be used as recorders.

Equipment. Standard 48-inch targets, bows, arrows, arm guards, and finger tabs. The number of bows should be at least double the number of targets so two archers can be tested on one target simultaneously. The number of arrows should be at least 6 times the number of archers shooting at one time. Preparation equipment includes a measuring tape, line markers, stakes, and chalk. Scoring equipment includes a whistle, score cards or recording sheets, and pencils.

Space. The maximum shooting distance to the targets is 20 yards. Targets should be placed at least 10 yards apart.

Test Item. Shooting arrows.

Preparation. Set up targets. Measure and mark two shooting lines 10 and 20 yards from the target and the safety line at 25 yards. Score cards must be prepared.

Directions. Each archer shoots four ends of six arrows (24) from 10 yards and four ends of six arrows from 20 yards at a standard 48-inch target. Each archer shoots 48 arrows.

Scoring. The score is the total points from the 48 arrows: gold = 9; red = 7; blue = 5; black = 3; and white = 1. Arrows outside the white don't score. Arrows that pass through or bounce off a target are scored as 7. A perfect score is 432.

Norms. Not established.

AAHPER Archery Skills Test (AAHPER, 1967)

Purpose. To evaluate arrow shooting ability in archery.

Validity and Reliability. Face validity was assumed because the item is the same as the skill tested. The test manual does not provide a reliability estimate but states that no test item has a reliability less than .70.

Age Level and Sex. Junior high school and senior high school students.

Personnel. Single tester. Nonshooting students can be used as recorders.

Equipment. Standard 48-inch targets, bows, arrows, arm guards, and finger tabs. Bows should range from 15 to 40 pounds in pull, and arrows should be 24 to 48 inches long. Because four archers are allowed to shoot at one target at the same time, the number of bows should be 4 times the number of targets. The number of arrows should be at least 6 times the number of

archers shooting at one time. Preparation equipment includes a measuring tape, line markers, stakes, and chalk. Scoring equipment includes a whistle, score cards or recording sheets, and pencils.

Space. The maximum shooting distance to the target is 30 yards. Targets should be 50 feet apart.

Test Item. Shooting arrows.

Preparation. Set up targets. Measure and mark shooting lines at 10, 20, and 30 yards as shown in Figure 4.1. Prepare score cards.

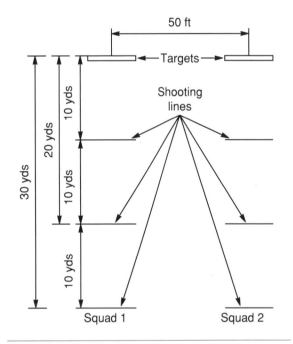

Figure 4.1 Field markings for the AAHPER Archery Test.
Note. From "AAHPER skills test manual for archery," by AAHPER, 1966, Washington DC. Copyright 1967 by AAHPER. Reprinted by permission.

Directions. Girls shoot two ends of six arrows (12) from distances of 10 and 20 yards, and boys shoot two ends of six arrows from distances of 10, 20, and 30 yards. Girls shoot 24 arrows and boys shoot 36 arrows. All archers begin at the 10-yard mark. When archers have completed two ends at the 10-yard mark, they move to the 20-yard mark. After completing shooting from the 20-yard mark, boys move to the 30-yard mark. Archers who do not score at least 10 points at one distance cannot move to the next distance. Archers are allowed to use any method of aiming and are allowed four practice shots at each distance. No more than four archers should be allowed to shoot at any one target at the same time.

Scoring. The score is the total points from 24 arrows for girls and 36 arrows for boys: gold = 9; red = 7; blue = 5; black = 3; and white = 1. Arrows outside the white don't score. Arrows that pass through or bounce off a target score 7. Arrows cutting through two colors score the higher color. A perfect score for girls is 216 and for boys 324. Score cards are available in the test manual.

Norms. Norms for girls appear in Table 4.1 and for boys in Table 4.2.

Table 4.1 Percentile Scores for Girls on the AAHPER Archery Test

Age	12-13			14			15			16			17-18		
Yards*	10	20	Tot.	10	20	Tot.	10	20	Tot.	10	20	Tot.	10	20	Tot.
100%	85	60	129	89	70	159	96	81	160	100	91	161	100	95	180
95	69	40	100	74	47	109	82	55	130	87	58	134	87	71	149
90	60	29	89	68	38	99	75	47	112	80	50	115	80	60	129
85	50	22	81	63	35	89	70	43	103	73	44	107	73	52	123
80	46	19	69	58	32	84	66	39	96	67	40	100	69	47	116
75	41	17	64	54	28	79	63	34	89	64	36	96	66	42	109
70	38	15	60	50	25	75	60	32	85	60	32	91	62	40	104
65	35	13	55	48	23	70	56	29	80	56	29	87	58	36	100
60	34	12	50	46	21	66	53	27	77	53	27	80	55	32	95
55	32	10	46	43	20	62	51	25	73	49	25	76	52	29	91
50	30	9	42	41	18	58	49	23	70	46	22	72	48	26	85
45	27	7	38	38	16	54	46	22	66	43	20	67	46	24	78
40	24	6	35	35	14	50	43	20	62	41	18	63	42	21	73
35	22	1	32	33	12	47	40	18	59	38	16	60	40	19	68
30	19	0	28	30	10	45	37	16	55	33	14	56	38	18	64
25	16	0	25	28	8	42	34	13	51	31	12	52	35	16	60
20	14	0	22	25	7	40	31	11	45	29	10	47	31	14	53
15	12	0	17	22	0	34	27	8	40	25	8	41	28	12	45
10	10	0	12	19	0	28	21	6	33	21	6	36	24	9	38
5	6	0	5	12	0	22	13	0	25	16	0	26	19	0	30
0	0	0	0	0	0	0	0	0	0	0	0	0	0	0	0

*10 yards = 9.15 meters; 20 yards = 18.29 meters.

Note. From ''AAHPER skills test manual for archery,'' by AAHPER, 1966, Washington DC. Copyright by AAHPER. Reprinted by permission.

Table 4.2 Percentile Scores for Boys on the AAHPER Archery Test

Age	12-13				14				15				16				17-18			
Yards*	10	20	30	Tot.	10	20	30	Tot.	10	20	30	Tot.	10	20	30	Tot.	10	20	30	Tot.
100%	91	70	45	195	96	75	50	210	100	90	81	270	100	100	95	270	100	95	85	270
95	83	53	28	156	88	61	34	179	97	77	50	215	99	78	56	220	98	78	64	222
90	78	44	24	138	80	48	28	160	94	70	41	195	97	71	47	205	96	72	53	206
85	73	38	22	128	78	45	24	150	90	66	35	187	96	67	43	197	93	67	47	197
80	70	34	18	122	75	41	21	146	88	63	31	177	91	63	40	189	90	63	42	190
75	67	31	16	112	72	38	18	143	84	58	28	167	90	59	36	181	88	59	39	184
70	64	28	14	103	70	36	16	139	80	54	25	158	88	56	32	173	86	55	37	176
65	61	26	12	98	68	33	15	136	78	51	22	149	86	54	30	163	84	52	35	166
60	59	24	11	93	67	30	13	130	76	47	20	149	84	54	28	160	82	49	31	158
55	57	23	9	87	65	28	11	124	73	42	17	130	80	48	25	154	79	45	28	151
50	54	22	8	81	63	26	10	119	69	39	15	120	79	45	23	148	77	43	26	144
45	50	20	7	74	60	24	8	114	65	36	14	114	77	43	22	142	74	40	24	136
40	48	13	6	67	57	22	7	110	62	34	13	107	75	41	20	136	71	37	21	130
35	45	16	4	60	55	20	5	106	59	31	12	100	72	38	18	129	68	34	20	125
30	42	14	0	54	52	18	4	98	55	28	11	94	70	36	16	123	63	32	17	119
25	38	12	0	47	45	16	0	87	51	24	10	87	67	33	13	117	59	29	16	112
20	34	10	0	38	40	14	0	77	48	21	9	79	61	28	11	110	55	25	11	109
15	31	8	0	28	36	12	0	69	43	18	7	70	51	25	9	103	48	20	9	96
10	26	6	0	21	31	10	0	61	36	15	6	62	50	20	6	80	40	17	6	86
5	16	3	0	15	25	6	0	43	25	9	2	43	40	14	2	61	27	11	3	65
0	0	0	0	0	0	0	0	0	0	0	0	0	0	0	0	0	0	0	0	0

*10 yards = 9.15 meters; 20 yards = 18.29 meters; 30 yards = 27.44 meters.

Note. From "AAHPER skills test manual for archery," by AAHPER, 1966, Washington DC. Copyright 1967 by AAHPER. Reprinted by permission.

Other Archery Tests

Bohn, R.W. (1962). *An achievement test in archery.* Unpublished master's thesis, University of Wisconsin, Madison.

Hyde, E.I. (1937). An achievement scale in archery. *Research Quarterly*, **8**, 108-116.

Ley, K.L. (1960). *Constructing objective test items to measure high school levels of achievement in selected physical education activities.* Unpublished doctoral dissertation, University of Iowa, Iowa City.

McKenzie, R., & Schifflett, B. (1986). *Skill evaluation in a coeducational beginning archery class.* Unpublished paper, San Diego State University.

Reichart, N. (1943). School archery standards. *Journal of Health and Physical Education*, **14**, 81, 124.

Schifflett, B., & Schuman, B.A. (1982). A criterion-referenced test for archery. *Research Quarterly for Exercise and Sport*, **53**, 330-335.

Zabick, R.M., & Jackson, A.S. (1969). Reliability of archery achievement. *Research Quarterly for Exercise and Sport*, **40**, 254-255.

Bowling Tests

Johnson, N.J. (1962). *Tests of achievement in bowling for beginning girl bowlers.* Unpublished master's thesis, University of Colorado, Boulder.

Martin, J.L. (1960). Bowling norms for college men and women. *Research Quarterly*, **31**, 113-116.

Martin, J.L., & Keogh, J. (1964). Bowling norms for college students in elective physical education classes. *Research Quarterly*, **25**, 325-327.

Olson, J.K., & Liba, M.R. (1967). A device for evaluating spot bowling ability. *Research Quarterly*, **38**, 193-201.

Phillips, M., & Summers, D. (1950). Bowling norms and learning curves for college women. *Research Quarterly*, **21**, 377-385.

Bowling

Bowling, one of the oldest games known, has been traced back as far as 7,000 years. The game, originally played with rounded stones, has been called tenpins and ninepins.

Bowling attracts nearly 60 million people, making it one of the most popular participant activities in the United States. Bowling is so popular because it can be done equally well by both sexes, requires little physical exertion, can be quickly learned, is relatively inexpensive, and is a great social mixer. Many bowling centers offer women's leagues in the morning, junior leagues in the afternoon, and competitive adult leagues in the evening. The popularity of bowling has caused many colleges and universities to build bowling centers on campus and offer bowling courses.

Bowling tests are not included in this text because the skills tests merely present norms appropriate only for college students. Bowling teachers should develop their own norms appropriate for their specific age group and skill level of their students.

Cycling

Even though the first bicycles were heavy, cumbersome, and inefficient, their advent in the 1800s changed transportation and recreation for millions of people. Bikes allowed people to travel faster and farther than on foot with a lot less wasted energy. Over the years bicycles have undergone numerous changes, so much so that the early pioneers probably would not recognize modern, 21-gear mountain bikes.

Cycling continues to grow as newer, lighter models and energy consciousness make it enjoyable for all family members. For individuals looking for alternative training techniques, biking is one of the best. If one rides hard enough, tremendous cardiovascular benefits occur without sore knee joints.

Cycling skills typically taught in physical education courses include starting, stopping, gear shifting, braking, turning, and steering. No objective cycling skills tests are available.

Dance

Skills tests to evaluate dance have been hard to develop because most people not only have a difficult time measuring rhythm but also have difficulty defining it. Wagslow (Johnson & Nelson, 1986) suggested criteria and provided ideas for dances that are popular in physical education curricula.

Folk Dance: Three criteria are style of execution and movement, knowledge of steps and sequence as related to music, and the student's rhythm in time with the music.

Square Dance: Three criteria are response to the caller, execution of the movement called for, and movement according to the music's rhythmic pattern.

Social Dance: Two methods of evaluating students in social dance are having students execute learned variations and having students execute variations not learned in class. It is important that students dance in time with the music's rhythm.

Tap Dance: Three criteria are proper execution of movements, memorization of the dance routine, and the student's rhythm in time with the music.

Modern Dance: Two methods of evaluating students in modern dance are having students learn the instructor's set patterns of movement in the preparation for self-expression and the performance of a dance to a poem or music. Students would be evaluated on difficulty, combination of movements, execution, and form.

Dance Tests

Ashton, D. (1953). A gross motor rhythm test. *Research Quarterly, 24,* 253-260.

Briggs, R.A. (1968). *The development of an instrument for assessment of motoric rhythmic performance.* Unpublished master's thesis, University of Missouri, Columbia.

Coppock, D.E. (1968). Development of an objective measure of rhythmic motor response. *Research Quarterly, 39,* 313-316.

Dvorak, S.E. (1967). *A subjective evaluation of fundamental locomotor movement in modern dance using a five-point scale.* Unpublished master's thesis, South Dakota State University, Brookings.

Fial, P.I. (1965). *Prediction of modern dance ability through kinesthetic tests.* Unpublished doctoral dissertation, University of Iowa, Iowa City.

Imel, E.C. (1963). *Construction of an objective motor rhythm skill test.* Unpublished master's thesis, University of Iowa, Iowa City.

Lange, L.M. (1966). *The development of a test of rhythmic response at the elementary level.* Unpublished master's thesis, University of Texas, Austin.

Lemon, E., & Sherbon, E. (1934). A study of the relationship of certain measures of rhythmic ability and motor ability in girls and women. *Research Quarterly Supplement, 5,* 82-85.

McCulloch, M.L. (1955). *The development of a test of rhythmic response through movement of first grade children.* Unpublished doctoral dissertation, University of Oregon, Eugene.

Smoll, F.L. (1973). A rhythmic ability analysis system. *Research Quarterly, 44,* 232-236.

Wagslow, I.F. (1953). An experiment in social dance testing. *Research Quarterly, 30,* 109.

Withers, M.R. (1960). *Measuring creativity of modern dancers.* Unpublished master's thesis, University of Utah, Salt Lake City.

Diving

Diving as we know it today began around the turn of the century in England and Germany. As equipment has improved, with the advent of fiberglass boards, for example, the sport has taken on an artistic element, with divers often performing as quasi gymnasts.

As enclosed, encapsulated, and retractable-roof pools become more common, the once summer-only sports of swimming and diving are becoming year-round sports. And as school physical education programs make greater use of community facilities, more schools are adopting swimming and diving as parts of their curriculum. Since diving became an Olympic event in 1904, Americans have won more gold medals in the springboard and platform events than athletes from any other nation.

It is difficult to develop a skills test in diving because scoring is completely subjective. Subjective scales may work for diving experts, but few physical education teachers fit that description. Rating scales rather than skills tests may be more practical for testing diving achievement. The author found only two diving skills tests.

Bennett Diving Test (Bennett, 1942)

Purpose. To evaluate diving ability.

Validity and Reliability. A validity coefficient of .94 was obtained by comparing test results with the ratings of three expert judges, and a reliability coefficient of .95 was determined by the split-half procedure followed by the Spearman-Brown Prophecy Formula.

Age Level and Sex. Originally conducted with college students. Appropriate for elementary school, junior high school, and senior high school students.

Personnel. Single tester. Nontesting students can be used as recorders and scorers.

Equipment. 1-meter and 3-meter diving boards. Score cards or reporting sheets and pencils.

Space. Swimming pool with a diving well.

Test Items. A series of diving tasks that become progressively more difficult.

1. Standing dive from the edge of the pool: Enter straight headfirst.
2. Standing dive from the edge of the pool with a return to the surface: Enter straight headfirst, keeping hands and arms in same relative position until return to surface.
3. Standing dive from the edge of the pool to the bottom of the pool: Enter straight headfirst and touch the bottom at an 11-foot depth.
4. Sitting tuck position with a fall into the water from the 1-meter board: Remain completely tucked (hands grasping shins and forehead on knees, which are drawn up to chest) until underwater. Any starting position.
5. Standing dive from the board: Enter straight headfirst.
6. Standing feetfirst dive: Body must be in the straight feetfirst position in air and at entry. Jump from board, do not step.
7. Forward approach: Must include at least three steps and a hurdle, landing on both feet. Accompanying arm motion must be smooth; no pauses in entire approach. Toes must be pointed to the board during the hurdle before landing on the end of the board.

8. Running feetfirst dive: Combine requirements of Numbers 7 and 6.
9. Springing the board: Rise from the board at least 6 inches with five consecutive jumps, using the arms to help in gaining height.
10. Rocking chair: Sit on the end of the board facing the water, and by rocking backward with feet over head, gain enough momentum to rock forward headfirst into the water. Enter headfirst.
11. Springing the board with a double tuck position: Same as Number 9 except that a tuck position must be assumed when in the air. Knees must be bent when hands touch shins in tuck position. Do four consecutive tucks.
12. Running front tuck dive: Enter straight headfirst after assuming a tuck position in the air (knees bent, hands on shins).
13. Forward dive over pole hip high: Enter straight headfirst clearing the pole.
14. Elementary front jackknife dive (standing): Bend enough at the hips to have the hands below the knees (though not necessarily touching the legs) at the time of the bend. Enter headfirst.
15. Running jackknife dive: Enter straight headfirst. Keep knees together and straight after leaving the board. Keep wrists below knees at time of jackknife bend.
16. Advanced jackknife dive: Same as Number 15 except that the diver must actually touch ankles or top of arch and must enter water within 6 feet of the end of the board.
17. Elementary back jackknife dive (taken at the side of the board): Enter headfirst with the head entering the water behind the starting point. Must have some bend at the hips.
18. Back jackknife dive: Same as Number 17 except that the dive is taken straight back from the end of the board.
19. Advanced back jackknife dive: Same as Number 18 except that there must be a straight headfirst entry and knees must be kept together and straight after leaving the board.
20. Back approach: Must include at least three steps, correct direction of turn (free leg swings out over the water, not over the board), and no hesitations.
21. Back spring to the water feetfirst: Use arms when springing up from the board; jump, do not step, from the board; and enter the water straight feetfirst.

22. Back spring to the board: From the back stance, spring upward from the board (using arms smoothly to assist) with knees straight and toes pointed to the board. Toes must be at least 6 inches above the board when in the air. Return to the board.

23. Back bend: From the back stance position, bend backward and enter the water headfirst.

24. Elementary back dive: Same as Number 23, but hold straight headfirst position in air and at entry.

25. Back dive: Same as Number 24 but use some preparatory spring with smooth use of arms.

26. Advanced back dive: Same as Number 25, but done in two parts.
    1. Keep head up, eyes forward, as body is rising from the board.
    2. Head is thrown back when the crest of the height is reached. Enter straight headfirst within 6 feet of the board (no twist). Keep toes pointed throughout the dive.

27. Standing forward dive with an arch: When in the air look distinctly forward and up. Look down just before entering straight headfirst. Lead with hands throughout the dive.

28. Butterfly dive: Same as Number 27, either running or standing, but with hands on hips when in the air. Enter straight headfirst.

29. Running swan dive: Must have body arched in the air. No body bends, arms above shoulder height and extended to sides, head up. The regular position of the swan dive in the air must be attained even if only for a moment. Enter headfirst.

30. Advanced running swan dive: Same as Number 29, entering straight headfirst.

31. Running forward half twist, feetfirst: Turn at least 180 degrees and enter straight feetfirst.

32. Quarter twist: Assume a distinct swan position in the air, followed by a turn on the long axis of the body of at least 90 degrees. (Shoulders determine degree of turn.) Enter headfirst.

33. Half twist: Same as Number 31, but turn at least 180 degrees.

34. Jackknife with a quarter twist: Assume a distinct jackknife position in the air, followed by a turn of at least 90 degrees. Enter headfirst.

35. Elementary jackknife with a half twist: Same as Number 34 but turn at least 180 degrees.

36. Neck stand: Lie with back to board and head at the water end of the board. Bring feet up over the head, aim them toward the water, and enter the water feetfirst. Hands must be at sides at time of feetfirst entry.

37. Handstand dive: Enter straight headfirst. Entire body must clear the board.

38. Handstand feetfirst dive: Enter feetfirst after assuming the handstand position on board and holding on until feet complete the arc and point toward the water.

39. Rocking chair (3-meter board): Enter headfirst, see Number 10.

40. Neck stand (3-meter board): Enter feetfirst, see Number 36.

41. Forward fall dive (3-meter board): From an erect, forward-standing position with arms extended over head, fall forward, entering the water headfirst. Remain perfectly still throughout the fall.

42. Backward fall dive (3-meter board): Same as Number 41 except that the fall is taken from a backward standing position.

43. Tuck and roll with a spring from edge of pool (a forward somersault in the air from the edge of the pool, turning in the tuck position): Turn at least far enough forward so that the head clears the water and the back strikes the water first.

44. Forward somersault (1-meter board): Turn a forward somersault in the air so that the feet hit the water first.

45. Backward somersault: Turn a backward somersault in the air so the feet hit the water first.

46. Half gainer: Only requirement is to enter headfirst.

47. Full gainer: Only requirement is to enter feetfirst.

48. Back half twist: From the back stance position, make a half twist, entering the water straight headfirst. Do not twist until after leaving the board.

49. Forward 1-1/2 somersault: Only requirement is to enter headfirst.

50. Perform any of the standard dives (including the handstand dive and the handstand feetfirst dive) from the 3-meter board. No requirements as to form except that the dive be recognizable to the judges and that it have a headfirst or feetfirst entry depending on

the dive selected. If, for example, a jackknife dive is done with very little bend at the hips, it would not be evident to the judges whether it was intended to be a jackknife or a plain forward dive.

Preparation. Secure the diving well so that non-divers are kept out of the testing area, prepare the diving board with a proper flex, and prepare score cards.

Directions. All students start with Dive 1 and move through the test as far as possible. Divers may skip dives. The following definitions clarify certain terms in the test item list:

Headfirst: Implies that hands, head, hips, knees, and feet enter the water in consecutive order.

Bellyflop: Occurs when hands, head, hips, knees, and feet enter the water simultaneously or nearly so.

Straight Headfirst: Means a near perfect vertical headfirst dive with the feet entering the same or nearly the same opening in the water as the head. The body should be straight with no bend.

Feetfirst: Implies feet, knees, hips, shoulders, and head enter the water in consecutive order.

Straight feetfirst: Means a near perfect vertical feetfirst entry with the head entering the same opening in the water as the feet. There should be no body bend, and the hands should touch the sides of the body.

Scoring. The successful completion of a dive is awarded 1 point; an unsuccessful dive earns no points. The final score is the total of points earned on the 50 test items completed.

Norms. Not available.

Another Diving Test

Foster, J.T. (1956). *Alternate procedures for judging and scoring competition diving.* Unpublished master's thesis, University of Iowa, Iowa City.

Figure Skating

Because figure skating requires unique facilities, it is seldom taught in junior or senior high schools. However the advent of artificial ice and the growth of heated ice rinks increase the possibility of adding it to the physical education curriculum. In cold northern climates, many communities flood a playground or clear snow from a lake or river for skating enthusiasts. Teachers looking for new activities that take them outside in winter are encouraged to add figure skating to their programs.

Carriere Skating Test (Carriere, 1969)

Purpose. To evaluate figure skating ability.

Validity and Reliability. A validity coefficient of .90 was determined by correlating judges' ratings and the number of items passed; a reliability coefficient of .97 was determined by the split-half method.

Age Level and Sex. Junior high school and senior high school students.

Personnel. Single tester. Nontesting students can be used as recorders and scorers.

Equipment. Ice skates. If an ice hockey rink is not used, preparation equipment would include a tape measure and marking material. Scoring equipment includes score cards or recording sheets and pencils.

Space. An ice hockey rink with official markings.

Test Items. A series of skating tasks that progress in difficulty. Use the following abbreviations:

R - right   F - forward   I - inside edge
L - left   B - backward   O - outside edge

Forward:

1. Skate 60 feet in any manner.
2. Stroke and parallel glide alternately for 60 feet; start with T push-off.
3. T push-off and cover 60 feet with three more strokes.
4. Take three strokes (R-L-R or L-R-L) and glide 30 feet on one skate with skating knee slightly bent and head up.

Backward Sculling:

Each sculling motion must start with feet less than 6 inches apart.

5. Scull with both feet for 60 feet in a straight line.
6. Scull around face-off circle with R scull and L glide. Repeat with L scull and R glide.
7. Scull straight with alternate feet for 60 feet; gliding skate must remain on red or blue line.
8. Scull straight with alternate feet and glide straight on either skate for 30 feet with skating knee slightly bent, back straight, arms down and out to the side.

Stops:

9. Skate five strokes forward and execute three consecutive stops using either snowplow, T, or side parallel stops.
10. Skate forward from one face-off circle and stop on the other face-off mark.

Turns:

11. Forward-to-backward turn on two feet; skate four F strokes, parallel glide on both skates, half turn R, and stop. Repeat with half turn L.
12. Forward-to-backward three turn on both feet and backward-to-forward turn changing from one foot to the other around face-off circle. Preliminary strokes, parallel glide, clockwise (RFO and LFI), three turn to RBI and LBO, shift weight to left skate, and turn to RFO. Repeat counterclockwise.

Forward Curves:

13. Four alternate, parallel glide half-circles (10-foot radius): Push off on RFO from line; glide with feet parallel around half-circle and back to line; change at line to LFO and parallel glide; change again to RFO and LFO at line. Lean with body straight from ankles up.
14. Ten alternate single strokes along straight line: Push off on RFO, curve back to line, shift to LFO (and back) four times.
15. Ten alternate single FI strokes along straight line: Same as Item 14 but on single inside edges.

Backward Curves:

16. Four alternate, backward, parallel glide half-circles (5-foot radius): Like Item 13 but backward; push off on RBO from line, glide around half-circle with feet parallel, change at line to LBO, and parallel glide; repeat. No toe scratches.
17. Ten alternate single BO strokes along straight line: Push off on RBO and curve back to line, shift to LBO, and so on.
18. Ten alternate single BI strokes along straight line: Same as Item 17 but on single inside edges.

Forward Crossovers:

19. Five forward crossovers around face-off circle, clockwise and counterclockwise (preliminary strokes permissible), stop (no stepping).
20. T push-off, complete circuit of face-off with four (or fewer) crossovers, clockwise or counterclockwise. Must show a bent skating knee, outward thrust with trailing skate, outside arm and shoulder forward, and inside arm back.

Advanced Turns:

21. RFO three turn and LFO three turn: Start with two or three preliminary strokes, turn from RBO to RBI, and hold RBI for 3 seconds, then parallel glide, and stop. Repeat with LBO to LBI turn. Movement must be straight or around face-off circle.
22. Four consecutive, alternate, small three turns in a straight line and stop: T push-off, RFO to RBI to LFO and LBI and repeat, stop.
23. Controlled three turn, RFO to RBI or LFO to LFI: T push-off, glide for 3 seconds on RFO preparing to turn with arms and shoulders, turn to RBI and glide for 3 seconds going back to line, and stop. Skater must prepare for turn with arms and shoulders and come out strongly checked (free arm, shoulder, and hip back).
24. Forward inside open Mohawk: Start with three or four preliminary strokes from LFO, glide for 3 seconds on RFI, change to LBI (inside R), and glide for 3 seconds, then parallel glide, skate backward to starting line, and stop. May be done to opposite side.

25. Forward inside closed Mohawk: Start like Item 24, RFI glide, L goes behind to LBI and glide 3 seconds, then parallel glide, 3 backward strokes, and stop.

Advanced Stops:

26. Forward T stop: Skate 3 or 4 strokes, short glide, and stop, alternate R and L braking skate behind at R angle and parallel to shoulders. No angle dragging on inside edge of blade, arms held down and out to the side.
27. Parallel side stop (hockey stop): Take 10 to 15 strokes with increasing speed, parallel glide, and stop (hold position 1 second). Shoulders must face direction of travel; skates are parallel and knees strongly bent.

Jumps:

28. Three bunny hops: Executed consecutively or alternated with one or two strokes between each jump. Free leg thrown forward, landing on toe pick, then push from toe pick into that of skating foot blade, stroke, and stop.
29. Waltz jump: Start with preliminary strokes, glide on a FO, swing free leg forward, push up with skating foot, make half turn in air, land on opposite BO, glide and stop. Free arm forward and head facing the initial direction. The jump is done on a curve.

Spins:

30. Three complete two-foot spins and stop: Spin on the flat of the blades without traveling on ice.

Intermediate and Advanced:

31. Five backward crossovers around face-off circle, clockwise and counterclockwise. When skating counterclockwise the left foot never loses contact with the ice and vice versa for clockwise (no toe scratch).
32. Six alternate sequences of progressive and chasse steps along the blue line with a count of six for each sequence (2-1-3): Curves should be equal size and about a third of a circle of 10-foot radius.
33. Six alternate FO swing rolls: Same as Item 32 but the free leg is extended and swinging from the back to the front of the body. Free toe pointed down and turned slightly out.
34. Forward change of edges on one foot: A moving start or start from a rest may be used to change from RFO edge to RFI. Curves should be equal sizes and change on blue or red line.
35. Shoot the duck: Take as many preliminary strokes as desired before going into a sitting position with free leg extended in front, head up, back straight. Glide for 5 seconds and come back to initial upright position, stroke, and stop.
36. Forward spiral: Start with preliminary strokes, glide on one foot, bring extended free leg up and behind. Head and free foot should be at least at the level with the upper part of the seat. Arms are extended to the side of the body. Glide for 5 seconds; bring free foot on ice, stroke, and stop.
37. Four alternate FI curves along an axis (blue or red line): Push off from rest. Free shoulder and arm are held low and in leading position. Skating shoulder and arm are held back. The free foot is in front at the middle of the curve. Approaching the long axis, square shoulder to the line of travel. Size of the curves same as Item 32.
38. Four alternate BO curves along axis (red or blue line): Push off from rest. Free shoulder and arm in front. Skating shoulder and arm in leading position. Body rotates; free leg is behind at the middle of the curve. Approaching the long axis, free side is in open position. Size of curves same as Item 32.
39. Full circle on one foot (outside edge): Push off from rest position to a forward outside edge, complete the face-off circle circuit on one foot, and stop.
40. Forward outside eight: Push off a right forward outside complete circle and stroke into the left forward outside edge crossing the transverse axis. Stay close to the marker on the ice (a 1-foot range is allowed only). Diameter of circles: 15 feet.

Preparation. No special facility preparation is needed if conducted on a hockey rink. You must prepare score cards.

Directions. Each student should execute as many test items as possible. All items are of equal value and may be attempted in any order and any number of times. Students must understand the following abbreviations and terms:

R - right   F - forward   I - inside edge
L - left   B - backward   O - outside edge

1. Inside shoulder: Shoulder toward the inside of the curve.
2. Employed skate: Skate on the ice.
3. Free skate: Skate off the ice.
4. Free arm: Arm that is forward when the free leg is back.
5. Leading leg: When skating backwards, the free leg is extended in back of the body.
6. Continuous axis: An imaginary line running the length of the rink.
7. Lobe: Any step or sequence of steps on one side of the continuous axis.
8. Transverse axis: An imaginary line intersecting the continuous axis at a right angle.

Scoring. Each item completed earns the skater 1 point. The final score is the total of points on the 40-item test. An attempt is considered failed for these mistakes: falling or having to recover, not covering distance in specified time, not holding stop for 3 seconds, using a toe pick when not allowed, and not changing feet on the line when specified.

Norms. Not available.

Other Figure Skating Tests

Leaming, T.W. (1959). *A measure of endurance of young speed skaters.* Unpublished master's thesis, University of Illinois at Urbana-Champaign.

Moore, K.F. (1967). *An objective evaluation system for judging free skating routines.* Unpublished master's thesis, Michigan State University, East Lansing.

Recknagel, D. (1945). A test of beginners in figure skating. *Journal of Health and Physical Education,* **16**, 91-92.

Golf

Golf, one of the oldest of the modern sports, is believed to have begun in Scotland about 500 years ago with St. Andrew's as the first course. The original "links" were tracts of land that linked the waterline of the seashore with lands further inland.

The organization of golf clubs in the United States began in the late 1700s, but golf as we know it today began in the early 1900s. The popularity of golf is evident. Each year the number of new golf enthusiasts grows, and new golf courses are developed. Many colleges and universities own golf courses.

Golf is a fitting activity for physical education programs. First, golf offers lifelong pleasure because it can be enjoyed at any age. Second, golf is challenging yet offers a handicapping system to equalize the skills of various players. Third, golf provides a unique social atmosphere on courses that are markedly different in variety and beauty. Finally, golf can be an inexpensive physical education activity because most of the equipment can be borrowed from students' parents.

Four skills are tested in golf: pitching, driving, middle iron, and putting. Outdoor tests for driving and middle iron play require large open spaces, while putting tests require putting greens. Schools often have neither large open spaces nor putting surfaces, which presents a testing roadblock. Tests described here include all skills except putting.

Nelson Golf Pitching Test (Nelson, 1967)

Purpose. To evaluate short iron ability in golf.

Validity and Reliability. Validity coefficients of .79 and .86 were obtained with test scores compared with actual scores and with judges' ratings, respectively. A reliability coefficient of .83 was found using the odd-even approach.

Age Level and Sex. Originally conducted with college students. Appropriate for junior high school and senior high school students.

Personnel. Two people are needed at each testing station. One person spots and calls where balls land, and the second person records scores.

Equipment. Golf clubs (8 iron, 9 iron, or wedge), golf balls, and baskets. Preparation equipment includes a measuring tape, marking material (chalk), a flag stick, and two cones. Scoring equipment include score cards or recording sheets and pencils.

Space. A testing area approximately 60 yards by 25 yards.

Test Item. The short iron pitch shot.

Preparation. Each testing station should be set up as shown in Figure 4.2. Measure and mark a restraining line 20 yards from a hitting line and target that has its center 20 yards from the

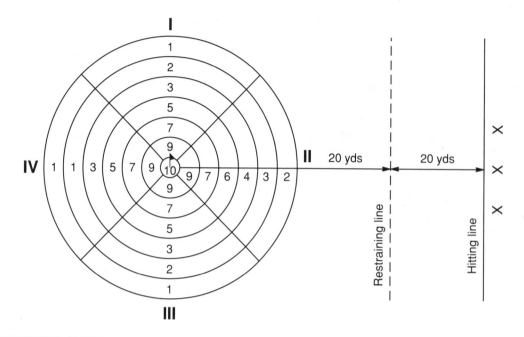

Figure 4.2 Field and target markings for the Nelson Golf Pitching Test.
Note. From ''An achievement test for golf,'' by J.K. Nelson, 1967, unpublished study, Louisiana State University, Baton Rouge, LA. Copyright 1967 by author. Reprinted by permission.

restraining line. The target is a series of concentric circles with each circle's diameter 10 feet larger than the previous circle. The inside circle is 6 feet in diameter and has a flag stick as its center. Subsequent circles have diameters of 16, 26, 36, 46, 56, and 66 feet. Additionally, the target is divided in four equal segments. Point values are shown in Figure 4.2.

Directions. As many as four students at a time can line up at the hitting line and take the test. Each student is permitted to hit three practice balls and then 10 test shots. Students try to hit shots as close to the flag stick as possible. Whiffs are counted as test shots. To be a legal hit, the ball must be in the air until it passes the restraining line. Shots that land before the restraining line and roll to the target count as attempts but earn no points.

Spotters are assigned to each student being tested. It is a spotter's responsibility to call out to the recorder where shots land. Spotters and recorders should be located near the target so they can easily communicate. Hitters should be encouraged not to hit at the same time.

Scoring. Points are awarded according to where golf balls come to rest in the target area. Balls resting on lines are awarded the higher point value. The final score is the total point value for 10 trials. A perfect score is 100 points.

Norms. Not available.

Schick-Berg Indoor Golf Test (Schick & Berg, 1983)

Purpose. To evaluate 5-iron ability in golf.

Validity and Reliability. A validity coefficient of .84 was reported using a measure of the best of three scores. Reliability coefficients of .91 and .97 were found for test-retest and single test administration.

Age Level and Sex. Originally conducted with junior high school boys. Appropriate for junior high school and senior high school students.

Personnel. Two people are needed at each testing station. One person spots and calls where balls land, and the second person records scores.

Equipment. 5-iron golf clubs, plastic golf balls, and hitting mats. Preparation equipment includes a measuring tape, marking tape, and a cone. Scoring equipment includes score cards or recording sheets and pencils.

Space. Testing stations require an area approximately 45 feet by 70 feet.

Test Item. The 5-iron shot.

Preparation. Each testing station should be prepared as shown in Figure 4.3. A hitting mat is placed in the center and 1 foot from the front edge of the testing grid. A target cone is placed at the other end, directly across the grid, 68 feet from the hitting mat. Beginning at the hitting mat end of the testing grid, the first row of three scoring rectangles are measured and marked at 15 feet by 23 feet each. The second, third, and fourth rows are measured and marked at 15 feet by 15 feet. The back side of the fourth row is left open. The rectangles and squares are given point values as shown.

Directions. Students being tested assume a hitting position on the hitting mat. They attempt to hit plastic golf balls as far and as straight as possible,

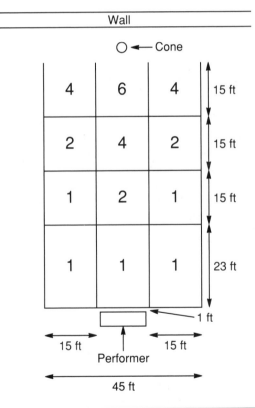

Figure 4.3 Testing grid for the Schick-Berg Indoor Golf Test.

Note. From "Indoor golf skill test for junior high school boys," by J. Schick and N.G. Berg, 1983, *Research Quarterly for Exercise and Sport,* **54**(1), 75-78. Copyright 1983 by AAHPERD. Reprinted by permission.

aiming for the target cone. Students are allowed two practice trials and then 20 consecutive test trials. Practice swings are permitted for each trial.

Scoring. Points are awarded according to where balls first land in the scoring grid. Balls landing on a line are awarded the higher point value. Balls traveling beyond the fourth row but in line with the scoring grid are awarded points as if those lines were extended. Topped balls that enter the scoring grid are awarded 1 point. Whiffs and balls landing outside the scoring grid earn no points. The final score is the total of the 20 trials. A perfect score is 120 points.

Norms. Not available.

Vanderhoof Golf Test (Vanderhoof, 1956)

Purpose. To evaluate driving and 5-iron ability in golf.

Validity and Reliability. Validity coefficients of .66 and .71 as reported for the 5-iron and drive tests, respectively, were computed by correlating test scores with subjective ratings of golf form and swing. Reliability coefficients of .84 and .90 as reported for the 5-iron and drive tests, respectively, were computed by the odd-even approach followed by the Spearman-Brown Prophecy Formula.

Age Level and Sex. Originally conducted with college women. Appropriate for junior high school and senior high school students.

Personnel. Two people are needed at each testing station. One person spots and calls where balls land, and the second person records scores.

Equipment. Woods, 5-irons, and plastic balls. Preparation equipment includes a measuring tape and marking tape, hitting mats, a cone, two standards, and rope. Scoring equipment includes score cards or recording sheets and pencils.

Space. The testing station requires an area 74 feet by 13 feet without overhead obstructions.

Test Items. The driving test and the 5-iron test.

Preparation. Testing stations should be prepared as shown in Figure 4.4. A restraining line is marked at one end of the testing station. Fourteen

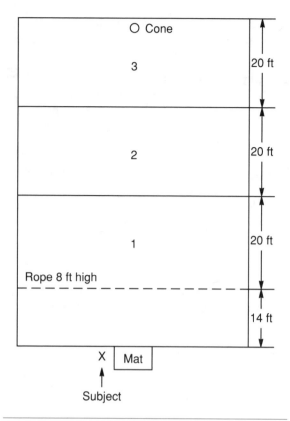

Figure 4.4 Scoring area for the Vanderhoof Golf Test. *Note.* From ''Beginning golf achievement test,'' by E.R. Vanderhoof, 1956, unpublished master's thesis, University of Iowa, Iowa City, IA. Copyright 1956 by the author. Reprinted by permission.

Table 4.3 Norms for the Vanderhoof Drive Test

T score	Raw score (Total of 15 trials)
75	45
70	41
65	38
60	33
55	28
50	24
45	19
40	13
35	9
30	7
25	4

*Based on scores of 110 college women.

Note. From ''Beginning golf achievement test,'' by E.R. Vanderhoof, 1956, unpublished master's thesis, University of Iowa, Iowa City, IA. Copyright 1956 by the author. Reprinted by permission.

feet from and parallel to the restraining line an 8-foot high rope is extended across the scoring grid. The scoring grid is marked into three scoring sections at 20-foot intervals. A target cone is placed at the far end of the scoring grid 74 feet from the restraining line. A hitting mat is placed behind the restraining line.

Directions. For both test items, students stand on the hitting mat, take as many practice swings as desired and, when ready, hit balls toward the target.

Scoring. Both the drive test and the 5-iron test are scored in the same manner. Zero to 3 points are awarded according to where balls originally land on the scoring grid. Balls must pass under the extended rope and land in the scoring grid to earn points. Two successive topped balls count as only one trial with a zero score. The final score is the number of points for 15 trials. A perfect score is 45 points.

Norms. T scores for the drive test appear in Table 4.3.

Benson Golf Test (Benson, 1963)

Purpose. To evaluate 5-iron ability in golf.

Validity and Reliability. A validity coefficient of .94 was obtained by correlating actual golf scores with distance and flight deviation scores. A reliability coefficient of .90 was computed using the odd-even approach followed by the Spearman-Brown Prophecy Formula.

Age Level and Sex. Appropriate for junior high school and senior high school students.

Personnel. Two people are needed at each testing station. One person spots and calls where balls land, and the second person records scores.

Equipment. Five-iron golf clubs, golf balls, and baskets. Preparation equipment includes a measuring tape and marking materials. Scoring equipment includes score cards or recording sheets and pencils.

Space. The testing area is approximately 150 yards by 100 yards.

Test Items. Hitting the 5-iron for distance and for accuracy.

Preparation. Testing stations should be prepared as shown in Figure 4.5. Distance markers should

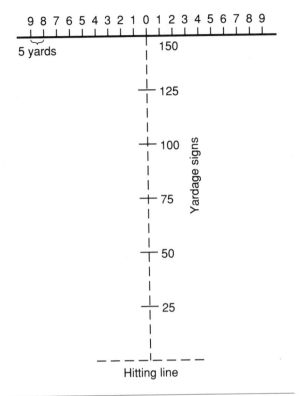

Figure 4.5 Field markings for the Benson Golf Test.
Note. From "Measuring golf ability through use of a number five iron test," by D.W. Benson, 1963, paper presented at the California Association for Health, Physical Education, and Recreation, Long Beach, CA. Copyright 1963 by the author. Reprinted by permission.

be placed in a line every 25 yards between the hitting line and the 150-yard line. On the 150-yard line, place nine "deviation signs" (numbered 1 through 9) every 5 yards on each side of the midpoint.

Directions. Subjects stand behind the hitting line with 25 golf balls each. Using a 5-iron, they take five practice shots. Following the practice, 20 shots are taken and scored. Students taking scores are located behind the hitters, in line with the 150-yard marker.

Scoring. For each of the 20 shots, scorers record two numbers. One is an estimate of how far the ball traveled in flight; the second is how far the ball deviates from the intended line of flight. Final scores are the averages for the 20 shots.

Norms. Not available.

Other Golf Tests

Autrey, E.B. (1937). *A battery of tests for measuring playing ability in golf.* Unpublished master's thesis, University of Wisconsin, Madison.

Brown, H.S. (1969). A test battery for evaluating golf skills. *Texas Association for Health, Physical Education and Recreation,* **May,** 28-29.

Clevett, M.A. (1931). An experiment in teaching methods of golf. *Research Quarterly,* **2,** 104-112.

Cochrane, J.F. (1960). *The construction of an indoor golf skills test as a measure of golfing ability.* Unpublished master's thesis, University of Minnesota, Minneapolis.

Coffey, M. (1946). *Achievement tests in golf.* Unpublished master's thesis, University of Iowa, Iowa City.

Cotton, D., Thomas, J.R., & Plaster, T. (1972, March). A plastic ball test for golf iron skill. Unpublished study presented at the American Association for Health, Physical Education, Recreation and Dance National Convention, Houston, TX.

Davis, C.M. (1960). *The use of the golf tee in teaching beginning golf.* Unpublished master's thesis, University of Michigan, Ann Arbor.

Green, K.W. (1974). *The development of a battery of golf skill tests for college men.* Unpublished doctoral dissertation, University of Arkansas, Fayetteville.

Green, K.N., East, W.B., & Hensley, L.D. (1987). A golf skills test battery for college males and females. *Research Quarterly,* **58,** 72-76.

Ley, K.L. (1960). *Constructing objective test items to measure high school levels of achievement in selected physical education activities.* Unpublished doctoral dissertation, University of Iowa, Iowa City.

McKee, M.E. (1950). A test for the full-swing shot in golf. *Research Quarterly,* **21,** 40-46.

Olson, A.C. (1958). *The development of objective tests of the ability of freshmen and sophomore college women to drive and to pitch a plastic golf ball in a limited indoor area.* Unpublished master's thesis, University of Colorado, Boulder.

Reece, P.A. (1971). *A comparison of the scores made on an outdoor golf test and the scores made on*

(continued)

Other Golf Tests (continued)

an indoor golf test by college women. Unpublished master's thesis, University of Colorado, Boulder.

Rowlands, D.J. (1974). *A golf skills test battery.* Unpublished doctoral dissertation, University of Utah, Salt Lake City.

Watts, H. (1942). *Construction and evaluation of a target on testing the approach shot in golf.* Unpublished master's thesis, University of Wisconsin, Madison.

West, C., & Thorpe, J.A. (1968). Construction and validation of an eight iron approach test. *Research Quarterly,* **39,** 1115-1120.

Wood, J.I. (1933). *A study for the purpose of setting up the specifications of a golf driving cage target and test for the mid-iron and the brassie clubs.* Unpublished master's thesis, University of Wisconsin, Madison.

Gymnastics

Gymnastics is judged subjectively and so the expertise of the teacher or test administrator affects scoring in this sport. Because of liability concerns and the lack of special gymnastics equipment, many junior and senior high schools elect to teach tumbling rather than gymnastics in their physical education programs. Still, many schools do teach gymnastics.

The impact of successful Olympians Olga Korbut and Mary Lou Retton has tremendously increased the number of gymnastic participants and gymnastic clubs. In many places gymnastic clubs have replaced physical education programs as the introduction site for gymnastics.

In coed physical education classes gymnastics testing may be difficult because of different events for males and females. For males, events include the floor exercise, pommel horse, still rings, long horse vaulting, parallel bars, and horizontal bar. For females, events include side horse vaulting, uneven parallel bars, balance beam, and floor exercise. The two tests listed in this text cover balance beam, floor exercise, uneven parallel bars, vault, and tumbling.

Ellenbrand Gymnastics Skills Test (Ellenbrand, 1973)

Purpose. To evaluate balance beam, floor exercise, uneven parallel bars, and vaulting ability in gymnastics.

Validity and Reliability. Concurrent validity coefficients, as determined by correlating scores of three judges of varied experience with the ratings of two experienced gymnastics judges, were reported to be .93, .97, .99, .88, and .97 for the balance beam, floor exercise, uneven parallel bars, vaulting, and the total test, respectively. Test-retest reliability coefficients of .99, .97, .99, .97, and .98 were reported for the balance beam, floor exercise, uneven parallel bars, vaulting, and the total test, respectively.

Age Level and Sex. Originally designed for college women. Appropriate for junior high school and senior high school students.

Personnel. One person is needed to record the difficulty rating for each skill. Spotters are needed for each event.

Equipment. A balance beam, 60-foot length of mats, uneven parallel bars, a vaulting horse, and a Reuther board. Preparation equipment includes a measuring tape, chalk for hands, crash pads for landing, and practice mats. Scoring equipment includes score cards or recording sheets and pencils.

Space. A gymnasium designed for gymnastics.

Test Items. Sixteen items performed on four gymnastic events: balance beam, uneven parallel bars, floor exercise, and vaulting.

Preparation. Set up equipment and prepare score cards.

Directions. Each event is scored separately, but all items in each event must be performed in the order given with a minimum of connecting movements between skills. Spotters should be present, but a student gets a zero if a spotter assists with a movement. A skill that is performed poorly or missed may be repeated immediately with no deduction. If a student falls, he or she should remount and continue the performance.

The administrator acting as recorder lists the difficulty rating of each item on the score sheet before each student begins. As a student performs, the recorder registers the execution rating.

Each student selects one skill under each item representative of his or her skills in that event. Events and test items are listed below.

Balance Beam Event: The beam may be approached from any direction and mounted with the aid of a Reuther board. Positioning of arms is optional, but arm movements are considered part of the form and may detract from the execution rating. Select one skill from each test item.

Test Item 1. *Mounts*

Difficulty	Skills
1.0	a. Front support mount
2.0	b. Single knee mount
3.0	c. Single leg squat on
3.0	d. Straddle on
4.0	e. Forward roll mount
5.0	f. Single leg step on (to stand)
6.0	g. Handstand mount

Test Item 2. *Locomotor Skills*

Difficulty	Skills
.5	a. Slide forward or sideward
1.0	b. Walk forward
2.0	c. Plie walk (dip step) forward
3.0	d. Step-hop forward (skip step)
4.0	e. Walk backward
5.0	f. Run forward
6.0	g. Cross-step sideward

Test Item 3. *Heights*

Difficulty	Skills
.5	a. Hop on one foot
1.0	b. Two-foot jump
2.0	c. Jump with change of legs
3.0	d. Hitch kick forward
3.0	e. Cat leap
4.0	f. Stride leap
4.0	g. Tuck or arch jump
5.0	h. Stag or split leap
6.0	i. Series of leaps or jumps

Test Item 4. *Turns*

Difficulty	Skills
.5	a. Half turn standing (both feet)
1.0	b. Half turn squat
2.0	c. Half turn on one foot
3.0	d. Full turn on two feet (walking turn)
4.0	e. Full turn on one foot
5.0	f. Jump with half turn
5.0	g. One-and-one-half turn on one foot
6.0	h. Leap with half turn

Test Item 5. *Tumbling Skills—On beam*

Difficulty	Skills
.5	a. Back lying position
1.0	b. Roll backward to touch toes over head and return
2.0	c. Back shoulder roll
2.0	d. Forward shoulder roll
3.0	e. Forward head roll to back lying
4.0	f. Shoulder stand
4.0	g. Forward head roll to feet
4.0	h. Bridge position (push to a back arch position)
4.0	i. Cartwheel off or walkover off
4.5	j. Handstand one-quarter turn dismount
5.0	k. Cartwheel on
5.0	l. Back walkover on
5.5	m. Handstand forward roll
5.5	n. Front walkover on
5.5	o. Free forward roll
6.0	p. Series of cartwheels or walkovers
6.0	q. One-handed cartwheel or walkover
6.0	r. Handspring on (forward or backward)
7.0	s. Aerials on

Floor Exercise Event: Lay out a length of mat on which to perform skills. A return trip may be used if necessary. Connecting skills may be added if needed for preparation of a selected skill. Extra steps and runs should be avoided because they detract from the execution rating.

Test Item 6. *Tumbling Skills—Rolls*

Difficulty	Skills
.5	a. Forward roll to stand
.5	b. Backward roll to knees
1.0	c. Back roll to stand
2.0	d. Pike forward or backward roll
2.0	e. Straddle roll (forward or backward)
3.0	f. Dive forward roll (pike)
4.0	g. Handstand forward roll
4.0	h. Back roll to headstand
4.5	i. Back extension
5.0	j. Dive forward roll (layout)

6.0	k. Back tuck somersault (aerial)
6.5	l. Back pike somersault
6.5	m. Forward tuck somersault
7.0	n. Back layout somersault
8.0	o. Somersault with a twist

Test Item 7. *Tumbling Skills—Springs*

Difficulty	Skills
1.0	a. Handstand snap-down
2.0	b. Round-off
2.5	c. Neck spring (kip)
3.0	d. Headspring
3.5	e. Front handspring to squat
4.0	f. Front handspring arch to stand
4.5	g. Front handspring walk-out
5.0	h. Back handspring
5.0	i. Front handspring on one hand or with a change of legs
5.5	j. Series of front handsprings
6.0	k. Series of back handsprings
6.5	l. Back handspring to kip (cradle)
6.5	m. Back handspring with twist

Test Item 8. *Acrobatic Skills*

Difficulty	Skills
1.0	a. Mule kick (three-quarter handstand)
1.0	b. Bridge (back arch position)
2.0	c. Handstand
2.0	d. Cartwheel
2.5	e. Backbend from standing
3.0	f. Front limber
3.0	g. One-handed cartwheel
4.0	h. Walkovers (forward and backward)
4.0	i. Dive cartwheel
4.0	j. Tinsica
4.5	k. Dive walkover
5.0	l. Handstand with half turn or straddle-down to a sit
5.0	m. One-handed walkovers
6.0	n. Butterfly (side aerial)
7.0	o. Aerial cartwheel or walkover

Test Item 9. *Dance Skills*

Difficulty	Skills
1.0	a. Half turn standing (one foot), run, leap
2.0	b. Half turn, step, hitch kick forward, step, leap
3.0	c. Half turn, slide, tour jeté, hitch kick
4.0	d. Full turn (one foot), step, leap, step, leap
5.0	e. Full turn, tour jeté, cabriole (beat kick forward)
6.0	f. One-and-one-half turn, step, leap, step, leap with a change of legs

Uneven Parallel Bars Event: Connecting stunts may be added as preparation for selected skills. Dismounting between items is allowed but not necessary.

Test Item 10. *Kips*

Difficulty	Skills
1.0	a. Single knee swing-up
2.0	b. Double leg stem rise to high bar
3.0	c. Single leg stem rise to high bar
4.0	d. Kip between bars from sit on low bar
4.5	e. Glide kip with single leg shoot-through
5.0	f. Glide kip
5.5	g. Glide kip, regrasp high bar
5.5	h. Drop, glide kip
6.0	i. Kip from long hang
6.5	j. Rear or reverse kip

Test Item 11. *Casts*

Difficulty	Skills
.5	a. Cast rearward off low bar to stand
1.0	b. Cast and return to bar
2.0	c. Cast to squat (one hand on low bar, one hand on high bar)

3.0	d. Cast, single leg shoot-through
4.0	e. Cast to long hang (from high bar)
4.5	f. Cast to squat, stoop, or straddle stand on either bar
5.0	g. Cast, half-turn to catch high bar
5.0	h. Eagle catch
5.5	i. From front support on high bar facing low bar, cast to handstand on low bar
6.0	j. Cast, full turn to regrasp either bar

Test Item 12. *Hip Circles*

Difficulty	Skills
1.0	a. Forward somersault over high bar to a hang
2.0	b. Back pullover on high bar or low bar
3.0	c. Back hip circle
4.0	d. Forward hip circle
5.0	e. Forward hip circle, regrasp high bar
5.0	f. Flying back hip circle (hands on high bar, circle low bar)
6.0	g. Free back hip circle to hang
6.0	h. From a seat circle backward on high bar, release to a front support on low bar

Test Item 13. *Underswings*

Difficulty	Skills
1.0	a. From sit on low bar, facing high bar, underswing dismount
2.0	b. From front support, half hip circle backward (underswing)
3.0	c. Half sole circle backward to dismount
3.5	d. Underswing on high bar to dismount over low bar
4.0	e. Sole circle backward or forward to regrasp high bar
4.5	f. Underswing on high bar to dismount over low bar with half twist

5.0	g. Straddle or sole circle backward, half turn to regrasp high bar in a hang
5.5	h. Straddle or flank cut on return swing of half seat circle backward
6.0	i. Straddle cut-and-catch

Vaulting Event: Two different vaults with varying difficulty values must be selected for performance. The Reuther board should be used for take-off, and may be adjusted to any distance from the horse.

Test Item 14. *Vault*

Difficulty	Skills
1.0	a. Knee mount
2.0	b. Squat mount
2.5	c. Straddle mount
3.0	d. Squat vault
3.5	e. Flank vault
4.0	f. Straddle vault
4.0	g. Wolf vault
4.5	h. Rear vault
5.0	i. Front vault
6.0	j. Thief vault
6.5	k. Headspring vault
7.0	l. Straddle half twist
9.0	m. Horizontal squat
9.5	n. Horizontal straddle
10.0	o. Horizontal stoop
11.0	p. Layout squat
11.5	q. Layout straddle
12.0	r. Layout stoop
13.0	s. Handspring vault
13.0	t. Giant cartwheel
14.0	u. Hecht vault
15.0	v. Yamashita
15.0	w. Handspring with half twist (on or off)

Test Item 15. *Vault Number 2*

(Select from previous list)

Scoring. Score sheets are prepared as shown in Figure 4.6, page 60. Students are scored on each test item by performing the one skill that best

Name: _____ Class period : _____ Date: _____

Balance beam event

   Item   Difficulty   Execution

    1. _____ × _____ = _____

    2. _____ × _____ = _____

    3. _____ × _____ = _____

    4. _____ × _____ = _____

    5. _____ × _____ = _____

        Balance beam total _____

Floor exercise event

   Item   Difficulty   Execution

    6. _____ × _____ = _____

    7. _____ × _____ = _____

    8. _____ × _____ = _____

    9. _____ × _____ = _____

        Floor exercise total _____

Uneven parallel bars event

   Item   Difficulty   Execution

   10. _____ × _____ = _____

   11. _____ × _____ = _____

   12. _____ × _____ = _____

   13. _____ × _____ = _____

        Bars total _____

Vaulting event

   Item   Difficulty   Execution

   14. _____ × _____ = _____

   15. _____ × _____ = _____

        Vault total _____

Event totals

B.B. _____

F.X. _____

Bars _____

Vault _____

Final test score _____

Figure 4.6 Score sheet for the Ellenbrand Gymnastics Skills Test.
Note. From "Gymnastics skills test for college women," by Deborah (Ellenbrand) Kutner, 1973, unpublished master's thesis, Indiana University, Bloomington, IN. Copyright 1973 by the author. Reprinted by permission.

demonstrates their ability in that area. Minor variations of these skills are acceptable if difficulty is not altered.

The score for each item is the product of the difficulty value and the execution rating. The sum of all test items in each event is the score for that event. The final test score is the sum of all events or all test items. Here is a description of the rating scale.

3 points Correct performance; proper mechanics; executed in good form. Performer shows balance, control, and amplitude in movements.

2 points Average performance; errors evident in either mechanics or form; may show some lack of balance, control, or amplitude in movements.

1 point Poor performance; errors in both mechanics and form. Performer shows little balance, control, or amplitude in movement.

0 points Improper or no performance; incorrect mechanics or complete lack of form; no display of balance, control, or amplitude in movements.

There is no deduction for falls or repeated skills. However, a stunt that is executed with assistance receives a zero rating.

Norms. Not available.

Bowers Gymnastics Skills Test (Bowers, 1965)

Purpose. To evaluate tumbling, floor exercise, uneven parallel bars, balance beam, and vaulting ability in gymnastics.

Validity and Reliability. Face validity was assumed because the items are the same as the skills tested. Reliability coefficients of .98, 1.00, .98, .99, and .97 were reported for tumbling, uneven parallel bars, balance beam, vaulting, and free exercise, respectively.

Age Level and Sex. Appropriate for junior high school and senior high school students.

Personnel. One judge; students act as spotters.

Equipment. A balance beam, uneven parallel bars, Reuther board, vaulting horse, and mats. Preparation equipment includes a measuring tape, marking tape, and chalk. Scoring equipment includes score cards or recording sheets and pencils.

Space. A gymnasium designed for gymnastics.

Test Items. Tumbling, uneven parallel bars, balance beam, vaulting, and free exercise.

Preparation. Preparation for the test items includes setting up the equipment and preparing score cards.

Directions. For an explanation of scoring, see page 62.

Event 1. *Tumbling*

1. Rolls
a. Forward		3, 2, 1
b. Backward		3, 2, 1
c. Backward extension		3, 2, 1

2. Cartwheels in Rhythm
a. To the right side		3, 2, 1
b. To the left side		3, 2, 1

3. Kip Progression (either movement a or b)
a. From headspring off a rolled mat		4
b. From shoulder-hand support		3, 2, 1

Event 2. *Uneven Parallel Bars*

1. Bar Snap

One line is marked on the landing mat 18 inches away from the bar, with a second line marked 12 inches beyond the first, then four additional lines each 6 inches farther away from the bar. If subject lands in the area between the bar and the first line, no points are awarded. Successive scores are based on the point and distance chart below.

Inches	18	30	36	42	48	54
Points	0	2	4	6	8	10

2. Progressive Movement to the Kip
a. One leg swing up		1, 2, 4
b. Walk out		4, 5, 6
c. Glide		5, 6, 8

3. Backward Hip Pullover   0, 2, 4

If subjects are given only slight assistance during any portion of the pullover, 2 points are awarded.

Event 3. *Balance Beam*

1. Locomotor Items
a. Three-step-turn		1, 2, 4
b. Step, hops on both feet		1, 2, 4
c. Step, leap		1, 2, 4
d. Scale		1, 2, 4

The score is determined by adding points accumulated on the four movements.

2. Arm Support   0, 1, 2, 4

3. Rolling
a. Backward shoulder roll		1, 2, 3, 4, 5, 6, 7

Points accumulated without the aid of a spotter constitute the official score.

Event 4. *Vaulting Event*

1. Vaulting Items

Floor items for body control of basic vault positions and flexibility. The scoring system is the same for each item. A solid line is constructed on the gymnasium floor. On one side of the line are three parallel lines marked 12, 6, and 3 inches away. On the opposite side is another parallel line 3 inches from the original line. Students place their hands on the solid line with the body extended in a front support over the line 12 inches away. The landing is measured from the heel. Points are awarded on a 0, 2, 4, 6, 10, 12 basis as shown on the point and distance chart below.

Inches Away	12	9	6	3	3	→
Points			0	2	4	6	10	12

a. Front support to straddle stand

b. Front support to stoop stand

2. Approach test for the run, hurdle, and take-off

a. Run, take-off   1, 2, 3, 4

A regulation Reuther board that has a black stripe on the front end is used. Lines are drawn on the board that are 5, 13, and 17 inches from the black stripe. The area where the ball of the foot hits is the scoring area. No points are scored for hitting the area between the back of the board to the first line. Three, 4 and 2 points are scored for the next three areas with 0 points given for the black part of the board. This score is added to the wall score minus the height score, which is discussed below.

b. Height measurement1, 2, 3, 4, 5, 6, 7

The Reuther board is placed beside a wall that is marked with 3-inch, alternating colored stripes of tape beginning at the 5-foot level. The stripes are numbered one through seven beginning with the bottom stripe. The score is the height of the sub-

ject's jump (in stripes) minus the height of the subject while standing.

Event 5.   *Free Standing Floor Exercise*

1. Tumbling total (points from event 1)   0-21

2. Continuity (routine)   0-10

a. Body wave

b. Leg leading turn

c. Scale

d. Concentric arm
circles

e. Final pose

One point is deducted for each stop in the flow of movement or a break in form.

Scoring. Score sheets are prepared as shown in Figure 4.7. The number or numbers after each item represent the scoring scale for that item. The highest numerical value, naturally,

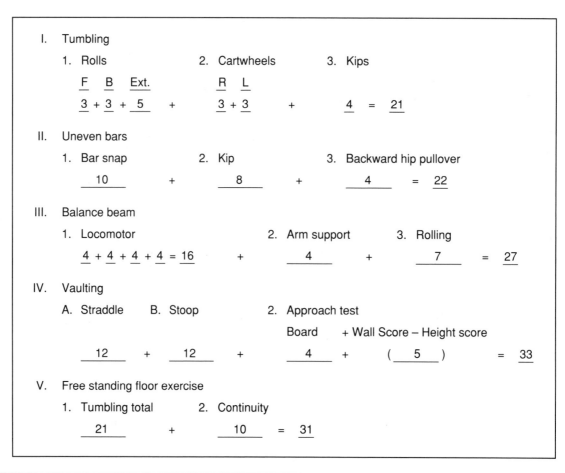

Figure 4.7   Score sheet for Bowers Gymnastics Skills Test.

Note. From ''Gymnastics skill test for beginning to low intermediate girls and women,'' by C.O. Bowers, 1965, unpublished master's thesis, Ohio State University, Columbus, OH. Copyright 1965 by the author. Reprinted by permission.

represents a well-executed item. Subjects may repeat a particular event to improve their score, but the second attempt is also recorded. If a skill cannot be completed, a zero is recorded. The skills tested are scored from zero to a maximum number of points with the highest score signify-

ing perfect execution in body rhythm and form with grace and poise.

Norms. Not available.

Other Gymnastics Tests

Barrow, H.M., & McGee, R. (1965). *Gymnastics skill test for beginning to low intermediate girls and women.* Unpublished master's thesis, Ohio State University, Columbus.

Faulkner, J., & Loken, N. (1962). Objectivity of judging at the National Collegiate Athletic Association gymnastic meet: A ten-year follow-up study. *Research Quarterly*, **33**, 485-486.

Fisher, R.B. (1950). *Tests in selected physical education service courses in a college.* Unpublished doctoral dissertation, University of Iowa, Iowa City.

Harris, J.P. (1966). *A design for a proposed skill proficiency test in tumbling and apparatus for male physical education majors at the University of North Dakota.* Unpublished master's thesis, University of North Dakota, Grand Forks.

Johnson, B.L., & Boudreaux, P.D. (1971). *Basic gymnastics for girls and women.* Englewood Cliffs, NJ: Appleton-Century Crofts.

Johnson, M. (1971). Objectivity of judging at the National Collegiate Athletic Association gymnastic meet: A 20-year follow-up study. *Research Quarterly*, **42**, 454-455.

Landers, D.M. (1965). *A comparison of two gym-nastic judging methods.* Unpublished master's thesis, University of Illinois at Urbana-Champaign.

Larson, R.F. (1969). Skill testing in elementary school gymnastics. *The Physical Educator*, **26**, 80-81.

Nelson, J.K. (1986). The Nelson balance test. Unpublished study. In B.L. Johnson & J.K. Nelson, *Practical measurements for evaluation in physical education.* (4th ed.). pp. 247-249. Edina, MN: Burgess International.

Scheer, J. (1973). Effect of placement in the order of competition on scores of Nebraska high school students. *Research Quarterly*, **44**, 79-85.

Schwarzkoph, R.J. (1962). *The Iowa Brace Test as a measuring instrument for predicting gymnastic ability.* Unpublished master's thesis, University of Washington, Seattle.

Wettstone, E. (1938). Test for predicting potential ability in gymnastics and tumbling. *Research Quarterly*, **9**, 115.

Zwarg, L.F. (1935). Judging and evaluation of competitive apparatus for gymnastic exercises. *Journal of Health and Physical Education*, **6**, 23.

Snow Skiing

Skiing began in Scandanavia as a form of travel for hunting and warfare. In the early 1800s equipment improvements transformed skiing into a recreational and competitive sport, although it did not become popular in the United States until the late 1800s.

Snow skiing can be of two types, alpine or cross-country. Traditionally, alpine skiing has been more popular but with alpine's spiraling costs and America's growing interest in fitness, cross-country skiing has become increasingly popular. Cross-country requires only snow, but alpine skiing also requires a mountain, a geographical feature not found everywhere.

The skills typically taught in alpine skiing include stopping, snow plowing, walking, schussing, and turning. Cross-country skills include striding, poling, turning, traversing, and snow plowing. Few skiing tests exist. The alpine skiing test included here tests climbing, turning, and stopping.

Rogers Skiing Test (Rogers, 1954)

Purpose. To evaluate downhill skiing ability.

Validity and Reliability. Face validity was claimed for each item. Reliability coefficients of .80, .87, and .87 for climbing, turning, and stopping, respectively, were computed by correlating scores of the first two trials with scores of the second two trials.

Age Level and Sex. Originally conducted with high school students. Appropriate for junior high school and senior high school students.

Personnel. Two people are needed to administer the test: a starter and a timer/recorder. Students can be point judges.

Equipment. Skis, ski poles, and ski slalom poles. Preparation equipment includes a measuring tape and slalom poles. Scoring equipment includes a stop watch, score cards or recording sheets, and pencils.

Space. A beginning ski slope at a public ski facility. The minimum amount of space is a length of 130 feet and a width of 45 feet. The ski slope should have a 25- to 30-degree incline with at least 25 feet of level space at its base.

Test Items. Climbing, turning, and stopping.

Preparation. Measuring and placing ski slalom poles for the three test items. The climbing test course is prepared as shown in Figure 4.8. This test should be given in an area with a 25-foot level base and a slope that increases in steepness as the skier climbs. The turning test course is prepared as shown in Figure 4.9, and the stopping test course is prepared as shown in Figure 4.10.

Directions.

Climbing: To begin, the student stands below the starting gate with ski tips behind the first gate. On the ''go'' signal, the student walks the first 25 feet (level base of the slope) to Gate 1. At Gate 1, the student performs a step turn to the right and half steps the 50 feet to Gate 2. At Gate 2 a kick turn to the left is performed followed by half steps covering 50 feet to Gate 3. From Gate 3 to Gate 4 the student performs a herringbone step. At Gate 4 a step turn to the

left is performed followed by a side step to Gate 5. At Gate 5 a kick turn is performed followed by a side step to the finish line with the left ski leading.

Proper climbing technique requires proper use of the ski poles. If poles are used incorrectly during the herringbone step, one point is deducted. Students who fall may get up and continue. The only penalty for falling is lost time. If skills are performed incorrectly, students must go back to the last gate passed and repeat the skill.

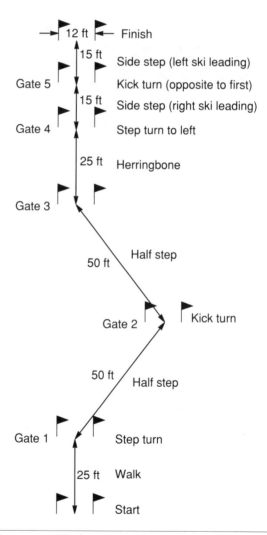

Figure 4.8 Climbing course for the Rogers Skiing Test. *Note.* From ''Construction of objectively scored skill tests for beginning skiers,'' by M.W. Rogers, 1954, unpublished master's thesis, University of Washington, Seattle, WA. Copyright 1954 by the author. Reprinted by permission.

Turning: The student assumes a starting position with ski tips behind the starting line. On the "go" signal, the student skis toward the first slalom gate 30 feet away, then proceeds through Gates 2, 3, 4, 5, and 6 and crosses the finish line.

Stopping: The student assumes a starting position with ski tips behind the starting line and on the "go" signal, skis straight down the fall line for 30 feet. When ski tips reach the stop line, the student executes a snow plow stop and stops completely as quickly as possible. Three trials are allowed. Trials are repeated if a student falls or begins to stop before reaching the stop line.

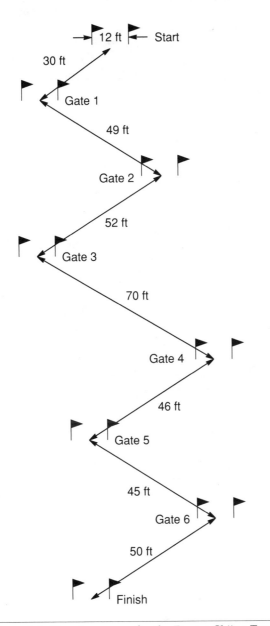

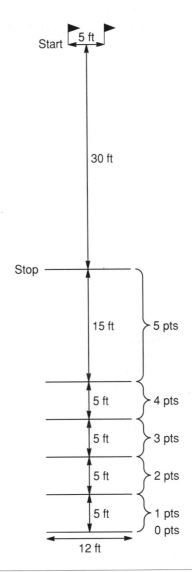

Figure 4.9 Turning course for the Rogers Skiing Test. *Note.* From "Construction of objectively scored skill tests for beginning skiers," by M.W. Rogers, 1954, unpublished master's thesis, University of Washington, Seattle, WA. Copyright 1954 by the author. Reprinted by permission.

Figure 4.10 Stopping course for the Rogers Skiing Test. *Note.* From "Construction of objectively scored skill tests for beginning skiers," by M.W. Rogers, 1954, unpublished master's thesis, University of Washington, Seattle, WA. Copyright 1954 by the author. Reprinted by permission.

Scoring.

Climbing: A student's score is the total time spent climbing the course. Timing begins with the ''go'' signal and ends when the skier passes the finish line. The final score is the best of two timed trials.

Turning: Two trials are given. The student starts with 9 points at the beginning of each trial. Two points are deducted if a skier falls while making a turn through a gate. One point is deducted if a skier falls after completing a turn or during a traverse. The final score is the total points for both trials.

Stopping: Each trial is scored on a point basis, depending on the distance it takes a skier to stop. Point values are shown in Figure 4.10. One point is deducted for each 5-foot line crossed. The location of the ski tips determines the value of the stop. The final score is the best of three trials.

Norms. Not available.

Other Skiing Tests

McGinnis, P.M. (1980). *Skills tests for discrimination of alpine skiing ability.* Unpublished master's thesis, University of Illinois at Urbana-Champaign.

Street, R.H. (1957). *Measurement of achievement in skiing.* Unpublished master's thesis, University of Utah, Salt Lake City.

Wolfe, J.E., & Merrifield, H.H. (1971). *Predictability of beginning skiing success from basic skill tests in college age females.* Paper presented at the American Association for Health, Physical Education, and Recreation Convention in Detroit.

Swimming

People swam as early as 9000 B.C., and the first book on swimming appeared in 1538. Swimming may be the most important activity for school-age children to master. Not only is swimming one of the best activities for developing overall fitness at any age, but it could save someone's life. Technologies in the development of swimming facilities make swimming proficiency a must. Enclosed pools, wave pools, lap pools, and man-made beach facilities are springing up at an increasing rate throughout the United States.

Skills that are developed in swimming include floating, breaststroke, elementary backstroke, butterfly stroke, sidestroke, front crawl, and back crawl. All swimming skills tests include at least one of these strokes, some testing endurance and power, others speed.

Fronske Swimming Test (Fronske, 1988)

Purpose. To evaluate swimming ability for the breaststroke, front crawl, butterfly, elementary backstroke, and sidestroke.

Validity and Reliability. Validity coefficients of .69, .67, .68, .63, and .60 for the breaststroke, front crawl, butterfly, elementary backstroke, and sidestroke, respectively, were computed by using time, number of strokes, subjective expert rating, and a checklist based on American Red Cross criteria. Reliability coefficients of .85, .93, .97, .96, and .93 for the breaststroke, front crawl, butterfly, elementary backstroke, and sidestroke, respectively, were computed using the same four variables.

Age Level and Sex. Originally conducted with university coed classes. The test can be used for any swimmer who can swim one or more of the front crawl, breaststroke, elementary backstroke, sidestroke, and butterfly.

Personnel. One person as starter/timer and one person as recorder. Students act as partners, one holding the subject stationary in the water. Students can also count the number of strokes for 25 yards.

Equipment. A swimming pool, lane dividers, a stop watch, score cards or score sheets, and pencils.

Space. 25-yard swimming pool.

Test Items. Time to swim 25 yards for the front crawl, butterfly, and breaststroke; and the number of strokes used to swim 25 yards for the sidestroke and elementary back stroke.

Preparation. Placing the lane dividers.

Directions. The student is taught starting positions for these swimming tests.

Front Crawl Start: The student starts from a stationary prone floating position, legs straight, toes touching the wall, both arms reaching straight out parallel with the body. The elbows should be close to the ears. A partner holds the swimmer at the waist, with one hand on the abdomen and one on the back. On the "ready, go" signal, the holder releases the swimmer and steps back. The swimmer swims the front crawl stroke as fast as possible.

Butterfly Stroke Start: The student starts from a stationary prone floating position, legs straight, toes touching the wall, both arms straight above the head. A partner holds the swimmer at the waist, with one hand on the abdomen and one on the back. On the "ready, go" signal, the holder releases the swimmer and steps back. The swimmer swims the butterfly as fast as possible.

Breaststroke Start: The student starts from a stationary prone floating position, legs straight, toes touching the wall, both arms straight above the head. A partner holds the swimmer at the waist, with one hand on the abdomen and one on the back. On the "ready, go" signal, the holder releases the swimmer and steps back. The swimmer swims the breaststroke as fast as possible or in as few strokes as possible, as directed for that particular test.

Elementary Backstroke Start: The student starts from a stationary position floating on his or her back, legs straight, toes touching the wall, both arms straight down along the side of the body. A partner holds the swimmer at the waist, with one hand on the abdomen and one on the back. On the "ready, go" signal, the holder releases the swimmer and steps back. The swimmer swims the elementary backstroke in as few strokes as possible.

Sidestroke Start: The student starts on his or her side in a floating position, legs straight, toes touching the wall, one arm straight above the head, the other arm down along the side. A partner holds the swimmer with one hand on each side of the waist. On the "ready, go" signal, the

holder releases the swimmer and steps back. The swimmer swims the sidestroke in as few strokes as possible.

Scoring. The final score is the time to swim 25 yards for the front crawl, butterfly, and breaststroke and the number of strokes needed to complete 25 yards for the sidestroke and backstroke.

Norms. Not available.

Twelve-Minute Swim Test (Jackson, Jackson, & Frankiewicz, 1979)

Purpose. To evaluate swimming endurance using the crawl stroke.

Validity and Reliability. Construct validity was reported to be .89 between the 12-minute swim and the tethered swim test. Test-retest produced a reliability coefficient of .98.

Age Level and Sex. Originally conducted with college males. Appropriate for junior high school and senior high school students.

Personnel. One person to act as starter and recorder. Students can act as counters.

Equipment. Swimming pool, lane dividers, a measuring tape, marking material, a stop watch, score cards or recording sheets, and pencils.

Space. 25-yard swimming pool.

Test Item. The 12-minute swim using the crawl stroke.

Preparation. Place the lane dividers and mark the poolside in 5-yard distances.

Directions. The student begins the test in the pool and is instructed to swim in an individual lane. On the "go" signal, the student pushes off from the end of the pool and begins swimming the crawl stroke, covering as much distance as possible in 12 minutes. A partner on the deck counts laps. On the "stop" signal, the partner records the yardage closest to the swimmer's hand and the number of full laps the swimmer completed.

Scoring. The final score is the distance covered in the alloted 12 minutes.

Norms. Not available.

Other Swimming Tests

Anderson, C.W. (1930). Achievement records in swimming. *Journal of Health and Physical Education*, **1**, 40.

Arrasmith, J.L. (1967). *Swimming classification test for college women.* Unpublished doctoral dissertation, University of Oregon, Eugene.

Burris, B.J. (1964). *A study of the speed-stroke test of crawl stroking ability and its relationship to other selected tests of crawl stroking ability.* Unpublished master's thesis, Temple University, Philadelphia.

Chapman, P. (1965). *A comparison of three methods of measuring swimming stroke proficiency.* Unpublished master's thesis, University of Wisconsin, Madison.

Conner, D.J. (1962). *A comparison of objective and subjective testing methods in selected swimming skills for elementary school children.* Unpublished master's thesis, Washington State University, Pullman.

Cureton, T.K. (1935). A test for endurance in speed swimming. *Research Quarterly*, **6**, 106-112.

Cureton, T.K. (1938). *Objective scales for rating swimming performance and diagnosing fault.* Springfield College, Springfield, MA.

Durrant, S.M. (1964). An analytical method of rating synchronized swimming stunts. *Research Quarterly*, **9**, 25-31.

Fisher, R.B. (1950). *Tests in selected physical education service courses in a college.* Unpublished doctoral dissertation, University of Iowa, Iowa City.

Fox, M.G. (1957). Swimming power test. *Research Quarterly*, **28**, 233-237.

Fried, M.G. (1983). *An examination of the test characteristics of the 12-minute aerobic swim test.* Unpublished master's thesis, University of Wisconsin, Madison.

Hewitt, J.E. (1948). Swimming achievement scales for college men. *Research Quarterly*, **19**, 282-289.

Hewitt, J.E. (1949). Achievement scale scores for high school swimming. *Research Quarterly*, **20**, 170-179.

Jackson, A.S., & Pettinger, J. (1969). *The development and discriminant analysis of swimming profiles of college men.* Paper presented at the 72nd annual meeting of the National College Physical Education Association for Men.

Kilby, E.J. (1956). *An objective method of evaluating three swimming strokes.* Unpublished doctoral dissertation, University of Washington, Seattle.

Munt, M.R. (1964). *Development of an objective test to measure the efficiency of the front crawl for college women.* Unpublished master's thesis, University of Michigan, Ann Arbor.

Parkhurst, M.G. (1934). Achievement tests in swimming. *Journal of Health and Physical Education*, **5**, 34-36, 58.

Rosentswieg, J. (1968). A revision of the power swimming test. *Research Quarterly*, **39**, 818-819.

Scott, M.G. (1940). Achievement examinations for elementary and intermediate swimming classes. *Research Quarterly*, **11**, 104-111.

Wilson, C.T. (1934). Coordination tests in swimming. *Research Quarterly*, **5**, 81-88.

Wilson, M.R. (1962). *A relationship between general motor ability and objective measurement of achievement in swimming at the intermediate level for college women.* Unpublished master's thesis, Women's College of the University of North Carolina, Greensboro.

Track and Field

Once every 4 years when the Olympic Games are conducted, track and field becomes the most popular sport in the world. Between the Games, track and field loses some of its luster, as few meets are covered on television, and big-name participants cut back on competition. Recently, however, record-setting performances by Carl Lewis and Mike Powell, among others, at the World Games in Japan attracted international attention. In addition, the number of marathons conducted in the United States has increased and the Boston and New York City marathons are covered on television from start to finish. Because of its universal appeal and because it includes a number of events, track and field is one of the best activity units to include in a physical education program. Running, jumping, and throwing are covered in a wide variety of specific events.

A typical track and field unit includes sprinting, hurdling, relays, distance running, long jumping, triple jumping, high jumping, shot putting, and discus throwing. Other events often included are pole vaulting and race walking. Skills tests are not available for track and field but they are not really needed because the results of competition reflect achievement.

Weight Training

As weight training equipment has become cheaper, easier to maintain, and smaller, and as the fitness movement has made more people aware of muscular strength and endurance development, many junior and senior high schools are adding weight training rooms. In many schools the demand for weight room scheduling is at a premium as physical education classes and athletic teams vie for space and time.

People weight train for a variety of reasons: to develop greater size, to develop better endurance, to rehabilitate or prevent injuries, to look and feel better, and to improve athletic performance. Lifts for each body segment are virtually endless.

A review of literature failed to reveal any objective weight training skills test. Most fitness texts, however, contain muscular strength and endurance tests. That no weight training skills tests are available is not too surprising because people lift weights for a variety of reasons and teachers find it difficult to judge individual performance based on a skills test.

Weight Training Tests

Allsen, P.E., Harrison, J.M., & Vance, B. (1989). *Fitness for life*. Dubuque, IA: Brown.

Corbin, C., & Lindsey, R. (1990). *Concepts of physical fitness*. Dubuque, IA: Brown.

Hoeger, W.W.K. (1989). *Lifetime physical fitness and wellness*. Englewood, CO: Morton.

McGlynn, G. (1990). *Dynamics of fitness*. Dubuque, IA: Brown.

Prentice, W. (1991). *Fitness for college and life*. St. Louis: Mosby Year Book.

Chapter 5

Tests for Dual Sports

Dual sports, as individual sports, are becoming increasingly popular in public schools because they can be played throughout life. Although called dual sports, many also can be played with three or four players.

This chapter includes skills tests for badminton, fencing, handball, racquetball, squash, table tennis, and tennis. No objective skills tests are available for horseshoes, pickle-ball, shuffleboard, and wrestling, but horseshoes and shuffleboard skills can be tested similarly to bowling (see page 44).

Badminton

Badminton is relatively easy to learn, uses inexpensive equipment, and can be played inside or out. The game has been played in America for about 100 years, booming during the 1920s. Badminton is not as popular as it once was, but it has held its own as new racquet sports have developed.

Badminton instruction usually includes short and long serves; forehand and backhand drives and clears; and lob, smash, and drop shots. All badminton tests cover at least one of these components.

Poole Forehand Clear Test (Poole & Nelson, 1970)

Purpose. To evaluate the ability to hit a forehand clear shot from the back court.

Validity and Reliability. A validity coefficient of .70 was found using tournament play as a criterion measure. Using a test-retest approach, a reliability coefficient of .90 was found.

Age Level and Sex. Originally conducted with college students. Appropriate for junior high school and senior high school students.

Personnel. Each testing station requires a person to act as an opponent and judge the clears as ''good'' or ''low,'' and one to act as recorder/scorer. An additional person could be used to gather and return shuttlecocks that clear the net.

Equipment. Badminton nets and standards, badminton racquets, and shuttlecocks. Individuals being tested must have 12 shuttlecocks each. Preparation equipment includes a measuring tape and floor tape. Scoring equipment includes scorecards or recording sheets and pencils.

Space. Regulation-sized badminton court for each testing station.

Test Item. The overhead clear.

Preparation. Each testing station should be prepared as shown in Figure 5.1. Markings include two lines running parallel to the short service line and two 15 inch by 15 inch squares. One parallel line is located between the short service line and the doubles long service line. A second parallel line is located 6 inches beyond the back boundary. One 15 inch by 15 inch square is placed in the middle of the center line 11 feet

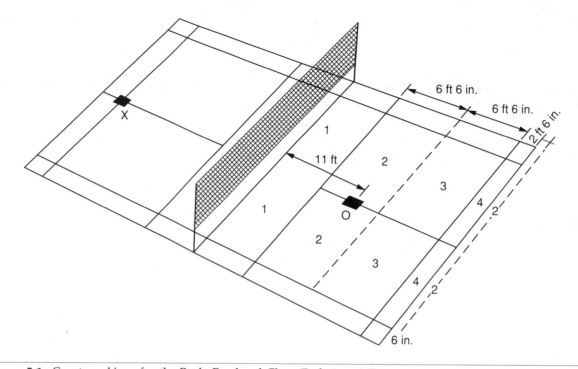

Figure 5.1 Court markings for the Poole Forehand Clear (Badminton) Test.
Note. From "Construction of a badminton skills test battery," by J. Poole and J.K. Nelson, 1970, unpublished manuscript, Louisiana State University, Baton Rouge, LA. Copyright 1970 by the authors. Reprinted by permission.

from the net on the target side. A second square is placed at the intersection of the doubles long service line and center line on the serving side of the net.

Directions. A performer stands with the right foot in the serving-side square (if left-handed, with the left foot in the square), and the opponent stands in the target-side square with the racquet extended high overhead. With a forehand grip the student holds the racquet head parallel to the floor. The shuttlecock is held with the left hand with the thumb and forefinger gripping the rubber end of the shuttlecock and the feather end facing the floor. The student tosses the shuttlecock high into the air. As the shuttlecock descends, the student hits a forehand clear to the target side of the net. For the student to score, the shuttlecock must clear both the net and the opponent's extended racquet. The hitter must keep the foot in the square until the shuttlecock is struck. The opponent calls out "low" if the shuttlecock fails to pass over the extended racquet.

Scoring. Each subject performs 12 forehand clear shots and earns the point value of the zone in

which the shuttlecock lands. To obtain the test score, count the best 10 of 12 shots. A shuttlecock landing on a line is given the higher point value. One point is subtracted for each shuttlecock that fails to clear the opponent's extended racquet. Only legal serves are scored. A perfect score is 40 points.

Norms. A scoring scale for the forehand clear appears in Table 5.1.

Table 5.1 Forehand Clear Scoring Scale for the Poole Forehand Clear Test

Preliminary skill test	Performance level	Final skill test
20 and above	Good	24 and above
13-19	Fair	16-23
0-12	Poor	0-5

Note. From "Construction of a badminton skills test battery," by J. Poole and J.K. Nelson, 1970, unpublished manuscript, Louisiana State University, Baton Rouge, LA. Copyright 1970 by the authors. Reprinted by permission.

Lockhart-McPherson Badminton Wall-Volley Test (Lockhart & McPherson, 1949)

Purpose. To evaluate the ability to volley a badminton shuttlecock against a wall.

Validity and Reliability. Using criterion measures of judges' ratings and round-robin tournament rankings, validity coefficients ranged from .71 to .90. A reliability coefficient of .90 was determined by the test-retest approach.

Age Level and Sex. Originally developed for college women and later adapted for college men. Appropriate for junior high school and senior high school students.

Personnel. It is best to use three persons to administer this test, but it can be administered with as few as one assistant. If three persons are used, one is the timer (giving the start and stop signals), one the scorer (counting the number of legal hits), and one the recorder (marking the number of legal hits performed).

Equipment. Badminton racquets, shuttlecocks, and wall space at least 10 feet high and 10 feet wide. Preparation equipment includes a measuring tape and marking tape. Scoring equipment includes a stop watch, score cards or recording sheets, and pencils.

Space. Each testing station requires a smooth wall area at least 10 feet high and 10 feet wide and floor space of equal dimensions.

Test Item. The badminton volley.

Preparation. Each testing station is prepared as shown in Figure 5.2. The wall surface should be at least 10 feet high and 10 feet wide. A 1-inch net line is marked on the wall 5 feet above and parallel to the floor. The testing floor is approximately the same dimensions as the wall. Mark a starting line on the floor 6 feet, 6 inches from the base of the wall, and mark a restraining line on the floor 3 feet from the base of the wall. Both lines run parallel to the front wall.

Directions. The student starts (behind the starting line) holding a badminton racquet in one hand and a shuttlecock in the other. On the

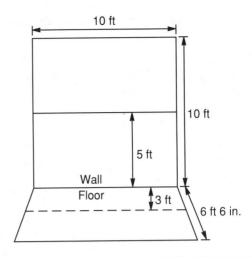

Figure 5.2 Floor and wall markings for the Lockhart-McPherson Badminton Wall-Volley Test.
Note. From "The development of a test of badminton playing ability," by A. Lockhart and F.A. McPherson, 1949, *Research Quarterly*, **20**, pp. 402-405. Copyright 1949 by AAHPER. Reprinted by permission.

"ready, go" signal, the shuttlecock is served in a legal manner against the wall on or above the 5-foot net line. The served shuttlecock is played against the wall as many times as possible in 30 seconds. The player gets three trials with a rest period between. A 15-second practice period is given before the first trial.

After serving the shuttlecock, the student may move to the restraining line and play there. If a student crosses the restraining line, the shuttlecocks remain in play but their hits are not counted. If shuttlecocks are missed or go out of control, the student may retrieve them and continue volleying by putting them back in play with a serve from behind the starting line. Fouls (such as carrying and double hitting) during the test are disregarded.

Scoring. The score is the number of legal shots made from behind the restraining line that hit on or above the 5-foot net line in three 3-second trials.

Norms. T scores appear in Table 5.2 and an achievement scale appears in Table 5.3

Table 5.2 T Scores for the Lockhart-McPherson Volleying Test

Raw score	T score	Raw score	T score	Raw score	T score
148	78	108		68	46.5
147		107	62	67	46
146		106		66	
145	75	105	61.5	65	45.5
144		104	61	64	45
143	74	103	60.5	63	44.5
142		102		62	44
141		101	60	61	43
140		100	59.5	60	42.5
139		99		59	42.5
138	72	98		58	42
137		97		57	42
136	71	96	59	56	41.5
135		95	58.5	55	41.5
134		94	58	54	41
133		93	57.5	53	40.5
132		92	57	52	40
131	70	91	57	51	39.5
130		90	56.5	50	38.5
129		89	56	49	38
128	69.5	88	55.5	48	37.5
127	68.5	87	55	47	37
126		86	54	46	36.5
125		85	53.5	45	35.5
124		84	53	44	34.5
123	67.5	83	53	43	34
122	67	82	52.5	42	33
121		81	52	41	
120	66.5	80	51.5	40	
119		79	51.5	39	31.5
118		78	51	38	30.5
117		77	51	37	29
116		76	51	36	
115	66.0	75	50.5	35	
114	65	74		34	
113	64.5	73		33	
112	64	72	48.5	32	25.5
111	63	71	48	31	
110	63	70	47.5	30	
109	62.5	69	47	29	21.0

Note. From ''The development of a test of badminton playing ability,'' by A. Lockhart and F.A. McPherson, 1949, *Research Quarterly,* **20**, pp. 402-405. Copyright 1949 by AAHPER. Reprinted by permission.

Table 5.3 Achievement Scales for the Lockhart-McPherson Volleying Test

Rating	Test score (sum of three trials)
Superior	126 and up
Good	90 - 125
Average	62 - 89
Poor	40 - 61
Inferior	39 and below

Note. From ''The development of a test of badminton playing ability,'' by A. Lockhart and F.A. McPherson, 1949, *Research Quarterly, 20*, pp. 402-405. Copyright 1949 by AAHPER. Reprinted by permission.

French Short Serve (Scott, Carpenter, French, & Kuhl, 1941)

Purpose. To evaluate the ability to short-serve the badminton shuttlecock.

Validity and Reliability. With tournament rankings as the criterion measure, a validity coefficient of .66 was reported. Using the odd-even approach followed by the Spearman-Brown Prophecy Formula, reliability coefficients ranging from .51 to .89 have been reported on different occasions.

Age Level and Sex. Originally designed for college men and women. Appropriate for junior high school and senior high school students.

Personnel. The test can be administered with one person acting as recorder and scorer. Test time can be reduced if three assistants are located at each testing station (one person as scorer calling where the shuttlecocks land, one person as recorder, and one person to retrieve shuttlecocks).

Equipment. Badminton racquets, at least 20 shuttlecocks for each testing station, and badminton standards and nets. Preparation equipment includes a rope long enough to reach the length of the net, a measuring tape, and marking tape. Scoring equipment includes score cards or recording sheets and pencils.

Space. Regulation-sized badminton court for each testing station.

Test Items. The badminton short serve.

Preparation. Each testing station is prepared as shown in Figure 5.3. A rope should be extended

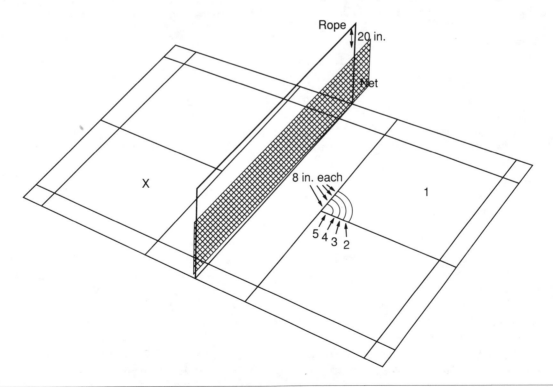

Figure 5.3 Court markings for the French Short Serve test.
Note. From ''Achievement examinations in badminton,'' by M.G. Scott, A. Carpenter, E. French, and L. Kuhl, 1941, *Research Quarterly, 12*, 242-253. Copyright 1941 by AAHPER. Reprinted by permission.

from standard to standard 20 inches above and parallel to the net. Four 2-inch lines in the form of an arc are placed from the midpoint of the intersection of the short service line and the center service line. The first arc line is 22 inches from the midpoint; the remaining three lines are then placed at 8-inch increments. The distances from the midpoint for the four lines are 22, 30, 38, and 46 inches. Each measurement includes the width of the 2-inch line. Zones are scored 1 through 5 with 5 being the smallest and most difficult zone to hit.

Directions. The student stands behind the service line in the service court diagonally opposite the target and tries 20 times to serve the shuttlecock so it travels between the net and the extended rope and lands in the 5-point scoring zone. Illegal serves must be re-served. Practice trials are permitted.

Scoring. The scoring zones are given point values as shown in Figure 5.3. Each serve is given the point value of the area in which it first lands. Serves that pass over the extended 20-inch rope or fall out of bounds count zero. Shuttlecocks that land on a division line get the higher value. Shuttlecocks that are illegally served or hit the rope do not count, but the server is allowed to

re-serve. The final score is the total for the 20 serves. A perfect score is 100 points.

Norms. T scores are shown in Table 5.4.

Table 5.4 T Scores for the French Short Serve Test

T score	Short serve	Short serve
80	68	86
75	66	79
70	59	73
65	53	66
60	44	59
55	37	52
50	29	46
45	22	39
40	13	32
35	8	26
30	4	19
25	1	12
20	0	6

Note. From ''Achievement examinations in badminton,'' by M.G. Scott, A. Carpenter, E. French, and L. Kohl, 1941, *Research Quarterly, 12*, pp. 242-253. Copyright 1941 by AAHPER. Reprinted by permission.

Other Badminton Tests

Beverlein, M.A. (1970). *A skill test for the drop shot in badminton.* Unpublished master's thesis, Southern Illinois University, Carbondale.

Bobrich, M. (1972). *Reliability of an evaluative tool used to measure badminton skill.* Unpublished master's thesis, George Williams College, Chicago.

Boldrick, E.L. (1945). *The measurement of fundamental skills in badminton.* Unpublished master's thesis, Wellesley College, Wellesley, MA.

Campbell, V.M. (1938). *Development of achievement tests in badminton.* Unpublished master's thesis, University of Texas, Austin.

Chang, C.J. (1980). *Tests of fundamental badminton skills for college students: Construction, analysis and norms.* Unpublished doctoral dissertation, University of Iowa, Iowa City.

Cotten, D.J., Cobb, P.R., & Fleming, J. (1987, April). *Development and validation of a badminton clear test.* Paper presented at the American Alliance for Health, Physical Education, Recreation and Dance National Convention in Las Vegas.

Davis, B. (1946). *The relationship of certain skill tests to playing ability in badminton.* Unpublished master's thesis, Wellesley College, Wellesley, MA.

Davis, P.R. (1968). *The development of a combined short and long badminton service skill test.* Unpublished master's thesis, University of Tennessee, Knoxville.

French, E., & Stalter, E. (1949). Study of skills tests in badminton for college women. *Research Quarterly*, **20**, 257-272.

Greiner, M.R. (1964). *Construction of a short serve test for beginning badminton players.* Master's thesis, University of Wisconsin, Madison. (Microcard PE 670, University of Oregon, Eugene.)

Hale, P.A. (1970). *Construction of a long serve test for beginning badminton players.* Master's thesis, University of Wisconsin, Madison. (Microcard PE 1133, University of Oregon, Eugene.)

Hicks, J.V. (1967). *The construction and evaluation of a battery of five badminton skill tests.* Unpublished doctoral dissertation, Texas Woman's University, Denton.

Johnson, R.M. (1967). *Determination of the validity and reliability of the badminton placement test.* Unpublished master's thesis, University of Oregon, Eugene.

Johnson, B.L., & Nelson, J.K. (1979). Badminton smash test. *Practical Measurements for Evaluation in Physical Education.* Edina, MN: Burgess International.

Kowert, E.A. (1968). *Construction of a badminton ability test for men.* Unpublished master's thesis, University of Iowa, Iowa City.

Lucey, M.A. (1952). *A study of the components of wrist action as they relate to speed of learning and the degree of proficiency attained in badminton.* Unpublished doctoral dissertation, New York University, New York.

McDonald, E.D. (1968). *The development of a skill test for the badminton high clear.* Master's thesis, Southern Illinois University, Carbondale. (Microcard PE 1083, University of Oregon, Eugene.)

Miller, F.A. (1951). A badminton wall volley test. *Research Quarterly*, **22**, 208-213.

Poole, J., & Nelson, J.K. (1970). *Construction of a badminton skills test battery.* Unpublished study, Louisiana State University, Baton Rouge.

Popp, P. (1970). *The development of a diagnostic test to determine badminton playing ability.* Unpublished master's thesis, University of Washington, Seattle.

Roger, M.J. (1950). Achievement tests in badminton for college women. Unpublished master's thesis, University of Iowa, Iowa City.

Sebolt, D. (1986). Sebolt short service test. In T.A. Baumgartner & A.S. Jackson (Eds.), *Measurement for evaluation in physical education.* (2nd ed.). Dubuque, IA: Brown.

Scott, J.H. (1941). *A study in the evaluation of playing ability in the game of badminton.* Unpublished master's thesis, Ohio State University, Columbus.

Scott, M.G., Carpenter, A., French, E., & Kuhl, L. (1941). Achievement examinations in badminton. *Research Quarterly*, **12**, 242-253.

Thorpe, J., & West, C. (1969). A test of game sense in badminton. *Perceptual and Motor Skills*, **27**, 159-169.

Washington, J. (1968). *Construction of a wall volley test for the badminton short serve and the effect of wall practice on court performance.* Unpublished master's thesis, North Texas State University, Denton.

Fencing

Fencing, a form of warfare made obsolete by gunpowder, is classified in the sport skills category of combatives. Although seldom taught in high school or college physical education programs, it is an excellent coeducational activity.

Skills typically taught in fencing physical education classes include the en guarde position, advance and retreat, lunge and recovery, attacks, and defense.

Bower Fencing Test (Bower, 1961)

Purpose. To evaluate offensive and defensive ability in fencing.

Validity and Reliability. A validity coefficient of .80 was found by comparing test results with round-robin tournament rankings. The test-retest approach obtained a reliability coefficient of .82.

Age Level and Sex. Originally designed for college men and women. Appropriate for senior high school students.

Personnel. One person to act both as judge and recorder/scorer.

Equipment. Fencing costume, gloves, jacket, mask, and foils. Preparation equipment includes a measuring tape and marking tape. Scoring equipment includes score cards or recording sheet and pencils.

Space. Each testing station requires an area about 5 feet by 15 feet.

Test Items. Offensive attack and defense.

Preparation. Before the test begins, a defensive fencer is positioned in an en guarde position with a rear foot against a wall. An offensive fencer will determine the length of his or her lunge by executing a full lunge so that the foil blade barely touches the defensive fencer. This action determines the correct attack distance, and a judge marks the inner border of the offensive fencer's rear foot. This becomes the starting line. A second line, 5 inches nearer the wall from the starting line, is designated the foul line.

Directions. The offensive fencer, using any acceptable attack, makes five attacks at his or her own pace against a defensive fencer. Each attack must begin behind the starting line. At the finish of each attack, the offensive fencer's rear foot must be on the floor behind the foul line. The defensive fencer may use any parry. After five attacks, fencers switch positions for five more attacks. New starting and foul lines must be measured and marked before the second five attacks may commence.

The judge should be positioned 1 yard behind and slightly to the right of the offensive fencer. The judge will determine if a point lands, if there is a complete miss, and if the offensive fencer's rear foot remains behind the foul line during an attack.

Scoring. One point is awarded to the offensive fencer for each disengage that lands on a target area. No points are awarded for an incorrect attack or for a disengage that lands off target and is not parried. One point is awarded to the defensive fencer for each successful counter parry. The defensive fencer earns 1 point if he or she parries the foil with a counter parry so that the offensive fencer's attack lands foul. No points are awarded for an incorrect parry or a

direct parry that stops an attack. Scores should be announced following each attack. Each test contains a possible 10 points, 5 on attack and 5 on defense.

Norms. Not available.

Schutz Fencing Test (Schutz, 1940)

Purpose. To evaluate lunging ability in fencing.

Validity and Reliability. Face validity was assumed. A reliability coefficient of .96 was determined by utilizing the test-retest approach.

Age Level and Sex. Originally designed for college women. Appropriate for senior high school students.

Personnel. One person is needed to act both as judge and recorder/scorer.

Equipment. Fencing foils, a target pad, a measuring tape, marking tape, materials to hang the target, a stopwatch, score cards or recording sheets, and pencils.

Space. Each testing station requires a space of about 5 feet by 20 feet.

Test Item. The Fencing lunge.

Preparation. A target should be hung on a wall at a height so that when the fencer lunges at the target his or her fully extended arm will be at the same level as the target. Additionally, a restraining line should be marked on the floor 15 feet from the target.

Directions. The student assumes an en guarde position behind the restraining line. With the start signal, the fencer moves forward and executes a lunge at the target followed by a recovery and retreat to the restraining line. After retreating to the restraining line, second and third lunges and retreats will be executed. The third lunge should be held in place with the foil on the target and the student in a balanced skill maneuver. The test is repeated if balance is lost. After a student retreats behind the restraining line, he or she must "call" (tap the front foot two times) before beginning the next advance. Two timed test trials are allowed. Retrials result if a student crosses his or her feet, uses a jumping action, or exhibits poor technique.

Scoring. Two timed trials are allowed with the better trial used as the final score. Timed trials begin with the start signal and end when the third foil touches the target. Times are recorded to the nearest 1/10 of a second.

Norms. Not available.

Other Fencing Tests

Busch, M.G. (1966). *The construction of a fencing test using a moving target.* Unpublished master's thesis, University of North Carolina, Greensboro.

Cooper, C.K. (1968). *The development of a fencing skill test for measuring achievement of beginning collegiate women fencers in using the advance, beat, and lunge.* Unpublished master's thesis, Western Illinois University, Macomb.

Emery, M.G. (1961). Criteria for rating selected skills of foil fencing. *DGWS Bowling-fencing guide 1960-1962,* Washington, DC: AAHPER.

Fein, J.T. (1964). *Construction of skill tests for beginning collegiate women fencers.* Unpublished master's thesis, University of Iowa, Iowa City.

Kuhajda, P.F. (1970). *The construction and validation of a skill test for the riposte-lunge in fencing.* Unpublished master's thesis, Southern Illinois University, Carbondale.

Safrit, M.J. (1962). *Construction of a skill test for beginning fencers.* Unpublished master's thesis, University of Wisconsin, Madison.

Swanson, A.H. (1967). *Measuring achievement in selected skills for beginning women fencers.* Unpublished master's thesis, University of Iowa, Iowa City.

Handball

Handball is one of the oldest sports played with a ball, appearing in Roman baths about 1000 B.C. The game was introduced in the United States during the middle 1800s. Originally played with four walls, the game was modified to one wall and brought outside in the early 1900s. The advent of racquetball in the late 1960s has led to a decline in the number of handball participants.

Skills taught in handball include the overarm stroke, sidearm stroke, underarm stroke, kill shot, back-wall shot, ceiling shot, passing shot, and serve. Skills tests usually contain tests for front-wall kill shot, back-wall shot, and volley.

Tyson Handball Test (Tyson, 1970)

Purpose. To evaluate kill shot and volley ability in handball.

Validity and Reliability. Validity coefficients of .87, .84, .76, and .92 were reported for the 30-second rally, front-wall kill, back-wall kill, and the three-item battery, respectively. Reliability coefficients of .82, .82, and .81 were reported for the 30-second rally, front-wall kill, and back-wall kill, respectively. Round-robin tournament results were used as the criterion measure.

Age Level and Sex. Originally tested on college men. Appropriate for junior high school and senior high school students.

Personnel. The test requires a scorer/timer, a recorder, and student assistants.

Equipment. Handballs and handball gloves, a measuring tape, marking tape, a stop watch, score cards or recording sheets, and pencils.

Space. Handball courts.

Test Items. The skills test battery includes three items: 30-second volley, front-wall kill with dominant hand, and back-wall kill with dominant hand.

Preparation. Preparation for the test includes measuring and marking front and back walls. Testing stations for the front-wall kill with dominant hand are prepared as shown in Figure 5.4, and the stations for the back-wall kill with dominant hand as shown in Figure 5.5.

Directions.

Thirty-Second Volley: The student stands, handball in hand, behind the short line. On the "go" signal, the student tosses a handball against the front wall to initiate the volley. The student volleys the handball against the front wall as many times as possible in 30 seconds. Legal volleys must be made from behind the short line. If a student crosses the short line or if the ball bounces twice or more, the return does not count. When ball control is lost, a student assistant quickly supplies a second or third ball as needed. Volleys may be executed with either hand.

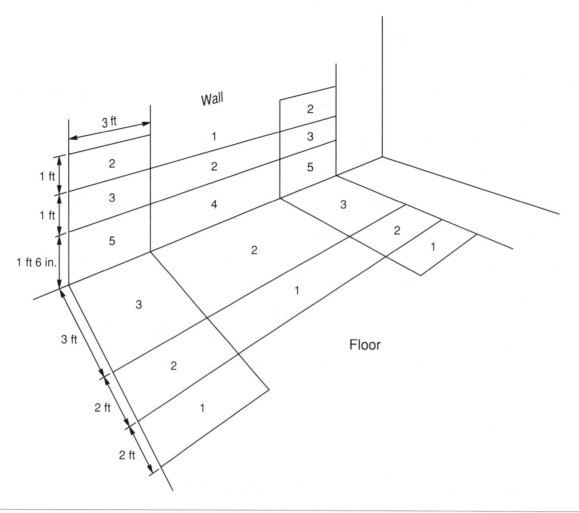

Figure 5.4 Court and wall markings for the Tyson Front-Wall Kill (Handball) Test.

Note. From "A handball skill test for college men," by K.W. Tyson, 1970, unpublished master's thesis, University of Florida, Gainesville, FL. Copyright 1970 by the author. Reprinted by permission.

Front-Wall Kill with Dominant Hand: The student stands in the doubles service box opposite of the dominant hand. If right-handed, the student starts on the left side, if left-handed, on the right side. A student assistant in the middle of the service zone begins the trial by tossing a handball against the front wall so that it rebounds to the dominant hand side of the student being tested. As the assistant releases the ball, the hitter is free to move into a better hitting position. When moving, the student should move behind (not in front of) the assistant. The hitter attempts to place the ball in the highest-scoring front wall target and have it rebound into the highest-scoring floor target. Five trials are allowed.

Back-Wall Kill with Dominant Hand: The student stands much as in the front-wall-kill-with-dominant-hand test. A student assistant is located in the center of the court, 6 feet behind the short line. The assistant tosses the handball against the front wall so that it rebounds and bounces 8 to 12 feet behind the short line and about 10 feet from the preferred side wall. The assistant should toss the handball 15 to 18 feet high on the front wall for best results. As the starting toss is made, the hitter may move into a better position for playing the ball as it rebounds off the back wall. The hitter may elect not to play a poorly tossed ball. The hitter attempts to place the ball in the highest-scoring front wall target and have it rebound into the

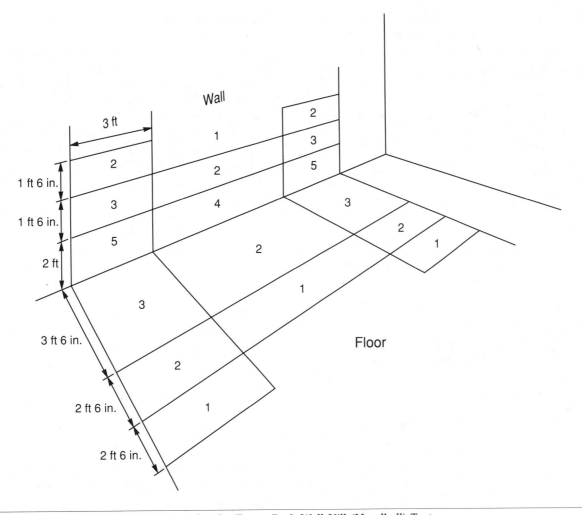

Figure 5.5 Court and wall markings for the Tyson Back-Wall Kill (Handball) Test.
Note. From "A handball skill test for college men," by K.W. Tyson, 1970, unpublished master's thesis, University of Florida, Gainesville, FL. Copyright 1970 by the author. Reprinted by permission.

highest-scoring floor target. Five trials are allowed.

Scoring.

Thirty-Second Volley: The final score is the number of legal volleys during the 30-second timed trial.

Front-Wall Kill with Dominant Hand: The final score is the number of points awarded on all five trials. A perfect score is 25 points.

Back-Wall Kill with Dominant Hand: The final score is the number of points awarded on all five trials. A perfect score is 25 points.

Norms. Not available.

Sattler Handball Battery (Sattler, 1973)

Purpose. To evaluate volleying and returning ability in handball.

Validity and Reliability. Validity coefficients of .81, .79, and .77 were reported for the dominant overhand return, 30-second alternate-hand volley, and 1-minute continuous back-wall volley, respectively. Round-robin tournament play was used as the criterion measure. The test-retest approach produced reliability coefficients of .89, .90, and .85 for the dominant overhand return, 30-second alternate-hand volley, and 1-minute continuous back-wall volley, respectively.

Age Level and Sex. Originally conducted with male college students. Appropriate for junior high school and senior high school students.

Personnel. Each test item can be administered by one person.

Equipment. Handballs, a measuring tape, marking tape, a stop watch, score cards or recording sheets, and pencils.

Space. Regulation-sized handball courts.

Test Items. Dominant overhand return, 30-second alternate-hand volley, and 1-minute continuous back-wall volley.

Preparation. Place marking tape across the front wall 2 feet above the floor and across the floor 6 feet from the back wall.

Directions.

Dominant Overhand Return: The student stands between the short and serve lines. After bouncing a ball on the floor high enough to contact the ball with an extended elbow, the student attempts an overhand delivery with the dominant hand. Balls must be hit hard enough to hit the front wall and rebound to the back wall without touching the floor. Sidearm hits or balls contacted without an extended elbow count as unsuccessful attempts. The hitter cannot cross the service line to hit the ball. Ten trials are counted, but only successful tries count.

Thirty-Second Alternate-Hand Volley: The test begins by having a student stand between the short and service line facing the front wall. On the signal ''begin,'' the student throws a ball to the front wall. After the ball bounces on its return from the front wall, the student tries to deliver the ball back to the front wall at an angle that causes the ball to return to the subject's op-

posite side for an alternate-hand return. If a ball is hit with the same hand on two successive returns, no point scores. If a ball is not returned to the front wall or is missed, the test examiner throws the subject a second ball. Points earned from volleys before the missed attempt will be added to successful points in succeeding attempts. A player cannot step across the service line to return a ball. At the end of the 30-second timed trial, the number of alternate hits will be recorded.

One-Minute Continuous Back-Wall Volley: The test begins by having the student stand between the short and service lines. On the signal ''begin,'' the student serves a ball to the front wall and attempts to return his or her own service after the ball bounces off the back wall. The return must be hit to the front wall hard enough that the ball rebounds into the back wall for another return. When a subject fails to successfully return a ball, he or she gets another ball and returns to the service area to begin again. After 1 minute, all successful attempts are recorded. A student can use the dominant hand exclusively.

Scoring.

Dominant Overhand Return: The final score is the number of successful attempts in 10 trials.

Thirty-Second Alternate-Hand Volley: The final score is the number of alternate hits in a 30-second timed trial.

One-Minute Continuous Back-Wall Volley: The final score is the number of successful attempts.

Norms. Not available.

Other Handball Tests

Cornish, C. (1949). A study of measurement of ability in handball. *Research Quarterly*, **20**, 215-222.

Griffith, M.A. (1949). *An objective method of evaluating ability in handball singles.* Unpublished master's thesis, Ohio State University, Columbus.

Leinbach, C.H. (1952). *The development of achievement standards in handball and touch football for use in the Department of Physical Training for Men at the University of Texas.* Unpublished master's thesis, University of Texas, Austin.

Malcomb, A.G. (1960). *Can we have an objective method for evaluating ability in handball singles?* Unpublished master's thesis, Ohio State University, Columbus.

McCachren, J.R. (1949). *A study of the University of Florida handball skill test.* Unpublished master's thesis, University of North Carolina, Chapel Hill.

Millonzi, F. (1974). *Development and validation of a handball skill test.* Unpublished master's thesis, University of Wisconsin, LaCrosse.

Montoye, H.J., & Brotzman, J. (1951). An investigation of the validity of using the results of a doubles tournament as a measure of handball ability. *Research Quarterly*, **38**, 247-253.

Pennington, G.G., Day, J.A., Drowatzky, J.N., & Hanson, J.F. (1967). A measure of handball ability. *Research Quarterly*, **38**, 247-253.

Schiff, F.S. (1938). *A test of skills performed in the game situation of handball.* Unpublished master's thesis, Ohio State University, Columbus.

Simos, T. (1952). *A handball classification test.* Unpublished master's thesis, Springfield College, Springfield, MA.

Horseshoes

Horseshoe pitching, long a popular recreational and competitive sport, has gained renewed interest during George Bush's presidency. Bush, a longtime horseshoe enthusiast, had a horseshoe pit built on the White House lawn and often pitches with celebrities. The game, played by two or four players, is inexpensive, can be played most anywhere, and can be enjoyed for a lifetime.

Horseshoe skills typically taught include the single turn delivery, the 1-1/4-turn delivery, the 1-1/2-turn delivery, and the 1-3/4-turn delivery. No objective horseshoe skills tests are available.

Pickle-Ball

Pickle-ball, created during the summer of 1965 in Seattle, was designed as a family game. It was originally played in a backyard without rules and was a modification of badminton and tennis. By 1967 official rules, a court, and strategies had been added. By 1972 the United States Pickle-Ball Association was formed to govern and promote the sport. By the mid-1970s the game spread to most high schools and colleges in the Seattle area. Pickle-ball is now often introduced at state and regional conventions.

Skills typically taught in pickle-ball include the forehand and backhand drives, serves, lobs, overhead slam, drop shots, and volley shots. No objective pickle-ball skills tests are available.

Racquetball

Racquetball, originally played with a wooden paddle, has evolved into a sport of high-tech graphite racquets. Racquetball as we know it is one of the youngest of our sports, born in the late 1960s. The game has grown steadily in popularity. There are now hundreds of racquetball clubs in the United States. Although racquetball is not taught in many physical education programs because of its need for special facilities, college courses tend to have full enrollments.

The skills taught and tested in racquetball are similar to those in handball. There are few racquetball tests, but that is understandable for a relatively new sport.

Hensley Racquetball Skill Test (Hensley, East, & Stillwell, 1979)

Purpose. To evaluate speed and power ability in racquetball.

Validity and Reliability. Validity coefficients of .79 and .86 for the short-wall volley and the long-wall volley, respectively, were obtained by using the instructor's rating of students as the criterion measure. Using the test-retest approach, reliability coefficients for the long-wall volley test were determined to be .82 for women and .85 for men. Coefficients for the short-wall volley test were .86 for women and .76 for men.

Age Level and Sex. Originally administered to college students. Appropriate for junior high school and senior high school students.

Personnel. One scorer and an assistant are required for each testing station.

Equipment. Racquets, eye protection, and four racquetballs at each testing station. A measuring tape, marking tape, stop watches, score cards or recording sheets, and pencils.

Space. Regulation-sized racquetball courts.

Test Items. A short-wall volley and a long-wall volley.

Preparation. Measure and mark a restraining line 12 feet behind and parallel to the short line for the long-wall volley test.

Directions. After receiving directions, students are allowed a 5-minute practice session in an adjacent court. Upon entering the testing court, students are allowed an additional minute of practice.

Short-Wall Volley Test: The student stands, two balls in hand, behind the short service line. An assistant, located within the court but near the backwall, holds two additional balls. To begin, the student drops a ball and volleys it against the front wall as many times as possible in 30 seconds. All legal hits must be made from behind the short line. The ball may be hit in the air after rebounding from the front wall or after bouncing. The ball may bounce as many times as the hitter wishes before it is volleyed back to the front wall. The student may step into the front court to retrieve balls that fail to return past the short line but must return behind the restraining line for the next stroke. If a ball is missed, a second ball may be put into play in the same manner as the first. (The missed ball may be put back into play or a new ball can be obtained from the assistant.) Each time a volley is interrupted, a new ball must be put into play by being bounced behind the short line. Any stroke may be used to keep the ball in play.

The scorer may be located either inside the court or in an adjacent viewing area. The 30-second count should commence the instant the student drops the first ball. Trial 2 should begin immediately after Trial 1.

Long-Wall Volley Test: The long-wall volley test is administered in the same manner as the short-wall volley test except for the positioning of the student being tested. The student must volley the ball from behind a restraining line 12 feet behind and parallel to the short line. Also, two additional balls are placed in the back wall floor crease. If possible, the scorer should be located outside the court, viewing either from above or through a glass back wall.

Scoring. Both tests are scored the same. One point is awarded each time the ball legally hits the front wall during two 30-second timed trials. The final score is the total of legal hits during the two trials. No points are awarded if a student steps on or over the restraining line to volley a ball or if the ball hits the floor (skips) on the way to the front wall.

Norms. T score values appear in Table 5.5.

Table 5.5 T score Norms for the Hensley Short Wall and Long Wall Volley Tests

| | Score | | | |
| | Short wall volley test | | Long wall volley test | |
T score	Men	Women	Men	Women
80	53	44	40	31
75	49	41	38	29
70	46	38	35	27
65	43	35	33	25
60	40	32	30	23
55	36	29	28	21
50	33	26	25	19
45	30	23	23	17
40	27	20	20	15
35	24	17	18	13
30	20	14	15	11
25	17	11	13	9
20	14	8	10	7

Note. From ''A racquetball skills test,'' by J.E. Hensley, W.B. East, and J.L. Stillwell, 1979, *Research Quarterly*, **50**, pp. 114-118. Copyright 1979 by AAHPERD. Reprinted by permission.

Other Racquetball Tests

Bartee, H. (1982). Tests of racquetball skills. *The Indiana Association HPERD Journal, 11,* 8-9.

Buschner, C.A. (1976). *The validation of a racquetball skills test for college men.* Unpublished doctoral dissertation, Oklahoma State University, Stillwater.

Chase, R.L. (1986). Racquetball testing. *Texas Association HPERD Journal, 55,* 17.

Collins, R. (1982). Racquetball skills test investigation. *Minnesota Journal for Health, Physical Education and Recreation, 10,* 10-13.

Epperson, S.W. (1977). *Validation of the Reznik racquetball test.* Unpublished master's thesis, Washington State University, Pullman.

Gorman, D.R. (1983). The predictive value of the Pennington skill test battery in assessing racquetball skill. *Arkansas Journal of Health, Physical Education and Recreation, 18,* 7-8, 10, 13.

Herman, M. (1991). *Johnson racquetball test.* Unpublished master's thesis, Bemidji State University, Bemidji, MN.

Karpman, M., & Isaacs, L. (1979). An improved racquetball skills test. *Research Quarterly, 50,* 526-527.

Peterson, A. (1989). Skill assessment for college racquetball classes. *Journal of Physical Education, Recreation and Dance, 69,* 71-73.

Reznik, J.W. (1975). Measure your proficiency. *Racquetball, 5,* 64.

Salmela, J.H. (1980). Measurement of racquet sport performance. *Perceptual and Motor Skills, 50,* 1074.

Valcourt, D.F. (1982). *Development of a racquetball skills test battery for male and female beginner and intermediate players.* Unpublished master's thesis, Springfield College, Springfield, MA.

Shuffleboard

Shuffleboard is played on a long, narrow court with triangular scoring areas at each end. The game is played by two or four people and can be adapted to any location. Shuffleboard is not strenuous, can be played for a lifetime, and is thoroughly enjoyed by many senior citizens at retirement centers. The only skill needed to play shuffleboard is the push thrust. No objective shuffleboard skills tests are available.

Squash

One form of squash is said to have originated in Greece or Rome. The modern game of squash is believed to have evolved in England among prisoners during the 1800s. Squash, like many other sports, became more popular after World War II. Squash, like tennis, had its greatest popularity during the 1970s.

Skills typically taught in a squash unit include the lob, drive, and angle serves; ground strokes; and crosscourt, down the line, pinch, and lob shots.

Cahill Squash Test (Cahill, 1977)

Purpose. To evaluate volley, serve, and forehand strokes in squash.

Validity and Reliability. Validity coefficients of .87 and .71 were reported for the 30-second rally and forehand crosscourt shot, respectively. Round-robin tournament play and coaches' rankings were used as criterion measures. Intraclass correlation produced reliability coefficients of .94 and .82 for the 30-second rally and forehand crosscourt shot, respectively.

Age Level and Sex. Originally conducted with male and female college students and varsity squash players. Appropriate for junior high school and senior high school students.

Personnel. One person.

Equipment. Squash racquets, squash balls, a measuring tape, marking tape, a stop watch, score cards or recording sheets, and pencils.

Space. Regulation-sized squash court.

Test Items. The 30-second rally and the forehand crosscourt shot.

Preparation. Each testing station for the forehand crosscourt shot test is prepared as shown in Figure 5.6. No preparation is required for the 30-second rally test.

Directions. Provide a warm-up period of at least 5 minutes before the test. Students should be allowed to practice for at least 30 seconds before each individual test.

Forehand Crosscourt Shot: The student stands midway between the center line and the side wall at the beginning of each trial. The student then hits a ball off the front wall and on the return directs the ball into the target area. The

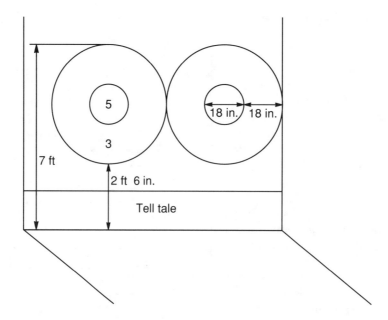

Figure 5.6 Target markings for the Cahill Forehand Crosscourt (Squash) Test.
Note. From ''The construction of a skills test for squash racquets,'' by P.J. Cahill, 1977, Doctoral Dissertation, Springfield College, Springfield, MA. Copyright 1977 by the author and Springfield College. Reprinted by permission.

ball is directed into the left-hand target for a right-handed player and the right-hand target for a left-handed player. After three practice shots, the student hits 10 forehand shots. The student can choose not to attempt a shot on a poorly hit setup. One trial is allowed.

Thirty-Second Rally: The student stands with both feet behind the service line holding one ball. Upon the command ''ready, go,'' the student starts rallying the ball against the front wall. The student can strike the ball after any number of bounces or with a volley stroke. The student can move across the service line to hit a ball that returns short but must return behind the line for the next shot. Until the student returns behind the line, no shots hit are counted. Three 30-second timed trials are allowed.

Scoring.

Forehand Crosscourt Shot: Points are awarded according to where balls strike the target. The innermost circle is worth 5 points, the middle circle worth 3, and anything outside the circles worth 1 point. The score is the total for 10 shots. Balls striking the side wall or floor first earn no points.

Thirty-Second Rally: Each correct hit is counted during a 30-second timed trial. The score for the test is the number of correct hits for the three trials.

Norms. Norms for the forehand crosscourt shot and the 30-second rally test are provided in Tables 5.6 and 5.7.

Table 5.6 Beginner T Scale Norms for the Forehand Crosscourt Test

Men		Women	
Score	T scale	Score	T scale
36	72	32	70
34	68	30	64
32	65	28	63
30	61	26	60
28	58	24	59
26	56	22	57
24	53	20	54
22	49	18	51
20	46	16	47
18	43	14	43
16	40	12	41
14	37	10	36
12	34	8	32
10	28	6	24

Note. From ''The construction of a skills test for squash racquets,'' by P.J. Cahill, 1977, Doctoral Dissertation, Springfield College, Springfield, MA. Copyright 1977 by the author and Springfield College. Reprinted by permission.

Table 5.7 Beginner T Scale Norms for the 30-Second Rally Test

Men		Women	
Score	T scale	Score	T scale
68	71	56	74
66	69	54	68
64	67	52	66
62	66	50	62
60	65	48	59
58	61	46	58
56	59	44	54
54	57	42	52
52	55	40	51
50	52	38	49
48	48	36	47
46	46	34	44
44	45	32	43
42	42	30	41
40	40	28	36
38	35	26	30
36	32	24	26
34	28		

Note. From ''The construction of a skills test for squash racquets,'' by P.J. Cahill, 1977, Doctoral Dissertation, Springfield College, Springfield, MA. Copyright 1977 by the author and Springfield College. Reprinted by permission.

Another Squash Test

Broadhead, G.D. (1967). *An assessment, at various levels of ability, of the respective contributions of stroking ability and physical condition to the outcome of a game of squash racquets.* Unpublished master's thesis, University of Wisconsin, Madison.

Table Tennis

Table tennis, originally known as Ping-Pong, began in the late 1800s. Its popularity in the United States peaked in the 1920s, but it still is popular. It is inexpensive and can be played in a small space such as a basement recreation room.

Mott-Lockhart Table Tennis Test (Mott & Lockhart, 1946)

Purpose. To evaluate volleying ability in table tennis.

Validity and Reliability. A validity coefficient of .84 was reported between test scores and subjective judges' ratings. The odd-even approach determined a reliability coefficient of .90.

Age Level and Sex. Originally administered to college females. Appropriate for junior high school and senior high school students.

Personnel. One central timer and one scorer at each testing station.

Equipment. Table tennis tables, balls, paddles, small cardboard box, tape or thumbtacks, a stop watch, score cards or recording sheets, and pencils.

Space. A low-ceilinged multipurpose room.

Test Item. The backboard volley.

Preparation. Fold a table tennis table so one half is perpendicular to the other half. Use the upright half as a backboard. A 6-inch net line is placed across the upright half of the table tennis table and a box to contain two balls is fastened to a side of the table.

Directions. The student takes a position, with paddle and ball in hand, at the end of a table. On the ''ready, go'' signal, the student bounces the ball on the table and strokes it toward the upright half of the table and continues rallying the ball as many times as possible in 30 seconds. There is no restriction on the number of times a ball can bounce before it is stroked. If a student loses control of a ball, he or she should grab a second ball from the box attached to the side of the table. When a new ball is put into play, the starting format is repeated. Shots do not count if a ball hits below the 6-inch line or if a student places a free hand on the table during or preceding a stroke. Provide a rest period between trials. Practice is allowed before the first timed trial.

Scoring. Points are awarded for each ball that hits above the 6-inch net line. A valid hit is one that is stroked after a bounce with no help from the free hand. Three 30-second timed trials are allowed. The final score is the best of the three trials.

Norms. T score values appear in Table 5.8.

Table 5.8 T Scores for the Mott-Lockart Table Tennis Test

T score	Raw score	T score	Raw score	T score	Raw score
77	60	59	45	41	29
76		58		40	
75		57	44	39	28
74		56		38	27
73	58	55	43	37	26
72		54	42	36	
71	55	53	41	35	25
70		52	40	34	24
69	54	51		33	23
68	52	50	39	32	22
67	51	49	38	31	
66	50	48	37	30	
65	49	47	36	29	21
64	48	46	34-35	28	
63		45	33	27	
62	47	44	32	26	20
61		43	31	25	
60	46	42	30	24	16

This article is reprinted with permission from the *Journal of Physical Education, Recreation and Dance*, 1946, **17**, pp. 550-552. The *Journal* is a publication of the American Alliance for Health, Physical Education, Recreation and Dance, 1900 Association Drive, Reston, VA 22091.

Tennis

Although some form of tennis has been played since 1300, modern tennis arrived in the United States in 1874 and spread throughout the country within 5 years. The boom years for tennis occurred during the 1970s as television brought Billy Jean King and Jimmy Connors into peoples' homes. Although interest has waned since then, tennis continues to attract people of both sexes and of all ages. Indoor tennis facilities have made tennis a year-round sport.

Tennis skills typically taught in a physical education unit include serves, groundstrokes, lobs, drop shots, and overhead smashes. Skills tests usually include groundstrokes, volleys, and serves.

Hewitt Tennis Achievement Test (Hewitt, 1966)

Purpose. To evaluate forehand, backhand, and service ability in tennis.

Validity and Reliability. Validity coefficients by ability level were reported as follows: for beginners, .67, .62, .72, and .89; for advanced players, .61, .61, .62, and .72; and for varsity players, .57, .52, .92, and .86 for forehand, backhand, service placement, and service speed tests respectively. The criterion measure for determining validity was round-robin tournament rankings. Through the test-retest approach, the following reliability coefficients were reported: .75, .78, .94, and .84 for the forehand, backhand, service placement, and service speed tests, respectively.

Age Level and Sex. Originally conducted with college students. Appropriate for junior high school and senior high school students.

Personnel. Each testing station requires a scorer/recorder, a ball retriever, and, for the forehand and backhand tests, a person to serve balls.

Equipment. Tennis racquets, balls, a measuring tape, marking tape, two 7-foot high poles at each station, a ladder, baskets for balls, a rope long enough to reach across the width of a tennis court, score cards or recording sheets, and pencils.

Space. Each testing station requires a regulation-sized tennis court.

Test Items. The service placement test, the speed of service test, and the forehand/backhand drive tests.

Preparation. Each testing station for the service placement test and the speed of service test is prepared as shown in Figure 5.7. A rope is stretched over and parallel to the net 7 feet high, a placement target is prepared in the right service court, and speed zones are located at the end of the tennis court. Each testing station for the forehand and backhand drive test is prepared as shown in Figure 5.8. A rope is stretched over and parallel to the net 7 feet high, and

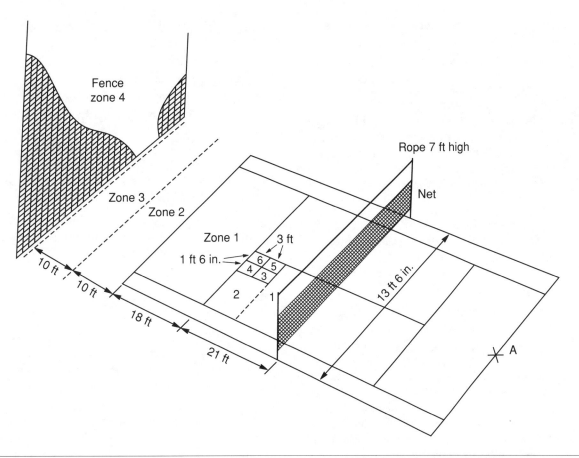

Figure 5.7 Court markings for the Hewitt Speed of Service and Service Placement (Tennis) Test.
Note. From ''Hewitt's tennis achievement test,'' by J.E. Hewitt, 1966, *Research Quarterly*, **37**, pp. 231-240. Copyright 1966 by AAHPER. Reprinted by permission.

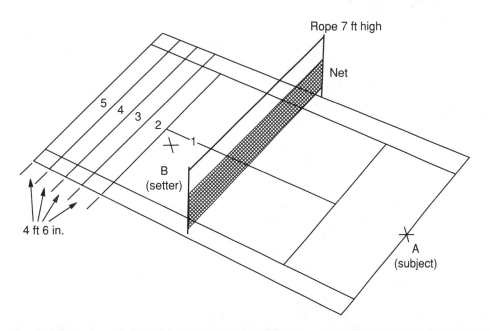

Figure 5.8 Court markings for the Hewitt Forehand and Backhand Drive (Tennis) Test.
Note. From ''Hewitt's tennis achievement test,'' by J. E. Hewitt, 1966, *Research Quarterly*, **37**, pp. 231-240. Copyright 1966 by AAHPER. Reprinted by permission.

placement zones are marked between the base-line and the service line.

Directions.

Service Placement Test: The student stands to the right of the center line behind the base line. Ten balls are served into the marked service court target. To be counted, served balls must pass between the net and the rope. Balls that hit the rope and net balls are repeated. Following a teacher's demonstration, the student is allowed a 10-minute warm-up on a different court.

Speed of Service Test: This test is administered simultaneously with the service placement. For each of the 10 good service placements (Service Placement Test) the score is the distance a ball bounces into the speed zones.

Forehand and Backhand Drive Tests: The student to be tested takes a receiving position at the center mark of the baseline. The setter takes a position across the net where center line and service line intersect. The setter hits to the student being tested balls that land just beyond the service line. Five practice trials are permitted before the 20 test trials are given. The student must return 10 shots with a backhand stroke and 10 with a forehand stroke. The student may choose which balls to return backhand and which to return forehand. Returned balls must pass between the net and the rope and land in target zones. Balls hit into the net or the rope are repeated.

Scoring.

Service Placement Test: Each of the 10 serves is scored from 0 to 6 points depending on where it lands in the service target. Served balls that go over the 7-foot rope and those wide or long are scored zero. Balls that land on a line earn the higher value. The final score is the point total for the 10 served balls. A perfect score is 60 points.

Speed of Service Test: Each of the 10 serves is scored from 0 to 4 points depending on where it lands in the speed zones after taking its first bounce in the service target zone. Served balls that go over the 7-foot rope and those wide or long are scored zero. Balls that land on a line

earn the higher value. The final score is the point total for the 10 served balls. A perfect score is 40 points.

Forehand and Backhand Drive Tests: Each of 20 returns is scored from 0 to 5 points depending on where it lands in the target zone. Returned balls that go over the rope but land in a target zone are awarded one-half the regular value. Balls that land on a line earn the higher value. The final score is the point total for 20 returned shots. A perfect score is 100 points.

Norms. Scoring scales for junior high school and senior high school students appear in Table 5.9 and for college students in Table 5.10.

Table 5.9 Achievement Scales for the Hewitt Tennis Test

Grade	Service placements	Service speed	Forehand placements	Backhand placements
	Junior varsity and varsity tennis (16 cases—5 S.D.)			
F	20-24	20-22	25-28	20-23
D	25-29	23-25	29-32	24-27
C	30-39	26-32	33-39	28-34
B	40-45	33-36	40-45	35-40
A	46-50	37-40	46-50	41-47
	Advanced tennis (36 cases—5 S.D.)			
F	11-14	8-9	24-25	22-26
D	15-19	11-13	26-29	27-30
C	20-30	14-21	30-39	31-37
B	31-37	22-25	40-44	38-42
A	38-44	26-30	45-48	43-46
	Beginning tennis (91 cases—5 S.D.)			
F	1-2	1-3	1-3	1-2
D	3-6	4-7	4-8	3-7
C	7-16	8-13	9-21	8-19
B	17-21	14-17	22-28	20-26
A	22-26	18-21	29-36	27-34

Note. From "Hewitt's tennis achievement test," by J.E. Hewitt, 1966. *Research Quarterly,* **37**, pp. 231-240. Copyright 1966 by AAHPER. Reprinted by permission.

Table 5.10 Scoring Scale for the Hewitt Service Placement Test

College men	Performance level	College women
20-60	Excellent	14-60
16-19	Good	10-13
7-15	Average	4-9
3-6	Poor	1-3
0-2	Very poor	0

Note. From "Hewitt's tennis achievement test," by J.E. Hewitt, 1966. *Research Quarterly,* **37,** pp. 231-240. Copyright 1966 by AAHPER. Reprinted by permission.

Jones Tennis Serving Test (Jones, 1967)

Purpose. To evaluate service ability in tennis.

Validity and Reliability. A validity coefficient of .76 was computed using rating scales as the criterion measure. A reliability coefficient of .92 was computed with the odd-even approach followed by the Spearman-Brown Prophecy Formula.

Age Level and Sex. Originally conducted with high school girls. Appropriate for junior high school and senior high school students.

Personnel. A minimum of three people: one timer and two scorer/recorders. If multiple stations are used, a scorer/recorder is needed at each station.

Equipment. Tennis racquets, tennis balls, a measuring tape, chalk, a basket for tennis balls, a stop watch, score cards or recording sheets, and pencils.

Space. Each testing station requires a regulation-sized tennis court.

Test Item. Serving a tennis ball.

Preparation. Each testing station is prepared as shown in Figure 5.9. Court markings are put down with chalk. Identical scoring grids should be prepared on both the right and left halves of one side of a tennis court.

Directions. To begin, students are paired as partners. One partner serves and the other retrieves

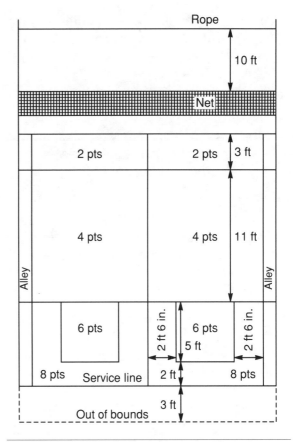

Figure 5.9 Court markings for the Jones Tennis Serving Test.

Note. From "A measure of tennis serving ability," by S.K. Jones, 1967, unpublished master's thesis, University of California, Los Angeles. Copyright 1967 by the author and UCLA. Reprinted by permission.

served balls. After one partner hits 10 serves to one side of the court, the second partner serves 10. When the second partner finishes, the first serves another 10 to the other half of the court. Then the second partner does likewise. Serves are made from behind the base line. Every trial counts. If a ball goes over the restraining rope, it counts half the point value of the zone it lands in. Let serves and serves striking the restraining rope are repeated without penalty. When a fault occurs during a serve, it counts as one of the 10 trials, whether it hit the net or went out of bounds. Subjects are allowed two trials for practice.

Scoring. Points are awarded according to where balls land in the scoring grid shown in Figure

5.9. If a served ball goes over the 10-foot rope, it is awarded half of what its point value would have been. The final score is the total points accumulated during the 20 trials.

Norms. Not available.

Kemp-Vincent Rally Test (Kemp & Vincent, 1968)

Purpose. To evaluate rallying ability in tennis under game conditions.

Validity and Reliability. Concurrent validity coefficients of .84 and .93 for beginners and intermediate players, respectively, were computed by comparing the rank difference between this test and the rank in a round-robin tournament. The test-retest approach reported reliability coefficients of .86 and .90 for beginners and intermediate players, respectively.

Age Level and Sex. Originally conducted with college students. Appropriate for junior high school and senior high school students.

Personnel. One person is needed to count the total number of strokes and two are needed to count each player's errors.

Equipment. Tennis racquets, tennis balls, a stop watch, score cards or recording sheets, and pencils.

Space. Regulation-sized tennis courts.

Test Item. Rallying a tennis ball.

Preparation. The only preparation involves score cards.

Directions. Two students of similar ability assume ready positions on opposite sides of the net on a singles tennis court. Each player has two tennis balls on his or her side of the court. On the "go" signal, one student bounces a ball behind the baseline and with a courtesy stroke puts the ball into play. The two students rally the ball as long as possible. When a ball is hit into the net or out of bounds, either player starts another ball into play with a courtesy stroke from behind the baseline. Any type of stroke may be used during a rally. If all four balls are hit out of play, the testing students are responsible for retrieving them to continue the test. One 3-minute timed trial is allowed.

Errors are recorded if a student fails to get the ball over the net on a courtesy stroke from behind the baseline; fails to get the ball over the net during a rally; fails to start a new ball from behind the baseline; fails to keep the ball within the singles court area; or fails to hit the ball before a second bounce.

Balls landing on boundary lines on a first bounce are good. Balls hitting the top of the net and going over into the opposite court are good and in play. Players may play a ball on which their test partner has committed an error if it is believed advantageous to keep the ball in play. A 1-minute warm-up period is permitted before the test.

Scoring. For a 3-minute rally, the combined number of hits for the two players are counted, including any erroneous hits. The courtesy stroke to put a ball in play counts as a hit. Errors committed by each player are counted. From the combined number of hits for both players, each individual player subtracts the number of his or her errors to arrive at a final rally score.

Norms. Not available.

Other Tennis Tests

American Alliance for Health, Physical Education, Recreation and Dance. (1989). *AAHPERD Tennis skills test manual.* Reston, VA: AAHPERD.

Avery, C.A., Richardson, P.A., & Jackson, A.W. (1979). A practical tennis serve test: measurement under simulated game conditions. *Research Quarterly,* **50,** 554-564.

Ballard, M.E. (1978). *The development of a test for assessing ability to serve in tennis.* Unpublished master's thesis, Southern Illinois University, Carbondale.

Broer, M.R., & Miller, D.M. (1950). Achievement tests for beginning and intermediate tennis. *Research Quarterly,* **21,** 303-313.

Butler, W.M. (1961). Comparison of two methods of measuring the degree of skill in the underarm serve. *Research Quarterly,* **33,** 261-262.

Cobane, E. (1962). Test for the serve. In *Tennis and badminton guide 1962-1964.* Washington, DC: AAHPER.

Cordon, C.J. (1941). *The development and evaluation of a battery of tennis skills as an index to ability in tennis.* Unpublished master's thesis, Springfield College, Springfield, MA.

DiGennara, J. (1969). Construction of forehand drive, backhand drive, and service tennis tests. *Research Quarterly,* **40,** 496-501.

Drowatsky, J.N., & Marcel, H. (1990). Simplification of the Talent-N-Timing tennis test for college students. *The Physical Educator,* **47,** 128-136.

Dyer, J.T. (1935). The backboard test of tennis ability. *Research Quarterly,* **6,** 63-74.

Dyer, J.T. (1938). Revision of the backboard test of tennis ability. *Research Quarterly,* **9,** 25-31.

Edwards, J. (1965). *A study of three measures of the tennis serve.* Master's thesis, University of Wisconsin, Madision. (Microcard PE 746, University of Oregon, Eugene.)

Felshin, J., & Spencer, E. (1963). Evaluation procedures for tennis. In D. Davis (Ed.), *Tennis and badminton articles.* Washington, DC: AAHPER.

Fiereck, L.M. (1969). *Assessments of velocity for the tennis serve of college women.* Unpublished master's thesis, Southern Illinois University, Carbondale.

Fonger, S.J. (1963). *The development of a reliable objective and practical tennis serve test for college women.* Unpublished master's thesis, University of Michigan, Ann Arbor.

Fox, K. (1953). A study of the validity of the Dyer Backboard Test and the Miller Forehand-Backhand Test for beginning tennis players. *Research Quarterly,* **24,** 1-7.

Hamer, D.R. (1974). *The "Mini-Match" as a measurement of the ability of the beginning tennis player.* Unpublished doctoral dissertation, Indiana University, Bloomington.

Hensley, L. (1979). *A factor analysis of selected tennis skill tests.* Unpublished doctoral dissertation, University of Georgia, Athens.

Hewitt, J.E. (1965). Hewitt revision of the Dyer backboard tennis test. *Research Quarterly,* **36,** 153-157.

Hewitt, J.E. (1968). Classification tests in tennis. *Research Quarterly,* **39,** 552-555.

Hubbell, N.C. (1960). *A battery of tennis skill tests for college women.* Unpublished master's thesis, Texas Woman's University, Denton.

Hulac, G.M. (1958). *The construction of an objective indoor test for measuring effective tennis serves.* Unpublished master's thesis, University of North Carolina, Greensboro.

Hulbert, B.A. (1966). *A study of tests for the forehand drive in tennis.* Master's thesis, University of Wisconsin, Madison. (Microcard PE 818, University of Oregon, Eugene.)

Johnson, J. (1957). Tennis serve of advanced women players. *Research Quarterly,* **28,** 123-131.

Malinak, N.R. (1961). *The construction of an objective measure of accuracy in the performance of the tennis serve.* Unpublished master's thesis, University of Illinois at Urbana-Champaign.

McAdams, L.B. (1964). *The use of rebound nets as a means of determining tennis skill.* Unpublished master's thesis, Washington State University, Pullman.

Murphy, W.E. (1941). *The measurement of some skills necessary to success in tennis.* Unpublished master's thesis, George Williams College, Chicago.

Mynard, V. (1938). *A preliminary analysis of the game of tennis, the reliability of certain tennis*

(continued)

Other Tennis Tests (continued)

skill tests, and the determination of practice board areas for serve and drive. Unpublished master's thesis, Wellesley College, Wellesley, MA.

Purcell, K. (1981). A tennis forehand-backhand drive skill test which measures ball control and stroke firmness. *Research Quarterly*, **52**, 238-245.

Recio, M., & Prestidge, C. (1972). *The overhead smash test utilizing the Johnson Tennis and Badminton Machine.* Unpublished study, Northeast Louisiana University, Monroe.

Reid, R. (1960). A tennis skills test. *DGWS Guide for tennis and badminton 1960-1962.* Washington, DC: AAHPER.

Ronning, H.E. (1959). *Wall tests for evaluation of tennis ability.* Unpublished master's thesis, Washington State University, Pullman.

Sanders, S. (1967). *A serving test for beginning tennis players.* Research project, Southern Illinois University, Carbondale.

Scott, M.G. (1941). Achievement examinations for elementary and intermediate tennis classes. *Research Quarterly*, **12**, 40-49.

Scott, M.G., & French, E. (1959). Scott-French revision of the Dyer wallboard test. In M.G. Scott & E. French, *Measurement and evaluation in physical education.* Dubuque, IA: Brown.

Shepard, G.J. (1972). The tennis drive skills test. *Tennis-badminton-squash guide.* Washington, DC: AAHPER.

Sherman, P. (1972). *A selected battery of tennis skill tests.* Unpublished doctoral dissertation, University of Iowa, Iowa City.

Swift, B.M. (1969). *A skill test and norms for the speed of the tennis serve.* Unpublished doctoral dissertation, University of Arkansas, Fayetteville.

Timmer, K.L. (1965). *A tennis test to determine accuracy in playing ability.* Unpublished master's thesis, Springfield College, Springfield, MA.

Varner, M. (1950). *A skill test for college women enrolled in beginner's tennis classes.* Unpublished master's thesis, Texas State University, Denton.

Wagner, M.M. (1935). An objective method of grading beginners in tennis. *Journal of Health and Physical Education*, **6**, 24-25.

Wrestling

Wrestling is both one of the oldest sports known and one practiced in many different countries: Greece, Egypt, Babylonia, and China. Wrestling, originally a test of manhood, became a means of training soldiers and developed into one of the original Greek Olympic events.

Typically taught wrestling skills in physical education include takedowns, reversals, up-position, down-position, breakdowns, rides, and pinning holds. A review of wrestling skill tests revealed just two tests, neither of which merit publication in this text.

Wrestling Tests

Sickels, W.L. (1967). *A rating test of amateur wrestling ability.* Unpublished master's thesis, San Jose State College, San Jose, CA.

Sievers, H.L. (1934). *The measurement of potential wrestling ability.* Unpublished master's thesis, University of Iowa, Iowa City.

Chapter 6

Tests for Team Sports

Team sports have long been the most common and popular activity units in physical education programs. They generally are introduced in middle school, emphasized in junior high school, and refined in high school (Annarino et al., 1980). Although team sports are usually not foreseen as lifetime activities, many adults continue playing basketball, softball, and volleyball into middle age and beyond.

This chapter includes skills tests for basketball, field hockey, football, ice hockey, lacrosse, soccer, softball, speedball, team handball, and volleyball. Skills tests for newer team sports—korfball, rugby, wallyball, and water polo—have yet to be developed.

Basketball

Basketball was born when James Naismith, a physical education teacher at Springfield (Massachusetts) College, secured the first hoop—a peach basket—to the balcony 10 feet above a gymnasium floor. The game originated to keep athletes interested and in shape during the winter.

Although basketball is a five-on-five team sport, it is played just as well one-on-one or two-on-two. Because it also is relatively inexpensive, basketball is the sport of choice among many of the nation's youth. Although basketball is generally not thought of as a lifetime sport, the substantial number of adult basketball leagues throughout the nation increases every year.

Skills typically taught in a physical education basketball unit include the chest, bounce, and baseball passes; pivoting; dribbling; lay-ups; jump and free throw shooting; rebounding; and defensive positioning. Basketball skills tests usually include at least two of the skill components.

AAHPERD Basketball Test (AAHPERD, 1984)

Purpose. To evaluate dribbling, passing, shooting, and defensive ability in basketball.

Validity and Reliability. Validity coefficients of .37 to .91 were reported for all ages on individual test items, and .65 to .95 for the test battery as a whole. A criterion measure of two subjective ratings of skill in shooting and game performance were used. The test-retest approach computed reliability coefficients of .84 to .97.

Age Level and Sex. Appropriate for junior high school and senior high school students.

Personnel. If the four tests are administered simultaneously, four testers are needed, one at each testing station.

Equipment. Basketballs, a measuring tape, marking tape, cones, a whistle, stop watches, score cards or recording sheets, and pencils.

Space. The passing test requires a smooth wall surface of 30 feet. The shooting, dribbling, and defensive tests require an area around the lane inside the 3-point line.

Test Items. Speed spot shooting, passing, control dribbling, and defensive movement.

Preparation. Each testing station for the speed spot shooting test is prepared as shown in Figure 6.1. Five markers, from which students must shoot, are placed on the floor. Fifth- and sixth-grade students shoot from 9-foot marks, seventh- through ninth-grade students shoot from 12-foot marks, and 10th-grade students through college age students shoot from 15-foot marks. Shooting spots A and E are measured from the middle of the backboard, those for B, C, and D are measured from the center of the basket. Each shooting spot marker should be 2 feet long and 1 inch wide.

Each station for the passing test is prepared as shown in Figure 6.2. A restraining line 26 feet long is placed 8 feet from and parallel to a smooth testing wall. The testing wall contains six 2 feet by 2 feet targets 2 feet apart. Moving from the left side of the testing wall, Targets A, C, and E have their base 5 feet from the floor while B, D, and F have their base 3 feet from the floor.

Each testing station for the control-dribble test is prepared as shown in Figure 6.3. Five cones are set up in the basketball lane, and one cone is set up outside of the lane. Cone A is placed along the outside of the left lane line halfway between the free throw line and the baseline. Cone

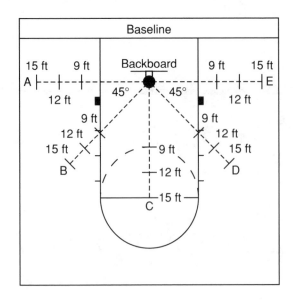

Figure 6.1 Court markings for the AAHPERD Basketball Speed Spot Shooting Test.
Note. From "AAHPERD skills test manual: Basketball for boys and girls," by AAHPERD, 1984, Reston, VA. Copyright 1984 by AAHPERD. Reprinted by permission.

B is placed in the middle of the lane halfway between the free throw line and the baseline and halfway between the two lane lines. Cones C, D, E, and F are placed in the four corners of the lane.

Each station for the defensive movement test is prepared as shown in Figure 6.4. Four floor markers, A, B, D, and E, are to be placed at the junctions of the free throw line and lane lines and

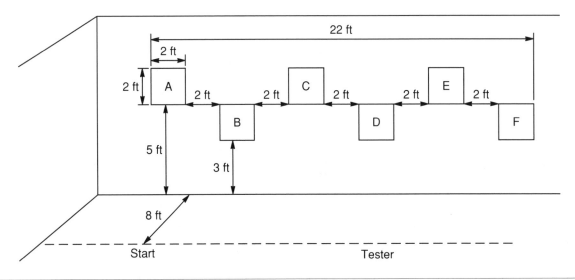

Figure 6.2 Wall markings for the AAHPERD Basketball Passing Test.
Note. From "AAHPERD skills test manual: Basketball for boys and girls," by AAHPERD, 1984, Reston, VA. Copyright 1984 by AAHPERD. Reprinted by permission.

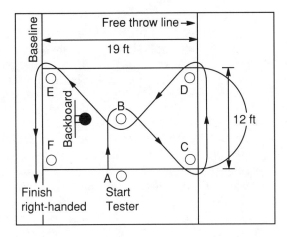
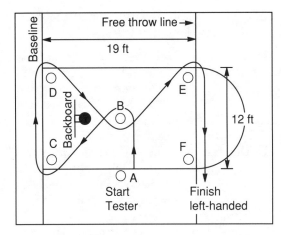

Figure 6.3 Court markings for the AAHPERD Basketball Control Dribble Test.
Note. From "AAHPERD skills test manual: Basketball for boys and girls," by AAHPERD, 1984, Reston, VA. Copyright 1984 by AAHPERD. Reprinted by permission.

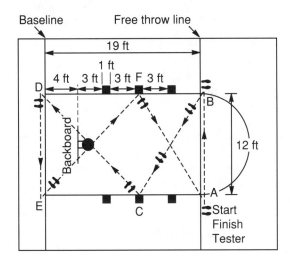

Figure 6.4 Court markings and foot positions for the AAHPERD Basketball Defensive Movement Test.
Note. From "AAHPERD skills test manual: Basketball for boys and girls," by AAHPERD, 1984, Reston, VA. Copyright 1984 by AAHPERD. Reprinted by permission.

the baseline and lane lines. The middle line markers on the free throw lanes serve as Targets C and F.

Directions.

Speed Spot Shooting: The student, basketball in hand, stands behind the shooting spots for his or her age. On the "ready, go" signal, the student shoots, retrieves or rebounds the ball, dribbles to another spot and shoots again. The student must attempt at least one shot from each of the five spots and must have at least one foot behind the marker on each shot. Four lay-up

shots may be attempted, but not two in succession. The student continues trying to score until "stop" is called. All students get three trials of 60 seconds each; the first trial is a practice trial.

Passing: The student stands behind the 8-foot restraining line, holding a basketball and facing the far left wall target (A). On the "ready, go" signal, the student performs a chest pass to the first target square (A), recovers the ball while moving to the second target square (B) and performs a chest pass to the second target (B). Students continue this action until they reach the last target (F). While at the last target (F), they throw two chest passes then repeat the sequence by moving to the left passing at targets E, D, C, and so on. Three 30-second trials are given, the first of which is practice. Only chest passes are allowed.

Control Dribble: The student starts, basketball in the nondominant hand on the nondominant-hand side of Cone A. On the "ready, go" signal the student dribbles, using the nondominant hand, to Cone B. The student circles Cone B and moves to Cone C. Students then proceed to Cone D, back to Cone B, to Cone E, and finish at Cone F. After circling Cone B the first time, students dribble with either hand. The course is completed when the student crosses the finish line with both feet at Cone F. A student who loses control of a ball must retrieve the ball and continue the test from that point. A student who fails to do this must return to the starting line and begin again. Ball-handling infractions (traveling, double dribbling, dribbling the ball either inside or over a cone) void the trial. A retrial is then allowed. Three timed trials are given, the first being a practice.

Defensive Movement: The student stands at Marker A facing away from the basket. On the "ready, go" signal, the student slides to the left toward Marker B. At Marker B, the student touches the floor outside the lane with the left hand. Following the execution of a dropstep, the student slides to Marker C and performs the same touching technique. This continues until the student touches all markers and arrives back at Marker A. Both feet must cross the finish line to end a trial. A student cannot cross his or her feet while sliding from marker to marker. The trial must be repeated if a student crosses the feet during the slide, fails to touch the hand to the floor outside the lane, or performs the dropstep before the hand touches the floor. Three timed trials are given, the first of which is practice.

Scoring.

Speed Spot Shooting: Two points are awarded for each shot that is made, either a shot from behind the shooting mark or a lay-up. One point is awarded for any unsuccessful shot that hits the rim from above either initially or after rebounding from the backboard. No points are awarded if a shot is preceded by a ball-handling infraction (traveling or double dribbling). If two lay-ups occur in succession, the second gets no points. Only four lay-ups may be attempted; any lay-up in excess of four will be scored as zero. Failure to attempt shots from all designated shooting spots voids a trial. Voided trials must be repeated. The test score is obtained by totaling the two trials.

Passing: Two points are awarded for each chest pass that hits in the target or on the target lines. One point is awarded for each pass that hits between the targets. No points are awarded if a student's foot is on or over the restraining line, or if a second pass is made at Targets B, C, D, or E, or if a pass other than a chest pass is used. The test score is obtained by totaling the two trials.

Control Dribble: The trial score is the time required to complete the course legally. Trial scores are recorded to the nearest 1/10 of a second. The test score is obtained by totaling the two trials.

Defensive movement: The trial score is the time required to complete the course legally. Trial scores are recorded to the nearest 1/10 of a second. The test score is obtained by totaling two trials.

Norms. Percentile norms for speed spot shooting are shown in Table 6.1, for passing in Table 6.2, for control dribble in Table 6.3, and for defensive movement in Table 6.4.

Table 6.1 Percentile Norms for the AAHPERD Basketball Speed Spot Shooting Test

	Age							
Percentile	10	11	12	13	14	15	16-17	College
				Girls				
95	18	19	22	22	25	23	23	35
75	11	11	13	13	15	15	14	21
50	8	8	10	10	11	11	11	17
25	5	5	7	8	9	8	7	13
5	2	2	3	4	4	4	3	8
				Boys				
95	23	25	27	28	30	27	28	30
75	17	18	19	19	23	20	22	25
50	13	14	15	15	18	16	16	22
25	10	10	11	12	13	11	12	19
5	7	6	7	7	9	6	7	14

Note. From ''AAHPERD skills test manual: Basketball for boys and girls,'' by AAHPERD, 1984, Reston, VA. Copyright 1984 by AAHPERD. Reprinted by permission.

Table 6.2 Percentile Norms for the AAHPERD Basketball Passing Test

	Age							
Percentile	10	11	12	13	14	15	16-17	College
Girls								
95	36	38	43	44	46	47	48	54
75	30	31	35	37	39	40	39	47
50	25	27	31	32	34	35	34	42
25	21	23	26	29	29	28	24	37
5	7	13	20	23	24	19	18	21
Boys								
95	41	43	48	54	55	55	57	70
75	35	36	40	43	45	48	49	58
50	31	32	35	39	40	39	41	53
25	25	28	30	35	35	23	25	47
5	8	18	22	23	23	18	21	35

Note. From ''AAHPERD skills test manual: Basketball for boys and girls,'' by AAHPERD, 1984, Reston, VA. Copyright 1984 by AAHPERD. Reprinted by permission.

Table 6.3 Percentile Norms for the AAHPERD Basketball Control Dribble Test

	Age							
Percentile	10	11	12	13	14	15	16-17	College
Girls								
95	10.8	10.3	8.8	8.7	8.4	8.2	8.2	7.6
75	12.3	11.8	10.6	10.0	9.6	9.7	9.8	8.5
50	14.3	13.2	11.9	11.0	10.7	10.7	10.7	9.3
25	16.6	15.0	13.3	12.4	12.0	12.0	12.2	10.4
5	21.7	20.5	19.0	17.8	18.1	15.8	15.0	13.8
Boys								
95	9.2	9.0	8.7	7.8	7.5	7.0	7.0	6.7
75	10.4	10.1	9.5	9.0	8.5	8.1	8.1	7.3
50	11.7	11.1	10.5	9.8	9.3	8.9	9.0	7.8
25	13.7	12.6	11.7	10.7	10.3	10.0	10.0	8.5
5	23.0	16.8	16.0	14.4	13.5	12.0	12.4	10.0

Note. From ''AAHPERD skills test manual: Basketball for boys and girls,'' by AAHPERD, 1984, Reston, VA. Copyright 1984 by AAHPERD. Reprinted by permission.

Table 6.4 Percentile Norms for the AAHPERD Basketball Defensive Movement Test

				Age				
Percentile	10	11	12	13	14	15	16-17	College
				Girls				
95	10.5	10.3	9.5	10.0	9.6	9.7	9.6	8.7
75	11.8	11.8	11.5	11.5	11.0	11.0	11.1	10.3
50	13.2	13.0	12.8	12.5	12.0	12.0	12.0	11.0
25	14.6	14.3	14.1	13.6	13.2	13.4	13.2	12.0
5	19.6	17.4	17.0	16.8	16.4	16.4	16.4	14.5
				Boys				
95	10.0	9.0	8.9	8.9	8.7	7.9	7.3	8.4
75	11.5	10.9	10.7	10.3	10.1	9.3	9.6	9.4
50	12.7	12.0	11.9	11.4	11.3	10.3	10.3	10.3
25	13.9	13.7	13.0	12.8	12.4	11.3	11.5	11.2
5	18.7	17.2	17.0	16.6	15.8	14.0	15.2	12.9

Note. From "AAHPERD skills test manual: Basketball for boys and girls," by AAHPERD, 1984, Reston, VA. Copyright 1984 by AAHPERD. Reprinted by permission.

Harrison Basketball Battery (Harrison, 1969)

Purpose. To evaluate shooting, passing, dribbling, and rebounding ability in basketball.

Validity and Reliability. A validity coefficient of .89 was obtained by using three criteria, the Johnson Basketball Test, peer ratings, and jury ratings. Using the test-retest approach, reliability coefficients for the test components ranged from .91 to .97.

Age Level and Sex. Originally conducted with high school students. Appropriate for junior high school and senior high school students.

Personnel. One person as timer for all four test items and one person at each testing station as recorder/scorer.

Equipment. At least one basketball at each testing station, a measuring tape, marking tape, five cones, a whistle, score cards or recording sheets, and pencils.

Space. The field goal and rebound tests both require the area around two baskets; the dribble test requires a 40 foot by 10 foot course; and the passing test requires an unobstructed wall surface and free space at least 15 feet out from the wall.

Test Items. Field goal shooting, speed pass, dribbling, and rebounding.

Preparation. Each dribbling station is prepared as shown in Figure 6.5. Five cones are placed 10 feet apart with Cone 1 located on the starting line. For the passing test a restraining line parallel to and 8 feet from the testing wall is marked on the floor. No special preparations are required for the field goal and rebound tests.

Directions. Two stations for each test item (eight stations) are set up throughout the gymnasium. Students move from station to station in squads. The instructor acts as a central timer; all tests last 30 seconds. Students are positioned at each station with one student ready to be tested. The timer gives a "ready" signal followed by a short whistle blast signaling the start of the test. The 30-second test ends when the timer gives a second whistle blast. Each student gets two trials. After a trial, that student moves to the end of the line to be ready for the second trial when all students have completed their first trial. A squad leader acts as recorder/scorer.

Field Goal Shooting: The student stands, basketball in hand, at any distance from a basket. On the whistle blast that starts the 30-second timed trial, the student shoots as many shots as possible in any way he or she wishes. Two trials are given.

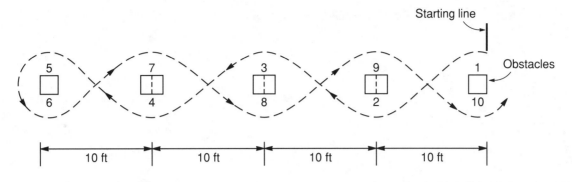

Figure 6.5 Floor plan for the Harrison Dribble Test.
Note. Courtesy of ''A test to measure basketball ability for boys,'' by E.R. Harrison, 1969, unpublished master's thesis, Temple University, Philadelphia, PA. Copyright 1969 by the author.

Speed Pass: The student stands, basketball in hand, with both feet behind the restraining line. On the start signal, the student continuously passes the ball against the wall for 30 seconds. The ball must be passed and received from behind the line using any type of pass. Two trials are given.

Dribbling: The student stands on the right side of the first cone. Upon hearing the whistle blast to start, the student dribbles around the cones alternately passing on the right side and then on the left. When the student reaches the fifth cone, he or she circles around and comes back passing on the right and then on the left. Students go through the course as many times as possible during the 30-second timed trial. Two trials are given.

Rebounding: The student stands, basketball in hand, at any distance from the backboard. On the start signal, the student tosses a basketball against the backboard. As the ball rebounds, the student jumps, catches the ball, and returns it

to the backboard before landing on the floor. If a student cannot execute this move, he or she may catch the ball and land on the floor before returning it to the backboard. Two trials are given.

Scoring.

Field Goal Shooting: One point is awarded for every basket made. A student's score is the better of the two trials.

Speed Passing: One point is awarded every time the ball hits the wall. A student's score is the better of two trials.

Dribbling: One point is awarded each time the student reaches the midpoint of a cone. A student's score is the better of two trials.

Rebounding: One point is awarded each time the ball hits the backboard. A student's score is the better of two trials.

Norms. T scores are shown in Table 6.5.

Table 6.5 T Scales for the Harrison Basketball Test

	Goal shooting				Speed pass				Dribble				Rebounding			
T scale	7th	8th	9th	10th	7th	8th	9th	10th	7th	8th	9th	10th	7th	8th	9th	10th
76					37	38	39	42	39	37	40	36	27	29	34	
75																
74																
73		17	18	18	5			41	38						33	32
72	14				34				37	36	39		26		32	

(continued)

Table 6.5 T Scales for the Harrison Basketball Test (*continued*)

T scale	Goal shooting				Speed pass				Dribble				Rebounding			
	7th	8th	9th	10th	7th	8th	9th	10th	7th	8th	9th	10th	7th	8th	9th	10th
71					33	37			36							
70								40				35	25	28	30	31
69											38				29	30
68		16	17	17		36	38	39	35					27		
67	13				32					35		34	24	26		
66				16	31	35		38	34		37				28	29
65	12	15	16											25		
64		14		15			37	37	33				23		27	
63			15	14	30	34				34	30	33				23
62		13					36	36	32						26	
61	11				29	33				33				24		
60				13			35	35				32				27
59			14		28				31	32	35		22			
58		12				32	34								25	26
57	10							34				31		23		
56		11	13			31	33		30	31	34		21			25
55				12	27						33	30			24	
54	9	10				30		33						22		
53			12						29	30	32		20		23	24
52				11			32				43	29				
51	8	9	11					32							22	
50					26	29			28	29		28	19			23
49			10	10			31				30			21		
48									27	28		27			21	
47		8	9	9		28	30	31		27	29	26	18	20		22
46					25		29									
45	6						29				28		17			21
44			8	8		27		30		26			25	19	20	
43		7			24		28				27		16			20
42				7				29		26					19	
41				7					25			24	15		19	
40			7		23	26	27					26		18		19
39		6						28				23	14			
38	4			6					24	25	25			17	18	18
37			6		22	25	26		23		24	22	13			
36				5	21		25	27	22			21	12	16	17	
35		5				24				24			11	15	16	17
34			5		20			26			23	20	10			
33		4		4			24		21		22	19				
32	3				19					23						16
31					18				20	22	21					
30			4	3		23	23						9	14		

T scale	Goal shooting				Speed pass				Dribble				Rebounding			
	7th	8th	9th	10th	7th	8th	9th	10th	7th	8th	9th	10th	7th	8th	9th	10th
29									19			18	8			
28	2	3	3		17				18	21	20		7		15	
27					16	22	22		17		17		6	13	14	
26							21		16		14		5			
25							20	25			11					
24	1		2	2	15		19		15	20	9	17	4	12		15

Note. Courtesy of ''A test to measure basketball ability for boys,'' by E.R. Harrison, 1969, unpublished master's thesis, Temple University, Philadelphia, PA. Copyright 1969 by the author.

Koski Basketball Test (Koski, 1950)

Purpose. To evaluate dribbling and field goal shooting ability in basketball.

Validity and Reliability. The validity coefficient for the test was .93, but individual items were .78 and .87 for dribbling and shooting, respectively. Using the test-retest approach, the reliability coefficient for the test was .88; individual items were .78 and .85.

Age Level and Sex. Originally conducted with college males. Appropriate for junior high school and senior high school students.

Personnel. The test administrator can start both tests at the same time. Students can be used to record each other's scores.

Equipment. Basketballs, 12 cones, a measuring tape, marking tape, a whistle, a stop watch, score cards or recording sheets, and pencils.

Space. The shooting test requires the area around a basket, and the dribbling test requires an area about 12 feet by 50 feet.

Test Items. Field goal dribbling and shooting.

Preparation. Each dribble test station is prepared as shown in Figure 6.6. Twelve cones are placed in two rows spaced 6 feet apart. (Measurements are made from the outside edge of one cone to the outside edge of the next cone.) Within the two rows, cones are spaced 8 feet apart. (Measurements are made from the front edge of one cone to the front edge of the next.) The start-

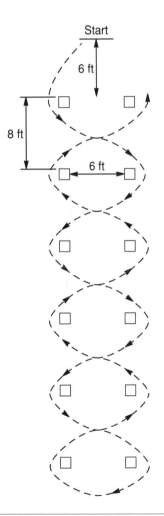

Figure 6.6 Floor plan for the Koski Dribble Test.
Note. From ''A basketball classification test,'' by W.A. Koski, 1950, unpublished master's thesis, University of Michigan, Ann Arbor, MI. Copyright 1950 by the author. Reprinted by permission.

finish line is centered in the middle of the two rows, 6 feet from the front edge of the first two cones.

Directions.

Dribbling: Holding a basketball in the right hand, a student waits behind the start-finish line. At the start signal, the student dribbles around the first cone on the right, continues around the left side of the second set of cones, continues around the right side of the third set of cones and so on. Students should go through the course as many times or as far as possible during the 30-second timed trial. It counts as a completed cone if a student is beside or beyond it.

Field Goal Shooting: While holding a basketball, the student stands in front of a basket. At the start signal, the student shoots a basket, rebounds the ball, continues to shoot and rebound. Rebounded shots may be taken from anywhere on the floor. The student shoots as many times as possible during the 30-second timed trial.

Scoring.

Dribbling: The number of cones passed during one 30-second timed trial is the score.

Field Goal Shooting: The number of goals made during one 30-second timed trial is the score.

Norms. Not available.

Other Basketball Tests

Barrow, H.M. (1959). Basketball skill test. *The Physical Educator*, **16**, 26-27.

Boyd, C.A., MacCachren, J.R., & Waglow, I.F. (1955). Predictive ability of a selected basketball test. *Research Quarterly*, **26**, 364.

Burr, W.P. (1948). *The development of a classification test of basketball ability*. Unpublished master's thesis, Springfield College, Springfield, MA.

Catlin, O.J. (1966). An individual skills test for basketball. *The NAIA Coach*, **1**, 6-7.

Chambers, D.E. (1952). Testing for basketball ability. *Scholastic Coach*, **22**, 36.

Culp, P. (1943). Basketball ability tests. *Scholastic Coach*, **12**, 11.

Cunningham, P. (1964). *Cunningham basketball test*. Unpublished doctoral dissertation, University of Iowa, Iowa City.

Davis, C.A. (1932). *An experiment in measuring ability and progress in basketball skills*. Unpublished doctoral dissertation, University of Iowa, Iowa City.

Dyer, J.T., Schurig, J.C., & Apgar, S.L. (1939). A basketball motor ability test for college women and secondary school girls. *Research Quarterly*, **10**, 128-147.

Edgren, H.D. (1932). An experiment in the testing of ability and progress in basketball. *Research Quarterly*, **3**, 159-171.

Fraser, D.C. (1934). *Motor ability test in basketball*. Unpublished master's thesis, Springfield College, Springfield, MA.

Friermood, H.T. (1934). Basketball progress tests adapted to class use. *Journal of Health and Physical Education*, **5**, 45-47.

Gaunt, S. (1979). *Factor structure of basketball playing ability*. Unpublished doctoral dissertation, Indiana University, Bloomington.

Gilbert, R.R. (1968). *A study of selected variables in predicting basketball players*. Unpublished master's thesis, Springfield College, Springfield, MA.

Glassow, R.B., Colvin, V., & Schwarz, M.M. (1938). Studies measuring basketball playing ability of college women. *Research Quarterly*, **9**, 60-68.

Grandstaff, G. (1969). *Grandstaff-Murphy basketball skills test for high school girls*. Unpublished master's thesis, Chadron State College, Chadron, NE.

Harrison, E.R. (1969). *A test to measure basketball ability for boys*. Unpublished master's thesis, University of Florida, Gainesville.

Hill, L.J. (1956). *Determining basketball ability through the use of basketball skill tests*. Unpublished master's thesis, Washington State University, Pullman.

Hopkins, D.R. (1977). Factor analysis of selected

basketball skill tests. *Research Quarterly*, **48**, 535-540.

Hopkins, D.R. (1979). Using skill tests to identify successful and unsuccessful basketball performers. *Research Quarterly*, **50**, 381-387.

Hughes, L. (1957). *Comparison of the validation of six selected basketball ability tests*. Unpublished master's thesis, Pennsylvania State University, University Park.

Jacobson, T.V. (1960). *An evaluation of performance in certain physical ability tests administered to select secondary school boys*. Unpublished master's thesis, University of Washington, Pullman.

Johnson, L.W. (1934). *Objective tests in basketball for high school boys*. Unpublished master's thesis, University of Iowa, Iowa City.

Jones, E. (1941). *A study of knowledge and playing ability in basketball for high school girls*. Unpublished master's thesis, University of Iowa, Iowa City.

Knox, R.D. (1937). *An experiment to determine the relationship between performance in skill tests and success in playing basketball*. Unpublished master's thesis, University of Oregon, Eugene.

Knox, R.D. (1947). Basketball ability tests. *Scholastic Coach*, **17**, 45-47.

Lambert, A.T. (1969). *A basketball skill test for college women*. Unpublished master's thesis, University of North Carolina, Greensboro.

Latchaw, M. (1954). Measuring selected motor skills in fourth, fifth, and sixth grades. *Research Quarterly*, **25**, 439-449.

Lehsten, N. (1948). A measurement of basketball skills in high school boys. *The Physical Educator*, **5**, 103-105.

Leilich, A.R. (1952). *The primary components of selected basketball tests for college women*. Unpublished doctoral dissertation, Indiana University, Bloomington.

Loose, W.A. (1961). *A study to determine the validity of the Knox basketball test*. Unpublished master's thesis, Washington State University, Pullman.

Matthews, L.E. (1963). *A battery of basketball skills tests for high school boys*. Unpublished master's thesis, University of Oregon, Eugene.

Miller, W.K. (1954). Achievement levels in basketball skills for women physical education majors. *Research Quarterly*, **25**, 450-455.

Money, C.V. (1933). Tests for evaluating the abilities of basketball players. *Athletic Journal*, **14**, 18-19.

Mortimer, E.M. (1951). Basketball shooting. *Research Quarterly*, **22**, 234-243.

Nelson, J.K. (1974). *The measurement of shooting and passing skills in basketball*. Unpublished study, Louisiana State University, Baton Rouge.

Peters, G.V. (1964). *The reliability and validity of selected shooting tests in basketball*. Unpublished master's thesis, University of Michigan, Ann Arbor.

Pimpa, U. (1968). *A study to determine the relationship between Burn's Basketball Skill Test and the writer's modified version of that test*. Unpublished master's thesis, Springfield College, Springfield, MA.

Randall, C.R. (1958). *Determining the validity of the Knox basketball test*. Unpublished master's thesis, Washington State University, Pullman.

Schwartz, H. (1937). Knowledge and achievement tests in girls basketball on the senior high school level. *Research Quarterly*, **8**, 143.

Stroup, F. (1955). Game results as a criterion for validating basketball skill tests. *Research Quarterly*, **26**, 353-357.

Stubbs, H.C. (1968). *An explanatory study of girls' basketball relative to the measurement of ball handling ability*. Unpublished master's thesis, University of Tennessee, Knoxville.

Thornes, M.A. (1963). *An analysis of a basketball shooting test and its relationship to other basketball skill tests*. Master's thesis, University of Wisconsin, Madison. (Microcard PE 694, University of Oregon, Eugene.)

Voltmer, E.F., & Watti, T. (1947). A rating scale for player performance in basketball. *Journal of Health and Physical Education*, **2**, 94-95.

Walter, R.J. (1968). *A comparison between two selected evaluative techniques for measuring basketball skill*. Unpublished master's thesis, Western Illinois University, Macomb.

Wilbur, C.D. (1959). Construction of a simple skills test. *DGWS Basketball guide 1959-1960*. Washington, DC: AAHPER.

Young, G., & Moser, H. (1934). A short battery of tests to measure playing ability in women's basketball. *Research Quarterly*, **5**, 3-23.

Field Hockey

Field hockey, an adaptation of ice hockey, became popular in the United States in the early 1900s when a physical education teacher visiting from England presented the game at eastern women's colleges. Men didn't care for the sport, but women did. Field hockey is still gaining popularity throughout the United States.

Field hockey skills typically taught in a physical education class include dribbling, driving, fielding, passing, dodging, tackling, and goalkeeping.

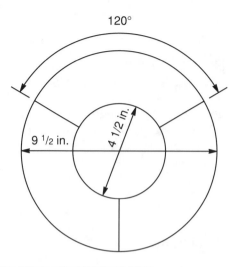

Chapman Ball Control Test (Chapman, 1982)

Purpose. To evaluate stick movement ability in field hockey.

Validity and Reliability. Logical validity and concurrent validity coefficients of .63 and .64 were reported. An intraclass reliability coefficient of .89 was computed.

Age Level and Sex. Originally conducted with women intercollegiate field hockey players. Appropriate for junior high school and senior high school students.

Personnel. The test requires two people: a timer and a scorer/recorder.

Equipment. Field hockey sticks, hockey balls, a measuring tape, marking tape, a stop watch, score cards or recording sheets, and pencils.

Space. Each testing station requires an area about 15 feet by 15 feet.

Test Item. Stick movement.

Preparation. Each testing station is prepared as shown in Figure 6.7. An inner circle with a 4-1/2-foot diameter and an outside circle with a 9-1/2-foot diameter are placed on the floor within the testing area. The area between the two circles is divided with 1/8-inch wide tape into three equal-sized sections of 120 degrees.

Figure 6.7 Target measurements for the Chapman Field Hockey Test.
Note. From ''Chapman ball control test—field hockey,'' by N.L. Chapman, 1982, *Research Quarterly for Exercise and Sport,* **53**(3), pp. 239-242. Copyright 1982 by AAHPERD. Reprinted by permission.

Directions. The student stands, with a field hockey stick in hand and a hockey ball on the floor, just outside the larger circle. On the ''ready, go'' signal the student taps a ball through or in and out of the center circle. Every time the ball is tapped out of or through the center circle, it must roll outside the larger circle. Legal hits are shown in Figure 6.8. Three 15-second timed trials are allowed. Both a brief practice period and rest between test trials are encouraged.

Scoring. One point is awarded each time a ball passes through or into the center circle and each time a ball passes from the center circle to outside the larger circle through a segment different from the one it entered. No points are awarded when a ball is tapped on the segment area or with the rounded side of the stick. The score is the number of points earned in three 15-second trials.

Norms. Not available.

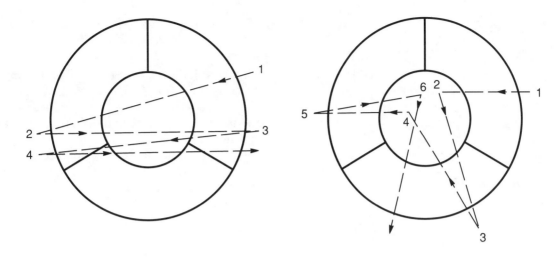

Figure 6.8 Examples of basic scoring techniques for the Chapman Field Hockey Test.
Note. From ''Chapman ball control test—field hockey,'' by N.L. Chapman, 1982, *Research Quarterly for Exercise and Sport*, **53**(3), pp. 239-242. Copyright 1982 by AAHPERD. Reprinted by permission.

Henry-Friedel Field Hockey Test (Henry, 1970)

Purpose. To evaluate dribbling, dodging, and shooting ability in field hockey.

Validity and Reliability. Validity coefficients computed through two judges' ratings were .70 to .89. Reliability coefficients, as determined through test-retest, were computed to be .71 to .81.

Age Level and Sex. Originally conducted with college and high school field hockey players. Appropriate for junior high school and senior high school students.

Personnel. Three people are required to administer the test: one to time and score the trials, one to roll balls to the student being tested, and a third to act as a stationary object.

Equipment. Field hockey sticks, hockey balls, a goal cage, a measuring tape, marking material, cones, a stop watch, score cards or recording sheets, and pencils.

Space. An area that is 25 yards by 10 yards.

Test Item. Dribbling, dodging, and shooting.

Preparation. Each testing station is prepared as shown in Figure 6.9. A 4-yard goal cage is placed on the starting line. Throw-in marks are placed on each side of the testing area 10 yards from the starting line, and a 3-yard restraining line is placed 7 yards from the starting line. A 2-yard by 2-yard target area is placed 15 yards from the starting line and in the center between the sidelines. Three-yard lane lines are placed 1-1/2 yards apart and connected to the target area. A 1-foot square is placed in the center of the 10-yard by 10-yard ball-handling area. Additionally, the cage goal is marked for scoring the accuracy test.

Directions. The student stands, with hockey stick in hand and ready to run, inside the goal cage but behind the starting line. On the ''ready, go'' signal the student runs toward the target area 15 yards away. As a student crosses the 7-yard mark, a ball is rolled from one of the 10-yard sideline marks. The ball should be rolled so that it will pass through the target within 1 foot in either direction of both corners, and come to a stop within 1 foot inside the sideline of the testing area. The student fields the ball on the run within the 2-yard square target area and dribbles toward a stationary person standing in the 1-foot square dodge area, making a right dodge around that person. The stationary person should leave the testing area as soon as a testing student moves by. The student continues dribbling to the end line, goes around the cone as if executing a circular tackle, and resumes dribbling back downfield moving within the 1-1/2-yard lane. Before getting to the restraining line, but within the lane line, the student drives the ball toward the goal area. The clock stops when a driven ball crosses the starting line (or the sideline if driven inaccurately) or when a ball stops within the testing area. Students get 10 scored time trials, 5

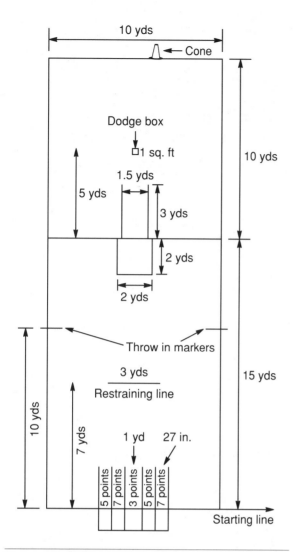

Figure 6.9 Field markings for the Henry-Friedel Field Hockey Test.

Note. From ''The validation of a test of field hockey skills,'' by M.E. Henry, 1970, unpublished master's thesis, Temple University, Philadelphia, PA. Copyright 1970 by the author. Reprinted by permission of the Department of Physical Education, Temple University.

the starting line or goes over the sideline earns no points. The accuracy score is the total points awarded for all 10 trials.

The score for a timed speed trial is the time in seconds and 1/10s of seconds from the ''go'' signal until the ball is driven across the goal line, the sideline, or stops within the testing area. One second is subtracted from the timed score for each of the following items: a) for incorrect right dodge or for omitting the dodge; b) for ''sticks'' on the drive; c) for using reverse sticks during the circular tackle; d) for the driven ball going over the sideline or not reaching the starting line; and e) for not fielding an accurately rolled ball within the target area. The speed score is the total time for all 10 trials.

Norms. Not available.

Other Field Hockey Tests

Illner, J.A. (1968). *The construction and validation of a skill test for the drive in field hockey.* Master's thesis, Southern Illinois University, Carbondale. (Microcard PE 1075, University of Oregon, Eugene.)

Kelly, E.D., & Brown, J.E. (1950). The construction of a field hockey test for women physical education majors. *Research Quarterly,* **23,** 322-329.

Lucey, M.A. (1934). *A study of reliability in relation to the construction of field hockey tests.* Unpublished master's thesis, University of Wisconsin, Madison.

Perry, E.L. (1969). *An investigation of field hockey skills tests for college women.* Unpublished master's thesis, Pennsylvania State University, University Park.

Schmithals, M., & French, E. (1940). Achievement tests in field hockey for college women. *Research Quarterly,* **9,** 84-92.

Stewart, H.E. (1965). *A test for measuring field hockey skill of college women.* Unpublished doctoral dissertation, Indiana University, Bloomington.

Strait, C.J. (1965). *The construction and evaluation of a field hockey skills test.* Unpublished master's thesis, Smith College, Northampton, MA.

with the ball rolled in from the left side and 5 with the ball rolled from the right side. A practice trial from each side is allowed. A retrial is allowed if a ball is inaccurately rolled so that it does not pass through the target area.

Scoring. Two scores are recorded: one for accuracy and one for speed. The cage goal is divided into five scoring lanes. Point values are shown in Figure 6.9. The accuracy score is determined by which scoring lane the ball passes through on the drive. Any ball passing outside the cage goal is awarded 1 point; any ball that does not reach

Football

Football, an American favorite, derives from soccer and rugby. Although contact football is too rough to be played without pads, it has been modified to touch and flag football for physical education classes and playgrounds.

Skills typically taught in physical education classes include passing and catching, stance, kicking and punting, blocking, and centering.

AAHPER Football Skill Test (AAHPER, 1966)

Purpose. To evaluate passing, running, catching, punting, and kicking ability in football.

Validity and Reliability. Face validity was claimed for each item. Reliability standards with a minimum level of .80 were established for distance events and .70 for accuracy or form events.

Age Level and Sex. Appropriate for junior high school and senior high school students.

Personnel. At least three individuals (timer, scorer, and starter) for the zigzag run and 50-yard dash test items. At least three individuals (scorer, marker, and ball retriever) for the forward pass, punt, and kick-for-distance test items. One person can administer the catching test.

Equipment. Footballs, kicking tees, marking stakes, a white towel, a measuring tape, cones, marking material, a canvas target, stop watches, score cards or recording sheets, and pencils.

Space. Regulation-sized football field.

Test Items. Forward pass for distance, forward pass for accuracy, catching the forward pass, 50-yard dash with football, ball-changing zigzag run, punt for distance, and kickoff. Additional items on the original test but not included here are the pullout, blocking, and dodging run.

Preparation.

Forward Pass for Distance: Two parallel lines placed 6 feet apart serve as a restraining area. (If testing on football field, one line would be the goal line and the second would be 6 feet behind the goal line.)

Forward Pass for Accuracy: A circular target is drawn on an 8 foot by 11 foot canvas. Three color-coded concentric circles are painted on the canvas. The center circle is 2 feet in diameter, the middle circle 4 feet in diameter, and the outside circle 6 feet in diameter. The target should be hung from the crossbar of a goalpost so that the bottom of the outer circle is 3 feet above the ground. A restraining line is placed 15 yards from the target.

Catching the Forward Pass: Each testing station is prepared as shown in Figure 6.10. End marks are placed on the line of scrimmage 9 feet either side of the center. Turning points are placed 30 feet downfield from the end marks, and passing points are placed 30 feet directly to the outside of the turning points (toward the "sidelines").

Ball-changing Zigzag Run: Each testing station is prepared as shown in Figure 6.11. Five cones are placed in a straight line 10 feet apart with a starting line marked 10 feet from the first cone.

Directions.

Forward Pass for Distance: Students get three trials to pass a football as far as possible while staying within the restraining lines. The student may take as many steps as needed before passing, without stepping over the front restraining line (goal line). The contact point of a thrown ball is marked with a wooden stake. The stake is moved to mark subsequent throws that travel farther. Three trials are given.

Forward Pass Accuracy: From behind the restraining line, the student takes two or three steps toward the target, turns, and passes the ball. Ten trials are given.

Catching the Forward Pass: The student lines up behind the right end mark. On the "go" signal, a ball is centered to a quarterback who takes one step back and passes the ball at head height directly over the passing point. At the same time, the test performer runs to the turning point, makes a 90-degree cut to the outside, and attempts to catch the pass arriving at the passing point. Poorly thrown passes are repeated. Ten trials are provided on each side.

50-Yard Dash: The student carries a football and runs as fast as possible for 50 yards. The starter shouts "go" and drops a white towel. The timer starts the watch as the towel drops and stops it as the student crosses the finish line. Two trials are allowed.

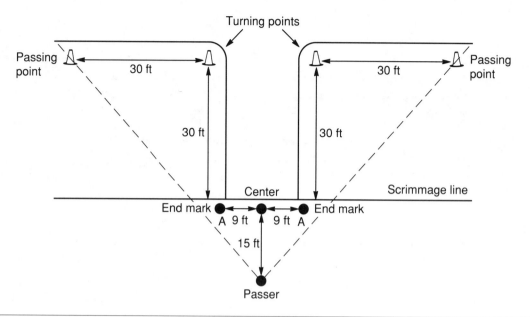

Figure 6.10 Field markings for the AAHPER Football Forward Pass Test.
Note: From ''AAHPER skills test manual for football,'' by AAHPER, 1966, Washington DC. Copyright 1966 by AAHPER. Reprinted by permission.

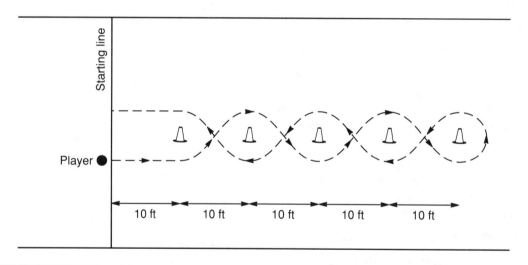

Figure 6.11 Field markings for the AAHPER Football Zigzag Run Test.
Note: From ''AAHPER skills test manual for football,'' by AAHPER, 1966, Washington DC. Copyright 1966 by AAHPER. Reprinted by permission.

Ball-Changing Zigzag Run: Football in hand, the student stands behind the starting line on the right side of the first cone. On the ''go'' signal, the student runs to the right side of the first cone, shifts the ball to the left hand, and proceeds around the left side of the second cone. The running pattern continues as the student circles the cones and returns to the starting line in the same circling manner. The ball must always be carried to the outside of the cones while the inside arm executes a stiff arm. Students are not permitted to touch the cones. Two trials are allowed.

Punt for Distance: The same restraining area as in the pass-for-distance test is used in the punt-for-distance test. The student may take as many steps as necessary in the restraining area before punting, but if a punter steps over the restraining line, the attempt does not count. Three trials are allowed.

Kickoff: The student places a ball on a kicking tee in the middle of a yard line, takes as many steps as needed, and kicks the ball as far as possible. Three trials are allowed.

Scoring.

Forward Pass for Distance: The score is the longest throw of the three trials. A tape measure is placed at a right angle to the restraining line to measure how far a student throws the football. The ball usually will be thrown either to the left or right of the tape measure. To measure the distance of the throw, line up where the ball landed at a right angle to the tape measure.

Forward Pass for Accuracy: The score is the number of points earned in 10 trials. One point is earned for hitting the outer circle, 2 points for the middle and 3 for the center. Passes that hit a line earn the higher point value. A perfect score is 30 points.

Catching the Forward Pass: One point is awarded for each pass caught. Twenty catches are attempted, 10 from both right and left sides. A perfect score is 20 points.

50-Yard Dash: The score is the best of two timed trials measured to the nearest 1/10 of a second.

Ball-Changing Zigzag Run: The score is the best of two timed trials measured to the nearest 1/10 of a second.

Punt for Distance: Scoring is the same as the forward pass for distance.

Kickoff: Scoring is the same as the forward pass and punt for distance.

Norms. Percentile norms for the forward pass for distance, forward pass for accuracy, zigzag run, catching the forward pass, 50-yard dash, punt for distance, and kickoff are shown in Tables 6.6 through 6.12.

Table 6.6 Percentile Scores for the AAHPER Football Forward Pass for Distance Test

Percentile	10	11	12	13	14	15	16	17-18	Percentile
100th	96	105	120	150	170	180	180	180	100th
95th	71	83	99	115	126	135	144	152	95th
90th	68	76	92	104	118	127	135	143	90th
85th	64	73	87	98	114	122	129	137	85th
80th	62	70	83	95	109	118	126	133	80th
75th	61	68	79	91	105	115	123	129	75th
70th	59	65	77	88	102	111	120	127	70th
65th	58	64	75	85	99	108	117	124	65th
60th	56	62	73	83	96	105	114	121	60th
55th	55	61	71	80	93	102	111	117	55th
50th	53	59	68	78	91	99	108	114	50th
45th	52	56	66	76	88	97	105	110	45th
40th	51	54	64	73	85	94	103	107	40th
35th	49	51	62	70	83	92	100	104	35th
30th	47	50	60	69	80	89	97	101	30th
25th	45	48	58	65	77	85	93	98	25th
20th	44	45	54	63	73	81	90	94	20th
15th	41	43	51	61	70	76	85	89	15th
10th	38	40	45	55	64	71	79	80	10th
5th	33	36	40	46	53	62	70	67	5th
0	14	25	10	10	10	20	30	20	0

Note: From "AAHPER skills test manual for football," by AAHPER, 1966, Washington DC. Copyright 1966 by AAHPER. Reprinted by permission.

Table 6.7 Percentile Scores for the AAHPER Football Forward Pass for Accuracy Test

Percentile	\<Age\> 10	11	12	13	14	15	16	17-18	Percentile
100th	18	26	26	26	26	26	28	28	100th
95th	14	19	20	21	21	21	21	22	95th
90th	11	16	18	19	19	19	20	21	90th
85th	10	15	17	18	18	18	18	19	85th
80th	9	13	16	17	17	17	17	18	80th
75th	8	12	15	16	16	16	16	18	75th
70th	8	11	14	15	15	15	15	17	70th
65th	6	10	13	14	14	14	15	16	65th
60th	5	9	12	13	13	13	14	15	60th
55th	4	8	11	13	13	13	13	15	55th
50th	3	7	11	12	12	12	13	14	50th
45th	2	6	10	11	11	11	12	13	45th
40th	2	5	9	11	10	11	12	12	40th
35th	1	5	8	10	9	9	11	12	35th
30th	0	4	7	9	8	9	10	11	30th
25th	0	3	6	8	8	8	9	10	25th
20th	0	2	5	7	7	7	8	9	20th
15th	0	1	4	5	5	6	7	8	15th
10th	0	0	3	4	4	5	6	7	10th
5th	0	0	1	2	2	3	4	5	5th
0	0	0	0	0	0	0	0	0	0

Note: From "AAHPER skills test manual for football," by AAHPER, 1966, Washington DC. Copyright 1966 by AAHPER. Reprinted by permission.

Table 6.8 Percentile Scores for the AAHPER Football Ball Changing Zigzag Run Test

Percentile	\<Age\> 10	11	12	13	14	15	16	17-18	Percentile
100th	7.2	7.4	7.0	6.0	6.5	6.0	6.0	6.0	100th
95th	9.9	7.7	7.8	8.0	8.7	7.7	7.7	8.4	95th
90th	10.1	8.1	8.2	8.4	9.0	8.0	8.0	8.7	90th
85th	10.3	8.6	8.5	8.7	9.2	8.3	8.4	8.8	85th
80th	10.5	9.0	8.7	8.8	9.4	8.5	8.6	8.9	80th
75th	10.7	9.3	8.8	9.0	9.5	8.6	8.7	9.0	75th
70th	10.9	9.6	9.0	9.2	9.6	8.7	8.8	9.1	70th
65th	11.1	9.8	9.1	9.3	9.7	8.8	8.9	9.2	65th
60th	11.2	10.0	9.3	9.5	9.8	8.9	9.0	9.3	60th
55th	11.4	10.1	9.5	9.6	9.9	9.0	9.1	9.4	55th
50th	11.5	10.3	9.6	9.7	10.0	9.1	9.3	9.6	50th
45th	11.6	10.5	9.8	9.8	10.1	9.2	9.4	9.7	45th

Percentile	10	11	12	13	14	15	16	17-18	Percentile
40th	11.8	10.6	10.0	10.0	10.2	9.4	9.5	9.8	40th
35th	11.9	10.9	10.1	10.2	10.4	9.5	9.7	9.9	35th
30th	12.2	11.1	10.3	10.3	10.5	9.6	9.9	10.1	30th
25th	12.5	11.3	10.5	10.3	10.7	9.9	10.1	10.3	25th
20th	12.8	11.6	10.8	10.8	10.9	10.1	10.3	10.5	20th
15th	13.3	12.1	11.1	11.1	11.2	10.3	10.6	10.9	15th
10th	13.8	12.9	11.5	11.4	11.5	10.6	11.2	11.4	10th
5th	15.8	14.2	12.3	12.1	12.0	11.5	12.2	12.1	5th
0	24.0	15.0	19.0	20.0	14.5	20.0	17.0	15.0	0

Note: From ''AAHPER skills test manual for football,'' by AAHPER, 1966, Washington DC. Copyright 1966 by AAHPER. Reprinted by permission.

Table 6.9 Percentile Scores for the AAHPER Football Catching the Forward Pass Test

Percentile	10	11	12	13	14	15	16	17-18	Percentile
100th	20	20	20	20	20	20	20	20	100th
95th	19	19	19	20	20	20	20	20	95th
90th	17	18	19	19	19	19	19	19	90th
85th	16	16	18	18	18	19	19	19	85th
80th	14	15	18	17	18	18	18	18	80th
75th	13	14	16	17	17	18	18	18	75th
70th	12	13	16	16	16	1	17	17	70th
65th	11	12	15	15	15	16	16	16	65th
60th	10	12	14	15	15	16	16	16	60th
55th	8	11	14	14	14	15	15	15	55th
50th	7	10	13	13	14	15	15	15	50th
45th	7	9	12	13	13	14	14	14	45th
40th	6	8	12	12	12	13	13	13	40th
35th	5	7	11	11	11	12	12	13	35th
30th	5	7	10	10	10	11	11	12	30th
25th	4	6	10	9	9	10	10	11	25th
20th	3	5	8	8	8	9	9	10	20th
15th	2	4	7	7	8	8	8	9	15th
10th	1	3	6	6	6	7	6	8	10th
5th	1	1	5	4	4	6	4	6	5th
0	0	0	0	0	0	0	0	0	0

Note: From ''AAHPER skills test manual for football,'' by AAHPER, 1966, Washington DC. Copyright 1966 by AAHPER. Reprinted by permission.

Table 6.10 Percentile Scores for the AAHPER Football 50-Yard Dash Test

Percentile	Age								Percentile
	10	11	12	13	14	15	16	17-18	
100th	7.3	6.8	6.2	5.5	5.5	5.5	5.5	5.0	100th
95th	7.7	7.4	7.0	6.5	6.5	6.2	6.0	6.0	95th
90th	7.9	7.6	7.2	6.8	6.6	6.3	6.1	6.1	90th
85th	8.1	7.7	7.4	6.9	6.8	6.4	6.3	6.2	85th
80th	8.2	7.8	7.5	7.0	6.9	6.5	6.4	6.3	80th
75th	8.3	7.9	7.5	7.1	7.0	6.6	6.5	6.3	75th
70th	8.4	8.0	7.6	7.2	7.1	6.7	6.6	6.4	70th
65th	8.5	8.1	7.7	7.3	7.2	6.8	6.6	6.5	65th
60th	8.6	8.2	7.8	7.4	7.2	6.9	6.7	6.6	60th
55th	8.6	8.3	7.9	7.5	7.3	7.0	6.8	6.6	55th
50th	8.7	8.4	8.0	7.5	7.4	7.0	6.8	6.7	50th
45th	8.8	8.5	8.1	7.6	7.5	7.1	6.9	6.8	45th
40th	8.9	8.6	8.1	7.7	7.6	7.2	7.0	6.8	40th
35th	9.0	8.7	8.2	7.8	7.7	7.2	7.1	6.9	35th
30th	9.1	8.8	8.3	8.0	7.8	7.3	7.2	7.0	30th
25th	9.2	8.9	8.4	8.1	7.9	7.4	7.3	7.1	25th
20th	9.3	9.1	8.5	8.2	8.1	7.5	7.4	7.2	20th
15th	9.4	9.2	8.7	8.4	8.3	7.7	7.5	7.3	15th
10th	9.6	9.3	9.0	8.7	8.4	8.1	7.8	7.4	10th
5th	9.8	9.5	9.3	9.0	8.8	8.4	8.0	7.8	5th
0	10.6	11.0	12.0	12.0	12.0	11.0	10.0	10.0	0

Note: From "AAHPER skills test manual for football," by AAHPER, 1966, Washington DC. Copyright 1966 by AAHPER. Reprinted by permission.

Table 6.11 Percentile Scores for the AAHPER Football Punt for Distance Test

Percentile	Age								Percentile
	10	11	12	13	14	15	16	17-18	
100th	87	100	115	150	160	160	160	180	100th
95th	75	84	93	106	119	126	131	136	95th
90th	64	77	88	98	110	119	126	128	90th
85th	61	75	84	94	106	114	120	124	85th
80th	58	70	79	90	103	109	114	120	80th
75th	56	68	77	87	98	105	109	115	75th
70th	55	66	75	83	96	102	106	110	70th
65th	53	64	72	80	93	99	103	107	65th
60th	51	62	70	78	90	96	100	104	60th
55th	50	60	68	75	87	94	97	101	55th
50th	48	57	66	73	84	91	95	98	50th
45th	46	55	64	70	81	89	92	96	45th

Percentile	Age								Percentile
	10	11	12	13	14	15	16	17-18	
40th	45	53	61	68	78	86	90	93	40th
35th	44	51	59	64	75	83	86	90	35th
30th	42	48	56	63	72	79	83	86	30th
25th	40	45	52	61	70	76	79	81	25th
20th	38	42	50	57	66	73	74	76	20th
15th	32	39	46	52	61	69	70	70	15th
10th	28	34	40	44	55	62	64	64	10th
5th	22	27	35	33	44	54	56	53	5th
0	11	9	10	10	10	10	10	10	0

Note: From ''AAHPER skills test manual for football,'' by AAHPER, 1966, Washington DC. Copyright 1966 by AAHPER. Reprinted by permission.

Table 6.12 Percentile Scores for the AAHPER Football Kickoff Test

Percentile	Age								Percentile
	10	11	12	13	14	15	16	17-18	
100th	88	110	120	129	140	160	160	180	100th
95th	69	79	98	106	118	128	131	138	95th
90th	64	72	83	97	108	120	125	129	90th
85th	59	68	78	92	102	114	119	124	85th
80th	58	64	74	86	97	108	114	119	80th
75th	55	60	70	81	94	104	108	113	75th
70th	53	58	67	78	90	100	104	108	70th
65th	50	56	65	75	86	96	99	105	65th
60th	47	54	64	72	84	93	97	103	60th
55th	46	52	60	69	81	90	95	98	55th
50th	45	50	57	67	77	87	93	95	50th
45th	43	48	54	64	74	83	90	92	45th
40th	40	46	52	62	71	79	87	88	40th
35th	39	44	48	59	68	76	83	84	35th
30th	37	42	45	56	65	72	79	79	30th
25th	35	40	42	52	62	69	75	74	25th
20th	32	37	38	48	58	64	70	70	20th
15th	30	34	34	42	52	59	65	64	15th
10th	26	30	29	36	45	50	60	57	10th
5th	21	24	22	26	38	40	47	43	5th
0	5	10	0	0	0	10	10	10	0

Note: From ''AAHPER skills test manual for football,'' by AAHPER, 1966, Washington DC. Copyright 1966 by AAHPER. Reprinted by permission.

Jacobson-Borleske Touch Football Test (Jacobson, 1960)

Purpose. To evaluate passing, punting, and running ability in football.

Validity and Reliability. A validity coefficient of .88 was reported for the three-item test. Reliability was not reported. Judges' ratings were used as the criterion measure.

Age Level and Sex. Originally administered to college males. Appropriate for junior high school and senior high school students.

Personnel. At least three individuals for each test item.

Equipment. Footballs, marking stakes, a measuring tape, marking material, a stop watch, score cards or recording sheets, and pencils.

Space. Regulation-sized football field.

Test Items. Forward pass for distance, punt for distance, and run for time.

Preparation. If you use a regulation-sized football field with line markings, no special preparations are required. A field plan for organizing the test is shown in Figure 6.12.

Directions.

Forward Pass for Distance: The student stands behind a restraining line, football in hand. When ready, the student passes the ball as far as possible downfield. As many preparation steps as necessary are allowed as long as the passer does not cross the restraining line. A 1-minute warm-up period preceding the three trials is allowed.

Punt for Distance: The student waits 7 yards behind a center, who is located at the restraining line. The center snaps a ball to a punter who must punt it within 2 seconds. A 1-minute warm-up period preceding the three trials is allowed.

Run for Time: The student is down in a 3-point backfield stance. Upon receiving a snap from a center who is 5 yards in front, the student immediately runs 50 yards while carrying the football. Bad snaps will be repeated. One trial is allowed.

Scoring.

Forward Pass for Distance: The score is the distance for the best of three passes measured to the nearest yard.

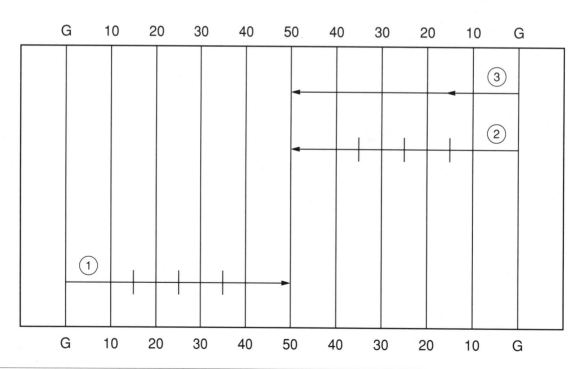

Figure 6.12 Field plan for the Jacobson-Borleske Football Test: 1. Pass for distance; 2. Punt for distance; 3. Run for Time.

Punt for Distance: The score is the distance for the best of three punts measured to the nearest yard.

Run for Time: The score is the time of one trial to the nearest 1/10 of a second. Timing begins when the student receives the ball and continues until he or she crosses midfield.

Norms. T scores and a grading scale are shown in Tables 6.13 and 6.14.

Table 6.13 T Scores for the Jacobson-Borleske Football Test

| T score | Pass for distance | | | Punt for distance | | | Run for Time | | | T score |
	7th grade	8th grade	9th grade	7th grade	8th grade	9th grade	7th grade	8th grade	9th grade	
85	41	48	53	38	43	47				85
80	39	45	50	36	40	44	6.3	5.8	5.7	80
75	36	41	46	33	37	41	6.7	6.2	6.0	75
70	34	38	43	31	34	38	7.0	6.6	6.3	70
65	31	35	39	28	31	34	7.3	7.0	6.7	65
60	28	32	36	26	28	32	7.7	7.4	7.0	60
55	25	29	33	23	25	28	8.0	7.7	7.3	55
50	23	26	29	20	22	25	8.3	8.1	7.6	50
45	20	23	26	18	19	22	8.6	8.5	7.9	45
40	18	20	23	16	16	19	9.0	8.9	8.3	40
35	15	17	19	13	13	16	9.3	9.2	8.6	35
30	13	14	16	11	10	13	9.6	9.6	8.9	30
25	10	10	13	8	7	10	10.0	10.0	9.2	25
20	8	8	10	6		7	10.3	10.4	9.5	20
15	5	6					10.6	10.7	9.9	15

Note. Courtesy of ''An evaluation of performance in certain physical ability tests administered to selected secondary school boys,'' by T.V. Jacobson, 1960, unpublished master's thesis, University of Washington, Seattle, WA. Copyright 1960 by the author and the University of Washington.

Table 6.14 Grading Scale for the Jacobson-Borleske Football Test

Event	Grade	7th grade	8th grade	9th grade
Pass for distance (measured in yards)	A	33 and over	38 and over	42 and over
	B	27 - 32	30 - 37	34 - 41
	C	21 - 26	23 - 29	26 - 33
	D	15 - 20	15 - 22	18 - 25
	E	14 and under	14 and under	17 and under
Punt for distance (measured in yards)	A	30 and over	34 and over	37 and over
	B	24 - 29	26 - 33	30 - 36
	C	18 - 23	19 - 25	22 - 29
	D	12 - 17	12 - 18	15 - 21
	E	11 and under	11 and under	14 and under

(continued)

Table 6.14   Grading Scale for the Jacobson-Borleske Football Test *(continued)*

Event	Grade	7th grade	8th grade	9th grade
Run for Time	A	7.1 and under	6.7 and under	6.4 and under
(measured in seconds)	B	7.2 - 7.8	6.8 - 7.6	6.5 - 7.1
	C	7.9 - 8.7	7.7 - 8.5	7.2 - 7.9
	D	8.8 - 9.5	8.6 - 9.4	8.0 - 8.7
	E	9.6 and over	9.5 and over	8.8 and over
Total test	A	195 and over	193 and over	195 and over
(measured in t scores)	B	166 - 194	165 - 192	165 - 194
	C	137 - 165	137 - 164	136 - 164
	D	108 - 136	108 - 136	106 - 135
	E	107 and under	107 and under	105 and under

Note. Courtesy of "An evaluation of performance in certain physical ability tests administered to selected secondary school boys," by T.V. Jacobson, 1960, unpublished master's thesis, University of Washington, Seattle, WA. Copyright 1960 by the author and the University of Washington.

Other Football Tests

Borleske, S.E. (1936). *A study of achievement of college men in touch football.* Unpublished master's thesis, University of California, Berkeley.

Brace, D.K. (1943). Validity of football achievement tests as measures of motor learning as a partial basis for the selection of players. *Research Quarterly, 14,* 372.

Brechler, P.W. (1940). *A test to determine potential ability in football (backs and ends).* Unpublished master's thesis, University of Iowa, Iowa City.

Cormack, H.P. (1940). *A test to determine potential ability in football (linemen).* Unpublished master's thesis, University of Iowa, Iowa City.

Edwards, R.L. (1960). *A method of selecting linemen for high school football.* Unpublished master's thesis, University of Utah, Salt Lake City.

Hatley, F.J. (1942). *A battery of functional tests for the prediction of football potentiality.* Unpublished master's thesis, University of Iowa, Iowa City.

Lee, R.C. (1965). *A battery of tests to predict football potential.* Unpublished master's thesis, University of Utah, Salt Lake City.

May, L.D. (1972). *A study of the measurement of potential football ability in high school players.* Unpublished master's thesis, Texas Tech University, Lubbock.

McDavid, R.F. (1978). Predicting potential in football players. *Research Quarterly, 49,* 98-104.

McElroy, H.N. (1938). A report of some experimentation with a skill test. *Research Quarterly, 9,* 82-88.

McGauley, T. (1959). *A scoring device for analyzing individual defensive football performance.* Unpublished master's thesis, South Dakota University, Brookings.

Micheli, R.P. (1977). *Development of a battery of tests to predict football ability at the college level.* Unpublished doctoral dissertation, University of Arkansas, Fayetteville.

Wallrof, P.J. (1965). *Methods for rating defensive proficiency of high school football players.* Unpublished master's thesis, University of Washington, Seattle.

Ice Hockey

Ice hockey began in Canada in 1850. Soldiers strapped skates to their boots, borrowed field hockey sticks, and hit at a ball on a frozen patch of ice. By 1917 the National Hockey League was formed, and in 1924 Boston was the first team from the United States to enter the league.

Skills typically taught in an ice hockey unit include forward and backward skating, starting and stopping, stick handling, puck control, passing, shooting, checking, and goaltending.

Merrifield-Walford Ice Hockey Skill Test (Merrifield & Walford, 1969)

Purpose. To evaluate skating and puck-carrying ability in ice hockey.

Validity and Reliability. Validity coefficients of .83, .79, .75, and .96 were reported for forward skating speed, backward skating speed, skating agility, and puck-carrying ability, respectively. The criterion measure was a coach's ranking of hockey playing ability. Using the test-retest approach, reliability coefficients of .74, .80, .94, and .93 were reported for forward skating speed, backward skating speed, skating agility, and puck-carrying ability, respectively.

Age Level and Sex. Originally conducted with college males. Appropriate for junior high school and senior high school students.

Personnel. A minimum of three timers and three recorders.

Equipment. Ice hockey sticks, hockey pucks, a goal cage, a measuring tape, 10 obstacles, stop watches, a whistle, score cards or recording sheets, and pencils.

Space. An ice hockey rink.

Test Items. Forward speed skating, backward speed skating, skating agility, and puck carrying.

Preparation. The rink is prepared with three testing stations as shown in Figure 6.13.

Directions. Any student who falls can repeat the trial. For all test items, students are required to carry the hockey stick with both hands below shoulder level. Students are allowed a practice trial in the skating agility and puck-carrying tests. Two trials are allowed for each item.

Forward Speed Skating: This test is conducted at Station 1 as shown in Figure 6.13. The student starts behind the starting line and faces the finish line. On the "go" signal, the student skates the distance as fast as possible.

Backward Speed Skating: Same as the forward speed skating item except students start with their backs to the starting line and skate backward.

Skating Agility: This test is conducted around obstacles at Station 2 as shown in Figure 6.13. The obstacles should be 30 inches high on a 2 inch by 4 inch base. The student starts behind the starting line facing the first obstacle. On the "go" signal, the student skates to the left of the first obstacle, loops the second obstacle by passing first on the right side, returns to loop the first obstacle, and continues to the 4-foot line in front of the goal cage. Following a stop at the goal line, the student continues to the next 4-foot line. The stop-start action is repeated. The student then passes behind the goal cage and continues to the far obstacle, there performing a turn to skate backward, skating backward, and turning to skate forward while on the way.

Puck Carry: This test is conducted at Station 3 as shown in Figure 6.13. The student stands behind a starting line, and a puck is placed on the starting line to the left of the obstacle. On the "go" signal, the student moves through the zigzag course, passing to the left of the first obstacle, to the right of the second obstacle and so on. The student skates around the farthest obstacle and zigzags back to the starting line. Students are required to keep control of the puck throughout the test. If puck control is lost or if two or more obstacles are knocked over, the student must repeat the test.

Scoring. For all test items, time is recorded to the nearest 1/10 of a second from the "go" signal until a skater's first skate reaches the finish line. The final score is the better of the two timed trials.

Norms. Not available.

Another Ice Hockey Test

Hache, R.E. (1967). *An achievement test in ice hockey.* Unpublished master's thesis, University of Massachusetts, Amherst.

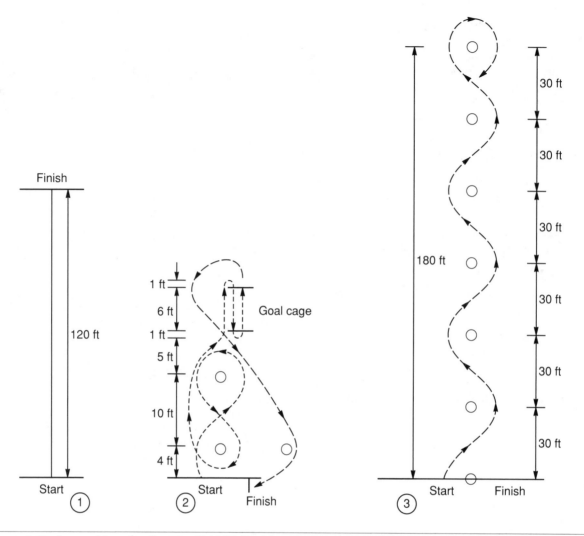

Figure 6.13 Ice markings for the Merrifield-Walford Ice Hockey Test: 1. Speed; 2. Agility; 3. Puck carry.
Note. From "Battery of ice hockey skill tests," by H.H. Merrifield and G.A. Walford, 1969, *Research Quarterly*, **40**, pp. 146-152. Copyright 1969 by AAHPER. Reprinted by permission.

Korfball

Korfball originated in 1902 as an outdoor recess game for boys and girls. The game caught on slowly partly because it was a coed game being played when sexes were not integrated in physical education classes. It eventually became internationally popular because American basketball was introduced overseas by the U.S. armed forces and because many indoor sports facilities were built. The sport was introduced in America by Nicolaas Moolenyzer at the 1970 National Conference of the American Association for Health, Physical Education, and Recreation.

Korfball skills typically included in a physical education unit are passing, shooting, guarding, defensive positioning, and lay-ups. No objective korfball skills tests are available.

Lacrosse

Lacrosse originated as a war-training activity for North American Indians. French settlers adopted the game and it eventually became the national sport of Canada in 1867. It was played professionally from 1920-1932. The game was introduced in the eastern United States in the 1870s and has remained a regional sport. Interest peaked in the 1970s.

Skills typically taught in a lacrosse unit include carrying the crosse, cradling, catching, passing, scooping, and goaltending.

Ennis Multi-Skill Test in Lacrosse (Ennis, 1977)

Purpose. To evaluate skill in lacrosse.

Validity and Reliability. A validity coefficient of .66 and a reliability coefficient of .89 were reported. The criterion measure was varsity lacrosse coaches rating their players into five categories using a revision of Hodges Rating Scale.

Age Level and Sex. Originally conducted with college students. Appropriate for junior high school and senior high school students.

Personnel. The test can be administered by one timer/scorer.

Equipment. Lacrosse sticks, balls, a goal, a measuring tape, marking materials, eight cones, a stop watch, score cards or recording sheets, and pencils.

Space. An area about 180 feet by 45 feet.

Test Items. Multiple components of running, stick handling, tossing, catching, and shooting.

Preparation. The testing field is prepared as shown in Figure 6.14.

Directions. The student begins near Cone 3. The student runs forward to pick up a stationary ball at Cone 1. Time begins as the ball is touched. After securing a ball, the student turns left and goes around Cone 1, runs to the right of Cone 2, to the left of Cone 3, and to the right of Cone 4. Once past Cone 4, the student performs two tosses and catches of the ball while running. The ball must be visible above the student's head or be repeated. After tossing and catching twice, the student shoots for goal. There is no penalty for a miss, but for successful shots, deduct 1 second from the final time. The shot may be taken from anywhere.

Without a ball, the student continues to the goal side of Cone 5, turns and runs backward to Cone 6, and then runs forward to pick up a ball beside Cone 7. The student continues to run

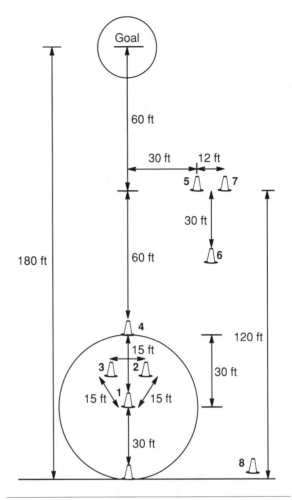

Figure 6.14 Field markings for the Ennis Lacrosse Test. *Note.* From "The development of a multi-skill test in lacrosse for college women," by Catherine D. Ennis, 1977, unpublished master's thesis, University of North Carolina, Greensboro, NC. Copyright 1977 by the author. Reprinted by permission.

around Cone 7 and throws the ball beyond Cone 8. The student may throw from anywhere, and the ball may bounce. If a ball stops before passing Cone 8, the student must use a stick to propel it again. Time will be recorded until the ball passes Cone 8.

Scoring. Time is recorded to the nearest 1/10 of a second. The score for a specific trial is the final time minus a 1-second deduction for a successful goal. The final score is the sum of the three trials.

Norms. Not available.

Other Lacrosse Tests

Hodges, C.V. (1967). *Construction of an objective knowledge test and skill test in lacrosse for college women.* Master's thesis, University of North Carolina, Greensboro. (Microcard PE 1974, University of Oregon, Eugene.)

Lutze, M.C. (1963). *Achievement tests in beginning lacrosse for women.* Unpublished master's thesis, University of Iowa, Iowa City.

McGowan, N. (1965). A skill test for the overarm pass. *Crosse Checks,* **1,** 23-24.

Waglow, I.F., & Moore, A. (1954). A lacrosse skill test. *Athletic Journal,* **34,** 4.

Wilkie, B.J. (1967). *Achievement tests for selected lacrosse skills of college women.* Unpublished master's thesis, University of North Carolina, Greensboro.

Soccer

Soccer, a game that millions play and watch, is the king of sport worldwide but still has a difficult time generating interest in the United States. The World Cup, played every 4 years, is the most followed sporting event in the world, rivaled only by the Olympic Games. As Americans become more familiar with soccer it is likely to become a popular physical education activity. It requires little equipment, is relatively safe compared to football, and allows many students a chance to participate regardless of size, strength, or sex.

Soccer skills typically taught in a physical education class include dribbling, passing, kicking, trapping, heading, tackling, goalkeeping, and throwing.

Mor-Christian General Soccer Ability Skill Test Battery
(Mor & Christian, 1979)

Purpose. To evaluate passing, dribbling, and shooting ability in soccer.

Validity and Reliability. Validity coefficients of .73, .78, and .91 were reported for dribbling, passing, and shooting, respectively. The criterion measure was a rating scale developed and used by three soccer experts. Using the test-retest approach, reliability coefficients for dribbling, passing, and shooting were .80, .96, and .98, respectively.

Age Level and Sex. Originally conducted with college males. Appropriate for junior high school and senior high school students.

Personnel. One individual at each of the three stations as recorder/scorer. Students retrieve and replace balls.

Equipment. Soccer balls, a soccer goal, a measuring tape, marking material, 17 cones, one 4-foot rope, two 10-foot ropes, four hoops, a stop watch, score cards or recording sheets, and pencils.

Space. Areas of 60, 45, and 45 feet are required for the dribble, pass, and shooting tests, respectively.

Test Items. Dribbling, passing, and shooting.

Preparation. Testing stations for the dribbling test are prepared as shown in Figure 6.15. A round course with a 20-yard diameter is measured and marked. Twelve 18-inch cones are located around the circle at 5-yard intervals. A 3-foot starting line is marked perpendicular to the outside of the circle.

Testing stations for the passing test are prepared as shown in Figure 6.16. A goal 1 yard wide and 18 inches high is prepared by placing two cones 1 yard apart with a 4-foot rope used as a crossbar. Two cones are placed at a 45-degree angle from the goal line, and one cone is placed at a 90-degree angle from the goal line. All three cones are located 15 yards from the goal.

Testing stations for the shooting test are prepared as shown in Figure 6.17. Two ropes suspended from the goal crossbar 4 feet from each goal post divide the soccer goal into two scoring areas. Each scoring area is further divided into two circular targets by two hoops 4 feet in diameter. A restraining line is marked 16 yards from and parallel to the goal.

Directions.

Dribbling: On the "go" signal, the student dribbles a ball, which has been placed on the starting line, around the course. The student dribbles between the cones as quickly as possible and back to the starting line. Three trials are allowed: the first clockwise, the second counterclockwise, and the third in the direction of the student's choice.

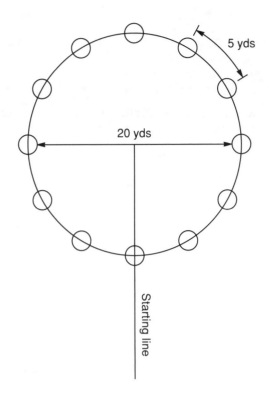

Figure 6.15 Field markings for the Mor-Christian Soccer Dribbling Test.

Note. From "The development of a skill test battery to measure general soccer ability," by D. Mor and V. Christian, 1979, *North Carolina Journal of HPE*, **15**, pp. 30-39. Copyright 1979 by the author. Reprinted by permission.

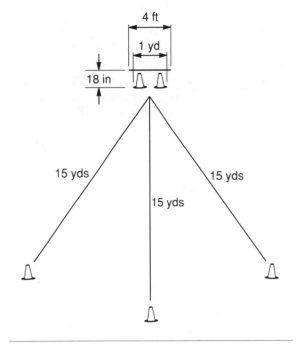

Figure 6.16 Field markings for the Mor-Christian Soccer Passing Test.

Note. From "The development of a skill test battery to measure general soccer ability," by D. Mor and V. Christian, 1979, *North Carolina Journal of HPE*, **15**, pp. 30-39. Copyright 1979 by the author. Reprinted by permission.

Passing: From each of the three cones students execute four passes into the goal (12 passes total). Students may use their preferred foot when passing. Two practice passes are allowed from each spot.

Shooting: From behind the restraining line, the student shoots stationary balls toward the target. The preferred foot may be used, and the ball may be placed anywhere behind the restraining line. Four practice trials are allowed followed by four consecutive attempts at each of the four target areas (a total of 16 shot trials).

Scoring.

Dribbling: The final test score is the combined time of the two best trials.

Passing: One point is awarded for each successful pass. Balls that hit the goal cones are considered successful. The final score is the total of 12 pass trials.

Shooting: Ten points are awarded for shots going through a proper target, and 4 points are

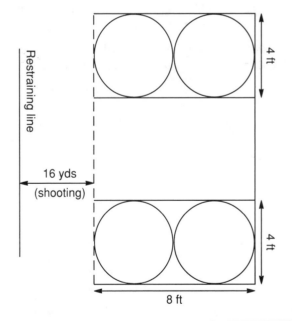

Figure 6.17 Field markings and target for the Mor-Christian Soccer Shooting Test.

Note. From "The development of a skill test battery to measure general soccer ability," by D. Mor and V. Christian, 1979, *North Carolina Journal of HPE*, **15**, pp. 30-39. Copyright 1979 by the author. Reprinted by permission.

awarded for shots going through a wrong target. For example, if a student is shooting for the upper right target and he or she successfully makes it, 10 points are awarded; if the shot goes through a bottom target, 4 points are awarded. Balls that hit a circular target count as good. Balls that bounce or roll through the target area are counted as unsuccessful. The final score is the total of 16 trials.

Norms. Not available.

Johnson Soccer Test (Johnson, 1963)

Purpose. To evaluate general ability in soccer.

Validity and Reliability. Validity coefficients of .98, .94, .58, .84, and .81 were reported for service class students, physical education majors, first-team varsity players, second-team varsity players, and third-team varsity players, respectively. Validity was determined by rank-difference between scores on the test and investigator rankings of soccer ability. A reliability of .92 was reported.

Age Level and Sex. Originally conducted with college males. Appropriate for junior high school and senior high school students.

Personnel. One person as recorder/scorer at each station. Students retrieve and replace balls.

Equipment. Soccer balls, a backboard with the same dimensions as a soccer goal, a measuring tape, marking material, a ball basket, a stop watch, score cards or recording sheets, and pencils.

Space. The testing area should allow for at least 30 feet directly in front of a backboard.

Test Item. A consecutive foot rally.

Preparation. A restraining line is placed 15 feet from a backboard that is 24 feet wide and at least 8 feet high. A ball basket containing extra balls is placed 15 feet behind the restraining line.

Directions. The student waits behind the restraining line holding a ball. On the "go" signal, the student kicks a ball against the backboard so that it rebounds back to him or her either on the fly or after bouncing. The student returns the ball against the backboard as many times as possible during a 30-second timed trial. Balls must be kicked from behind the restraining line using any

legal soccer kick. When balls go out of control, students may obtain spare balls from the ball basket rather than retrieve the loose ball. Three 30-second timed trials are given.

Scoring. The final score is the number of legal hits during the three timed trials.

Norms. A scoring scale is shown in Table 6.15.

Table 6.15   Scoring Scale for the Johnson Soccer Test

	Number of hits
Superior	42-over
Good	37-41
Average	31-36
Below average	25-30
Poor	24-below

Note. From "The development of a single item test as a measure of soccer skill," by J.R. Johnson, 1963, master's thesis, University of British Columbia, Vancouver. Copyright 1963 by the author. Reprinted by permission.

Yeagley Soccer Battery (Yeagley, 1972)

Purpose. To evaluate beginning soccer ability.

Validity and Reliability. Validity coefficients of .80, .81, and .74, obtained by comparing judges' ratings with test scores, were reported for the dribble, wall-volley, and juggling tests, respectively. Reliability coefficients of .92, .90, and .95 were reported for the dribble, wall-volley, and juggling tests, respectively.

Age Level and Sex. Originally conducted with college students. Appropriate for junior high school and senior high school students.

Personnel. Two assistants for each test.

Equipment. Soccer balls, a smooth wall surface, a measuring tape, marking tape, seven cones, stop watches, score cards or recording sheets, and pencils.

Space. A gymnasium.

Test Items. Dribbling, wall-volley, and juggling.

Preparation. Testing stations for the dribble test are prepared as shown in Figure 6.18.

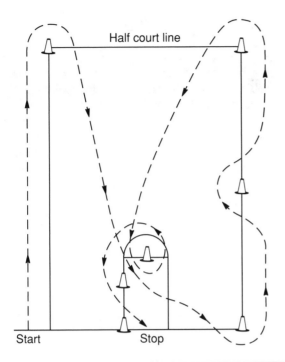

Half court line

Start   Stop

Figure 6.18 Court markings for the Yeagley Soccer Test. *Note.* From "Soccer skills tests," by J. Yeagley, 1972, unpublished paper. Copyright 1972 by the author. Reprinted by permission.

Wall-Volley: The area for this test consists of an 8 foot by 24 foot unobstructed wall and a restraining line marked 15 feet from the wall. The student stands, with a soccer ball at his or her feet, behind the restraining line. On the "go" signal, the student kicks the ball against the wall as many times as possible during a 30-second timed trial. To score, the nonkicking foot must be behind the restraining line; however, any type of kick and trap is allowed. Extra balls should be available in case students lose control of the original ball. Two trials are allowed.

Scoring.

Dribble: Time is recorded to the nearest 1/10 of a second. The final score is the best of two timed trials.

Juggling: The student's score is the number of legal juggles during the 30-second timed trial. The final score is the best of two trials.

Wall-Volley: The student's score is the number of legal volleys during the 30-second timed trial. The final score is the best of two trials.

Norms. Not available.

Directions.

Dribble: The test is administered on a basketball half court. The student stands behind the restraining line with a soccer ball at his or her feet. On the "go" signal, the student dribbles around the cones following the course as outlined in Figure 6.18. The test is completed when the student dribbles the ball across the finish line and brings the ball to a complete halt using only the feet. It is legal to touch, knock down, or move any cone with the ball or the feet so long as the course is followed. Two trials are allowed.

Juggling: The student stands in a testing area (a basketball half court) with a soccer ball in hand. On the "go" signal, the student bounces a ball on the floor and juggles the ball in the air with other body parts as many times as possible during a 30-second timed trial. All body parts except the arms and hands can be used to juggle the ball. Recommended body parts include the feet, thighs, head, shoulders, and chest. Balls may bounce on the floor without penalty during juggles. Juggles outside the half-court boundary do not count. Each time the hands or arms are used to control the ball, 1 point is deducted. Two trials are allowed.

Other Soccer Tests

Bontz, J. (1942). *An experiment in the construction of a test for measuring ability in some of the fundamental skills used by fifth and sixth grade children in soccer.* Unpublished master's thesis, University of Iowa, Iowa City.

Crawford, E.A. (1958). *The development of skill test batteries for evaluating the ability of women physical education major students in soccer and speedball.* Unpublished doctoral dissertation, University of Oregon, Eugene.

Crew, V.N. (1968). *A skill test battery for use in service program soccer classes at the university level.* Unpublished master's thesis, University of Oregon, Eugene.

Heath, M.L., & Rogers, E.G. (1932). A study in the use of knowledge and skill tests in soccer. *Research Quarterly,* **3,** 33-53.

Konstantinov, K.J. (1939). *The development and evaluation of a battery of soccer skills as an index of ability in soccer.* Unpublished master's

(continued)

Other Soccer Tests (continued)

thesis, Springfield College, Springfield, MA.

Lee, H.C. (1941). *An evaluation of Brock's Soccer Skill Test and a rating scale of physical endurance, tackling, and personality traits on the secondary school level.* Unpublished master's thesis, Springfield College, Springfield, MA.

MacKenzie, J. (1968). *The evaluation of a battery of soccer tests as an aid to classification of general soccer ability.* Unpublished master's thesis, University of Massachusetts, Amherst.

McDonald, L.G. (1951). *The construction of a kicking skill test as an index of general soccer ability.* Unpublished master's thesis, Springfield College, Springfield, MA.

McElroy, H.N. (1938). A report on some experimentation with a skill test. *Research Quarterly, 9*, 782-788.

Mitchell, J.R. (1963). *The modification of the McDonald Soccer Skill Test for upper elementary school boys.* Unpublished master's thesis, University of Oregon, Eugene.

Munro, J.B. (1941). *An evaluation of Brock's Soccer Skill Test and a rating scale of physical endurance, tackling, and personality traits in soccer on the college level.* Unpublished master's thesis, Springfield College, Springfield, MA.

Schaufele, E.F. (1940). *The establishment of objective tests for girls in the ninth and tenth grades to determine soccer ability.* Unpublished master's thesis, University of Iowa, Iowa City.

Streck, B. (1961). *An analysis of the McDonald Soccer Skill Test as applied to junior high school girls.* Unpublished master's thesis, Fort Hays State College, Fort Hays, KS.

Tomlinson, R. (1964). Soccer skill test. In *Soccerspeedball guide 1964-1966.* Washington, DC: AAHPER.

Vanderhoff, M. (1932). Soccer skills tests. *Journal of Health and Physical Education, 3*, 42.

Warner, F.H. (1941). *The development of achievement scales of fundamental soccer skills for high school boys.* Unpublished master's thesis, Springfield College, Springfield, MA.

Warner, G.F. (1950). Warner soccer test. *Newsletter of the National Soccer Coaches Association of America, 6*, 13-22.

Whitney, A.H., & Chapin, G. (1946). Soccer skill testing for girls. In *Soccer-speedball guide 1946-1948.* Washington, DC: AAHPER.

Softball

Softball developed as an offshoot of Abner Doubleday's baseball. Because players wanted to play baseball in winter, indoor baseball developed, and although it did not become popular (until the Astrodome was built), it led to softball. The 1930s, a time when many people were unemployed, were the growth years of softball as we know it. Today an estimated 30 million people play some form of the game.

Skills typically taught in physical education softball include hitting, pitching, catching fly balls, fielding grounders, throwing, and baserunning. Softball skills tests generally include at least two skill components.

Kehtel Softball Fielding and Throwing Accuracy Test (Kehtel, 1958)

Purpose. To evaluate fielding and throwing ability in softball.

Validity and Reliability. Using the scores of college students, validity coefficients were shown between .76 to .79 depending on which scoring system was used. Using the odd-even method followed by the Spearman-Brown Prophecy Formula, reliability coefficients were estimated at .90 and .91 for the two scoring systems.

Age Level and Sex. Originally conducted with college students. Appropriate for junior high school and senior high school students.

Personnel. The test is best administered with at least five people: one timer, one recorder, and three ball retrievers.

Equipment. Softball gloves, at least 10 softballs at each testing station, a box to hold balls, a measuring tape and marking tape, a stop watch, score cards or score sheets, and pencils.

Space. An area with two high walls at right angles to one another. Each testing station needs a minimum floor area of 45 feet by 45 feet.

Test Items. A softball fielding test and a throwing accuracy test.

Preparation. Each testing station is prepared as shown in Figure 6.19. The testing station must be located in an area that has two walls at right angles to one another. A 10-foot line with its center approximately 40 feet from Wall B and 4 feet above and parallel to the floor is placed on Wall A. A 5-foot starting line is placed 40 feet

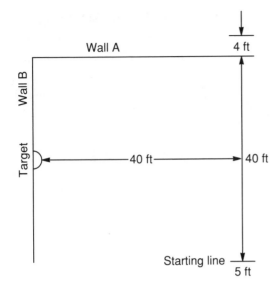

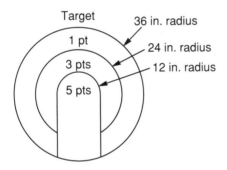

Figure 6.19 Floor and target markings for the Kehtel Softball Test.

Note. From "The development of a test to measure the ability of a softball player to field a ground ball and successfully throw it at a target," by E.H. Kehtel, 1958, unpublished master's thesis, University of Colorado, Boulder, CO. Copyright 1958 by the author. Reprinted by permission of the department of kinesiology, University of Colorado.

from and parallel to Wall A. The midpoint of the 5-foot starting line is 40 feet from Wall B. A circular target with a 36-inch radius is placed on Wall B so that its center is 20 feet from Wall A. The upper half of the target has a semicircle with a 12-inch radius and two straight lines extending down each end of the semicircle to the bottom of the target. An incomplete circle with a 24-inch radius is located around the oblong area.

Directions. The student waits behind the 40-foot starting line. At the start signal, the student throws a ball below the 4-foot line on Wall A. Balls are fielded as quickly as possible and thrown at the target on Wall B. The student may cross the starting line to make a recovery. Upon

completion of the throw, the student hurries behind the starting line, grabs a second softball, and repeats the action. This action continues for 2 minutes.

The thrower may take one step over the starting line. Balls that hit the floor before contacting Wall A are playable. An additional ball should be put into play as quickly as possible when a ball fails to reach Wall A because any such ball does not count. One practice trial is allowed.

Assistants supply students with additional balls. Two assistants should retrieve thrown balls and relay them to a third assistant, who places them in a ball box near the starting line. Assistants must not interfere with students who are testing.

Scoring. Two scoring methods can be used. Either method is acceptable as long as students are scored consistently. The final score for method one is the total score for each ball. Score is determined by where a ball hits within the target area. Figure 6.19 indicates the point values on the target. Balls striking a division line separating two sections earn the higher value. The final score for method two is the number of balls striking the target in a 2-minute period.

Norms. Not available.

Underkofler Softball Skills Test (Underkofler, 1942)

Purpose. To evaluate distance throwing and batting ability in softball.

Validity and Reliability. Validity coefficients of .81 and .72 were obtained for the distance throw and the batting test, respectively. Reliability coefficients of .95 and .79 were obtained for the distance throw and batting test, respectively.

Age Level and Sex. Appropriate for junior high school and senior high school students.

Personnel. The distance throw is best administered with three people: one marks where balls land, one records the distance balls are thrown, and one shags balls from retrievers. The batting test is best administered with at least three people: one pitcher, one umpire, and one score recorder. Nontesting students retrieve balls.

Equipment. Softballs, softball bats, a home plate, a measuring tape and chalk for field markings, score cards or recording sheets, and pencils.

Space. A regulation-sized softball field with a 45-foot diamond and 30-foot pitcher's mound. The outfield should be deep enough so that the longest throws can be measured.

Test Items. A softball distance throw and a batting test.

Preparation. Measure and mark 10-foot intervals in the outfield.

Directions. For the distance throw, three trials of three throws each are allowed (nine total throws). The best throw in each trial is recorded. When throwing, the student must stay behind the throwing line and may not take more than one step before throwing. The student may use any type of throw.

For the batting test, the student stands in a batter's box and tries to hit 10 legal underhand slow pitches. The umpire calls balls and strikes. Called strikes count as trials, but balls do not. Use the same pitcher and umpire throughout the test.

Scoring. The best of three throws in each of three trials constitutes the official score. Throws are measured to the nearest foot and represent the distance from the throwing line to the point where they first contact the ground.

Batted balls that land beyond the 45-foot softball diamond count as 5 points, and balls that initially land in the infield count as 3 points. Foul balls are counted as 1 point, and swinging and called strikes earn no points. The batting score is the number of points earned in the 10 trials.

Norms. T score values are shown in Table 6.16.

Table 6.16 T Scores for the Underkofler Batting Test

T score	Batting	T score	Batting
76	42	53	23
75		52	22
74		51	
73		50	21
72	40	49	20
71		48	19
70		47	
69		46	18
68	38	45	17
67		44	16
66	36	43	
65	35	42	15
64		41	14
63		40	
62	34	39	13
61		38	12
60	32	37	11
59	30	36	9
58	29	35	8
57	28	34	
56	27	33	
55	26	32	6
54	24	31	
		30	
		29	
		28	1

Note. From ''A study of skill tests for evaluating the ability of junior high school girls in softball,'' by A. Underkofler, 1942, unpublished master's thesis, University of Iowa, Iowa City, IA. Copyright 1942 by the author and the University of Iowa. Reprinted by permission.

Other Softball/Baseball Tests

American Alliance for Health, Physical Education, Recreation and Dance. (1991). *AAHPERD Softball skills manual.* Reston, VA: AAHPERD.

Broer, M.R. (1958). Reliability of certain skill tests for junior high school girls. *Research Quarterly,* **29,** 139-143.

Cale, A.A. (1962). *The investigation and analysis of softball skill tests for college women.* Unpublished master's thesis, University of Maryland, College Park.

Cobb, J.W. (1958). *The determination of the merits of selected items for the construction of a baseball skill test for boys of little league age.* Unpublished doctoral dissertation, Indiana University, Bloomington.

Davis, R. (1951). *The development of an objective softball battery test for college women.* Unpublished master's thesis, Illinois State University, Normal.

Elrod, J.M. (1969). *Construction of a softball skill battery for high school boys.* Unpublished master's thesis, Louisiana State University, Baton Rouge.

Fox, M.G., & Young, O.G. (1954). A test of softball battery ability. *Research Quarterly*, **25**, 26-27.

Fringer, M.N. (1961). *Fringer softball battery.* Unpublished master's thesis, University of Michigan, Ann Arbor.

Fry, J.B. (1958). *The relationship between a baseball skill test and actual playing in game situations.* Unpublished master's thesis, Pennsylvania State University, University Park.

Hooks, G.E. (1959). Prediction of baseball ability through an analysis of measures of strength and structure. *Research Quarterly*, **30**, 38-43.

Maver, D.J. (1986). *Maver softball skills test battery.* Unpublished paper, University of North Carolina, Greensboro.

Kelson, R.E. (1953). Baseball classification plan for boys. *Research Quarterly*, **24**, 304-307.

O'Donnell, D.J. (1950). *Validation of softball skill tests for high school girls.* Unpublished

master's thesis, Indiana University, Bloomington.

Rodgers, E.G., & Heath, M.L. (1931). An experiment in the use of knowledge and skill tests in playground baseball. *Research Quarterly*, **2**, 113.

Safrit, M.J., & Pavis, A. (1969). Overarm throw skill testing. In J. Felshin & O'Brian, *Selected softball articles*. Washington, DC: AAHPER.

Scott, M.G., & French, E. (1959). Softball repeated throws test. In M.G. Scott & E. French, *Measurement and evaluation in physical education*. Dubuque, IA: Brown.

Sheehan, F.E. (1954). *Baseball achievement scales for elementary and junior high school boys.* Unpublished master's thesis, University of Wisconsin, Madison.

Shick, J. (1970). Battery of defensive softball skills tests for college women. *Research Quarterly*, **41**, 82-87.

Sopa, A. (1967). *Construction of an indoor batting skills test for junior high school girls.* Unpublished master's thesis, University of Wisconsin, Madison.

Speedball

Speedball, which arrived in the United States after the Depression, is still relatively new to the catalog of sports available to physical education teachers. Elmer Mitchell was looking for a way to combine elements of basketball, soccer, and football when he developed speedball. Because students can use their hands in speedball (they cannot in soccer), the game is growing rapidly and is included in many physical education programs nationwide.

Skills typically included in a speedball unit are ground dribbling, goalkeeping, passing, overhead dribbling, kicking, catching, trapping, lifting, and heading.

Buchanan Speedball Test (Buchanan, 1942)

Purpose. To evaluate ability in speedball.

Validity and Reliability. Validity coefficients of .88, .79, .85, and .69 were reported for lift to others, throwing and catching while standing, kick-up, and dribbling and passing tests, respectively.

Three instructors' subjective ratings were used as the criterion measure. Reliability coefficients of .93, .92, .93, and .98 were reported for lift to others, throwing and catching while standing, kick-up, and dribbling and passing tests, respectively. Reliability was determined with the odd-even approach followed by the Spearman-Brown Prophecy Formula.

Age Level and Sex. Originally conducted with high school girls. Appropriate for junior high school and senior high school students.

Personnel. One person to score or time. Students assist.

Equipment. Soccer balls, goals, net, standards, cones, a stop watch, score cards or recording sheets, and pencils.

Space. A playing field and an unobstructed wall space.

Test Items. Lift to others, throwing and catching while standing, kick-up, and dribbling and passing.

Preparation. Testing stations for the lift-to-others test are prepared as shown in Figure 6.20. A net is stretched between two standards so that its

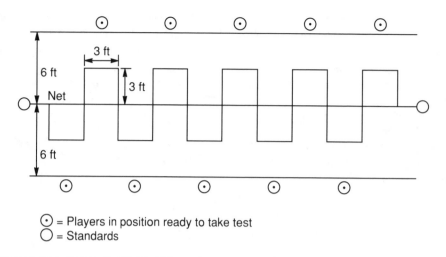

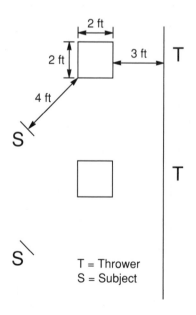

Figure 6.20 Field markings for the Buchanan Speedball Lift Test.
Note. From "A study of achievement tests in speedball for high school girls," by R.E. Buchanan, 1942, unpublished master's thesis, University of Iowa, Iowa City, IA. Copyright 1942 by the author. Reprinted by permission of the University of Iowa.

top is 2-1/2 feet above the surface. Located on each side of the net are 6-foot restraining lines and 3-foot squares.

Testing stations for the kick-up test are prepared as shown in Figure 6.21. A 2-foot square with its inner side 3 feet from and parallel to a sideline is marked. Following an imaginary extension of the diagonal of the square, a starting line is marked 4 feet from the outside corner of the square.

Figure 6.21 Field markings for the Buchanan Speedball Kick-Up Test.
Note. From "A study of achievement tests in speedball for high school girls," by R.E. Buchanan, 1942, unpublished master's thesis, University of Iowa, Iowa City, IA. Copyright 1942 by the author. Reprinted by permission of the University of Iowa.

Testing stations for dribbling and passing tests are shown in Figure 6.22. A starting line is marked 60 yards from and parallel to the end line of a field. Six-yard wide goal areas are marked on the end line. Cones are placed at 10-yard intervals between the starting line and the end line. Cone lines are placed 3 yards to the right and left of goal areas with a 10-yard space between goal areas.

Directions.

Lift to Others: The student stands, with a ball at his or her feet, behind the 6-foot restraining lines. With either foot the student lifts a ball and passes it over the net so that it lands within the 3-foot square. A partner recovers the ball and, in turn, becomes the test student lifting the ball back over the net into a 3-foot square. Partners alternate until each student completes 10 trials.

Throwing and Catching While Standing: A restraining line is marked 6 feet from and parallel to a clean wall space. The student stands, ball in hand, behind the restraining line. On the "ready, go" signal, the student throws a ball and catches the rebound as many times as possible in a 30-second timed trial. Five timed trials are allowed.

Kick-Up: Students work as partners, one student behind the starting line, the other behind the sideline. To begin, the student behind the sideline tosses a ball overhead so that it lands in the 2-foot square. The student who is to execute the kick-up begins behind the starting line. As a ball leaves the thrower's hand, the kicker runs forward and performs a kick-up to self. The

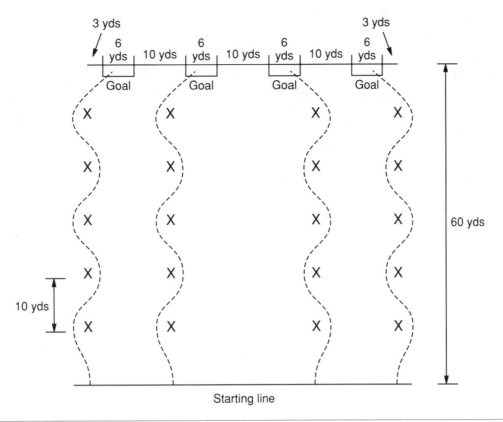

Figure 6.22 Field markings for the Buchanan Speedball Dribble and Pass Test.
Note. From "A study of achievement tests in speedball for high school girls," by R.E. Buchanan, 1942, unpublished master's thesis, University of Iowa, Iowa City, IA. Copyright 1942 by the author. Reprinted by permission of the University of Iowa.

trial is repeated if a ball does not land in the 2-foot square. Ten trials are allowed.

Dribbling and Passing: The student, with a soccer ball resting on the line directly in line with the cones, stands behind the starting line. On the "ready, go" signal, the student dribbles downfield toward the first cone. The student dribbles right of the first cone, left of the second cone, and so on the length of the course. After dribbling to the last cone, the student tries to kick the ball to the left into the goal area. Ten trials are allowed, five to the left and five to the right. Allow a rest period between attempts.

Scoring. Balls that hit the net but land in a square and balls that hit lines count as 1 point.

Lift to Others: One point is awarded for each pass that lands in the proper square. The final score is the total points for 10 trials.

Throwing and Catching While Standing: One point is awarded for each successful throw and catch. The final score is the average number of throws and catches in each of five timed trials.

Kick-Up: One point is awarded for each successful kick-up to self. The final score is the total points for 10 trials.

Dribbling and Passing: Three scores are obtained. The dribbling score is the total in seconds of 10 trials. The passing score is the number of accurate passes (into the goals) completed in 10 trials. The combined dribbling and passing score is the sum of the times for 10 trials recorded in seconds, minus 10 times the number of accurate passes on 10 trials. For example, if a student has a dribbling score of 600 and a passing score of 8, his or her combined score would be 600 minus 80 (10 × 8) or 520.

Norms. T score values and achievement scales are shown in Tables 6.17 and 6.18.

Table 6.17   T Scales for the Buchanan Speedball Test

T score	Lift to others[a]	Throwing and catching standing[b]	Throwing and catching standing[c]	Kick-ups[d]	Passing[e]	Passing[f]	T score
75		19.8-20.2					75
74							74
73							73
72		19.3-19.7	27.8-29.7	10			72
71	10					10	71
70							70
69		18.8-19.2					69
68					5		68
67		18.3-18.7					67
66				9		9	66
65		17.8-18.2	25.8-27.7				65
64							64
63	9						63
62		17.3-17.7				8	62
61							61
60		16.8-17.2					60
59				8		7	59
58		16.3-16.7					58
57	8		23.8-25.7			6	57
56		15.8-16.2					56
55							55
54		15.3-15.7		7			54
53	7						53
52			21.8-23.7				52
51		14.8-15.2			4	5	51
50				6			50
49							49
48			19.3-21.7				48
47	6			5			47
46		14.3-14.7				4	46
45			17.8-19.7				45
44							44
43	5	13.8-13.2		4	3		43
42		13.3-13.7					42
41		12.8-13.2	15.8-17.7				41
40		12.3-12.7				3	40
39	4	11.8-11.2					39
38				3			38
37			13.8-15.7				37
36		11.3-11.7					36
35					2	2	35
34	3			2			34
33			11.8-13.7				33
32							32
31							31
30	2						30
29				1			29
28					1		28

T score	Lift to others[a]	Throwing and catching standing[b]	Throwing and catching standing[c]	Kick-ups[d]	Passing[e]	Passing[f]	T score
27							27
26			9.8-11.7				26
25	1					1	25

Note. From "A study of achievement tests in speedball for high school girls," by R.E. Buchanan, 1942, unpublished master's thesis, University of Iowa, Iowa City, IA. Copyright 1942 by the author. Reprinted by permission of the University of Iowa.

[a] Ten trials
[b] Mean of five trials
[c] Mean of two trials
[d] Ten trials
[e] Five trials
[f] Ten trials

Table 6.18 Achievement Scales for the Buchanan Speedball Test

Rating	Lift to others	Throwing and catching	Passing	Kick-ups
Superior	10 and up	18.8 and up	10	9 and up
Good	8-9	16.3-18.7	7-9	7-8
Average	5-7	14.3-16.2	4-6	4-6
Poor	2-4	11.3-14.2	2-3	2-3
Inferior	1 and below	11.2 and below	1 and below	1 and below

N = 72, number of trials as specified in directions.

Rating	Lift to others	Throwing and catching	Passing	Kick-ups
Superior	10 and up	27.8 and up	6 and up	10
Good	8-9	23.8-27.7	5	8-9
Average	6-7	17.8-23.7	3-4	4-7
Poor	3-5	11.8-17.7	2	2-3
Inferior	2 and below	11.7 and below	1 and below	1 and below
	N = 262	N = 159	N = 190	N = 262
	10 trials	M of 2 trials	5 trials	10 trials

Note. From "A study of achievement tests in speedball for high school girls," by R.E. Buchanan, 1942, unpublished master's thesis, University of Iowa, Iowa City, IA. Copyright 1942 by the author. Reprinted by permission of the University of Iowa.

Smith Speedball Test (Smith, 1947)

Purpose. To evaluate kick-up-to-self ability in speedball.

Validity and Reliability. A validity coefficient of .54 and a reliability coefficient of .90 were reported for the kick-up-to-self test. Playing ability rating by three judges was used as the criterion measure.

Age Level and Sex. Originally conducted with female college physical education majors. Appropriate for junior high school and senior high school students.

Personnel. One person at each station to act as recorder and timer.

Equipment. Soccer balls, a measuring tape, marking tape, a stop watch, score cards or recording sheets, and pencils.

Space. An unobstructed wall and floor space at least 10 feet wide and 15 feet long.

Test Item. Kick-up to self.

Preparation. Testing stations are prepared as shown in Figure 6.23. The unobstructed wall should be at least 6 feet wide and 10 feet high. Floor space should be about the same. A restraining line 7 feet from and parallel to the wall is marked on the floor.

Directions. The student stands behind the restraining line with soccer ball in hand. On the "go" signal, the student tosses a ball against the wall and performs a kick-up to self on the rebound as many times as possible during a 30-second timed trial. A toss to the wall 2 to 3 feet above the floor works well. The student can cross the restraining line to recover the ball (use of hands acceptable) but must move behind the line for the next toss. The same is true if a ball gets out of control. Legal kick-ups are ones that go directly off a student's foot or instep to the hands, but do not roll up the shins or touch any part of the body except the hands. Six 30-second timed trials are allowed. Students can rest 1 minute between trials.

Scoring. One point is awarded for each legal kick-up to self. The final score is the number of legal kick-ups for six time trials.

Norms. Not available.

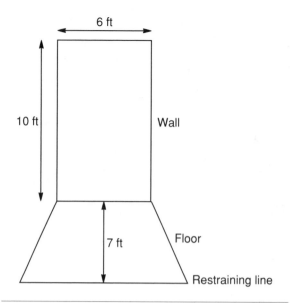

Figure 6.23 Markings for the Smith Speedball Test. *Note.* From "Speedball skill tests for college women," by G. Smith, 1947, National Section on Girls' and Women's Sports (an agency of AAPHER). Copyright 1947 by the author. Reprinted by permission.

Other Speedball Tests

Crawford, E.A. (1958). *The development of skill test batteries for evaluating the ability of women physical education major students in soccer and speedball.* Unpublished doctoral dissertation, University of Oregon, Eugene.

Miller, S.B. (1959). *A battery of speedball skill tests for college women.* Unpublished master's thesis, University of Nebraska, Lincoln.

Stephyns, O.R. (1947). *Achievement tests in speed-a-way for high school girls.* Unpublished master's thesis, Illinois State University, Normal.

Team Handball

Team handball is popular internationally, but has caught on slowly in the United States. Its addition to the Olympic Games (in 1972 for men and in 1976 for women) and its speed and excitement give team handball bright prospects for continued growth.

Skills typically taught in team handball classes include passing, shooting, dribbling, defensive positioning, and goalkeeping.

Zinn Team Handball Skills Battery (Zinn, 1981)

Purpose. To evaluate passing and throwing ability in team handball.

Validity and Reliability. Validity coefficients were reported to be .71, .77, and .76 for the dominant-hand speed pass, overhead pass, and 9-meter front throw, respectively. Judges' ratings were used as the criterion measure. Using the test-retest approach, reliability coefficients ranged from .82 to .89 for the three-item battery.

Age Level and Sex. Originally conducted with male and female high school members of a team handball squad. Appropriate for junior high and senior high school students.

Personnel. One tester.

Equipment. Team handballs, rope or string, a measuring tape, marking tape, a stop watch, score cards or recording sheets, and pencils.

Space. The 9-meter front throw test requires the area around a goal, and the dominant-hand speed and overhead pass tests require an unobstructed wall.

Test Items. Nine-meter front throw, dominant-hand speed pass, and overhead pass.

Preparation. Each testing station for the 9-meter front throw is prepared as shown in Figure 6.24. The front surface area of a team handball goal is divided with rope or string into eight parts. Each part is assigned a certain number of points reflecting the difficulty of throwing the ball into that area. The dominant-hand speed pass test requires that a restraining line be marked 2.5 meters from and parallel to a wall.

Stations for the overhead pass test are prepared as shown in Figure 6.25. A line is drawn 15 meters from and parallel to a wall. The target, located on the wall as shown, consists of three concentric circles. The inner circle is 45 cm in diameter, the second circle is 95 cm in diameter, and the outer circle is 150 cm in diameter. The bottom of the outer circle is 100 cm above the floor.

Directions.

Nine-Meter Front Throw: The student gets 10 throws, 5 when executing a jump throw and 5 when executing a set throw. The student can take three steps before releasing a ball but the last step must be executed outside the free throw line (9-meter line). If a ball hits the court surface before it reaches the goal, no points are scored.

Dominant-Hand Speed Pass: The student stands behind the restraining line. Upon the signal

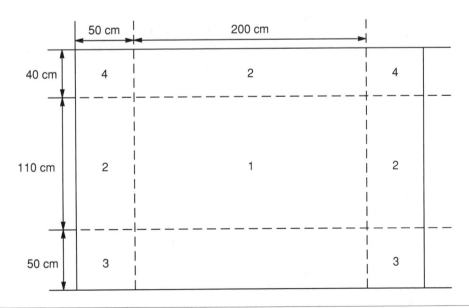

Figure 6.24 Target markings for the Zinn Team Handball 9 m Front Throw Test.

Note. From ''Construction of a battery of team handball skills test,'' by J.L. Zinn, 1981, unpublished master's thesis, University of Iowa, Iowa City, IA. Copyright 1981 by the author. Reprinted by permission of the University of Iowa.

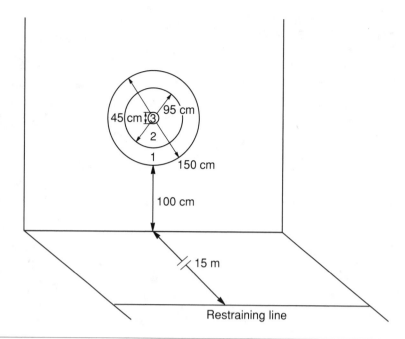

Figure 6.25 Target markings for the Zinn Team Handball Overhead Pass Test.
Note. From ''Construction of a battery of team handball skills test,'' by J.L. Zinn, 1981, unpublished master's thesis, University of Iowa, Iowa City, IA. Copyright 1981 by the author. Reprinted by permission of the University of Iowa.

''begin,'' the student uses the dominant hand to bounce a ball against the wall as rapidly as possible, catches the return bounce, and repeats until 10 bounces have hit the wall. All bounces must come from behind the restraining line, and the student must catch all passes with both hands. A stop watch is started as soon as the ball first contacts the wall and is stopped when the ball hits the wall on the 10th bounce. Two trials are given.

Overhead Pass: Subjects are positioned behind the restraining line. Using a one-armed throw, they throw a ball at the target. Ten passes are made and all must be executed from behind the restraining line. Points are awarded as shown. Passes hitting a line are awarded the higher score.

Scoring.

Nine-Meter Front Throw: The score for 10 trials is the sum of points awarded on each attempt. A maximum of 40 points is possible.

Dominant-Hand Speed Pass: Time for the better of two timed trials is the final score. Time is recorded to the nearest 1/10 of a second.

Overhead Pass: The score is the total for 10 throws. A maximum of 30 points is possible.

Norms. Not available.

Volleyball

Volleyball, invented in 1895 as an indoor winter game, is like basketball, truly an American sport. It is popular because it requires inexpensive equipment and few people to play. Volleyball is played on beaches, in backyards, and in gymnasiums nationwide. After volleyball became an Olympic sport in 1964, the game has evolved from one of recreation to one of power.

Skills included in physical education volleyball classes are passing, setting, serving, spiking, and blocking.

AAHPER Volleyball Skills Test (AAHPER, 1969)

Purpose. To evaluate fundamental volleyball ability.

Validity and Reliability. Face and content validity are claimed. The test manual does not provide a reliability estimate, but states that no test item has a reliability of less than .70.

Age Level and Sex. Appropriate for junior high school and senior high school students.

Personnel. The tests require scorers at each station, timers for the volley test, tossers for passing and setting, and student assistants to retrieve and set balls.

Equipment. Volleyballs, a measuring tape, marking tape, rope, nets, standards, a stop watch, score cards or recording sheets, and pencils.

Space. Regulation-sized volleyball courts.

Test Items. Passing, service, setting, and volleying.

Preparation. Testing stations for the passing test are prepared as shown in Figure 6.26. A rope 8 feet above the floor should extend across the testing area 10 feet from the volleyball net. A 10 foot by 6 foot passing zone is located near midcourt. A 4 foot by 4 foot tossing zone is located near the extended rope. Two scoring zones, 6 feet by 4 feet, are marked on the right and left sides of the court. Scoring zones are located 3 feet from the net and 3 feet from the extended rope.

Testing stations for the service test are prepared as shown in Figure 6.27. Point values on the scoring court are shown.

Testing stations for the setting test are prepared as shown in Figure 6.28. A rope 10 feet above the floor extends across the court 4 feet from the net. A 5 foot by 5 foot tosser's zone is located

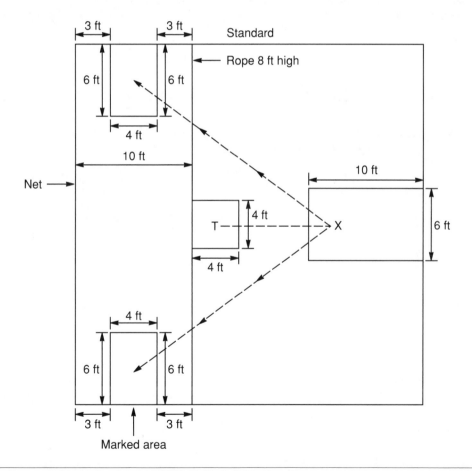

Figure 6.26 Court markings for the AAHPER Volleyball Passing Test.
Note: From ''AAHPER skills test manual—Volleyball for boys and girls,'' by AAHPER, 1969, Washington DC. Copyright 1969 by AAHPER. Reprinted by permission.

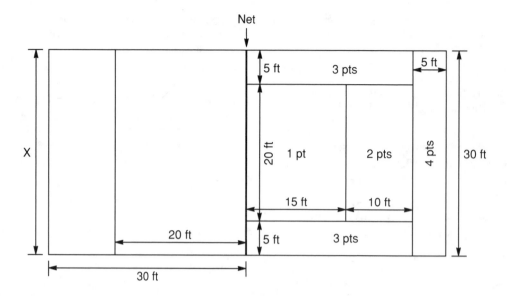

Figure 6.27 Court markings for the AAHPER Volleyball Service Test.
Note: From "AAHPER skills test manual—Volleyball for boys and girls," by AAHPER, 1969, Washington DC. Copyright 1969 by AAHPER. Reprinted by permission.

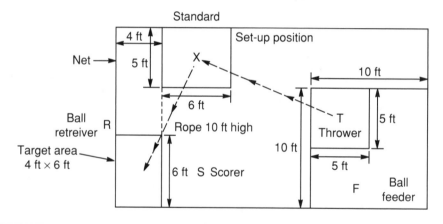

Figure 6.28 Court markings for the AAHPER Volleyball Setting Test.
Note: From "AAHPER skills test manual—Volleyball for boys and girls," by AAHPER, 1969, Washington DC. Copyright 1969 by AAHPER. Reprinted by permission.

near the back corner of the court. A 5 foot by 6 foot set-up zone is located near midcourt and next to the rope. A 4 foot by 6 foot scoring zone is located across the net near the sideline. An identical testing station is located on the other half of the same half-court.

Testing stations for the volley test are prepared as shown in Figure 6.29. A 5 foot by 4 foot target is marked on a wall 11 feet above the floor.

Directions.

Passing: To begin, a tosser in a tossing area tosses balls to a passer in the passing area. The passer tries to pass the ball over the 8-foot net into a scoring zone. Ten trials are given to the right scoring zone and 10 to the left. Balls that hit the rope, the net, or fall outside scoring zones earn no points.

Service: The server stands behind the endline in the proper service court. Using any legal serve, the student serves volleyballs over the net, attempting to have them land in the zones worth the most points. Ten trials are allowed. Balls that hit but do not go over the net count as a trial with no points. The service line for children under 12 is 20 feet from the net.

Setting: The thrower, located in a tossing zone, tosses high passes to a student in the set-up

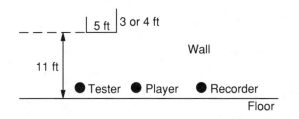

Figure 6.29 Court markings for the AAHPER Volleyball Volley Test.
Note: From "AAHPER skills test manual—Volleyball for boys and girls," by AAHPER, 1969, Washington DC. Copyright 1969 by AAHPER. Reprinted by permission.

zone. The receiver sets the ball over the rope into the scoring zone. Ten trials are given to the right and 10 to the left. Balls that touch the rope, the net, or hit outside the scoring zone earn no points. The tosser's throws that land in the set-up zone may be repeated.

Volley: The student waits with volleyball in hand, facing the wall. On the "go" signal, the student tosses a ball into the target area. As the ball rebounds the student volleys it into the target area. The test continues for 1 minute. Only legal volleys are counted. If a student catches or misses a ball, it is put back into play with a toss. Tosses do not count as volleys.

Scoring.

Passing. One point is awarded for each pass that lands in the marked scoring zones. The final score is the total points for 20 trials.

Service: Points are awarded according to where serves land within the marked court. The final score is the total points for 10 trials.

Setting: One point is awarded for each set that lands in the marked scoring zones. The final score is the total points for 20 trials.

Volley: One point is awarded for each legal volley that lands in the target area within the 1-minute trial. The final score is the total number of points.

Norms. Percentile norms for passing, service, setting, and volleying are shown in Tables 6.19 through 6.22

Table 6.19 Percentile Scores for the AAHPER Volleyball Passing Test

| | Boys | | | | | | | Girls | | | | | | | |
Percentile	10-11	12	13	14	15	16	17-18	10-11	12	13	14	15	16	17-18	Percentile
100	19	19	19	20	20	20	20	19	19	20	20	20	20	20	100
95	12	14	16	17	17	17	17	10	12	12	13	13	14	15	95
90	10	13	14	16	16	16	16	8	10	10	11	11	12	13	90
85	9	12	13	15	15	15	15	7	8	9	10	10	11	12	85
80	8	11	12	14	14	14	14	6	7	8	9	9	10	11	80
75	7	10	12	13	13	13	13	5	6	7	8	8	8	9	75
70	6	9	11	12	12	12	13	4	6	6	7	7	8	9	70
65	5	8	10	12	12	12	13	3	5	5	6	6	8	8	65
60	4	8	9	11	11	12	12	3	4	4	6	6	7	8	60
55	4	7	9	10	10	12	12	2	4	4	5	5	6	7	55
50	3	6	8	10	10	11	11	2	3	4	5	5	6	6	50
45	3	5	7	9	9	10	10	1	3	3	4	4	5	6	45
40	2	4	7	8	8	9	9	1	2	3	4	4	4	5	40
35	2	4	6	8	8	9	9	0	2	2	3	3	4	4	35
30	1	3	5	7	7	8	8	0	1	2	3	3	3	4	30
25	1	2	4	6	6	7	8	0	1	1	2	2	3	3	25
20	0	2	4	5	5	6	7	0	0	1	1	2	2	3	20
15	0	1	3	4	4	5	6	0	0	0	1	1	2	2	15
10	0	0	2	3	3	4	4	0	0	0	0	1	1	1	10
5	0	0	1	2	2	2	2	0	0	0	0	0	0	0	5
0	0	0	0	0	0	0	0	0	0	0	0	0	0	0	0

Note. From "AAHPER skills test manual—volleyball for boys and girls," by AAHPER, 1969, Reston, VA. Copyright 1969 by AAHPER. Reprinted by permission.

Table 6.20 Percentile Scores for the AAHPER Volleyball Serving Test

	Boys							Girls							
Percentile	10-11	12	13	14	15	16	17-18	10-11	12	13	14	15	16	17-18	Percentile
100	39	40	40	40	40	40	40	36	38	40	40	40	40	40	100
95	29	31	32	34	36	37	37	24	26	26	28	30	31	32	95
90	27	28	29	31	33	33	33	20	22	23	26	26	26	26	90
85	25	26	27	29	32	32	32	18	20	20	23	23	24	24	85
80	23	24	26	27	30	30	31	16	18	18	21	21	22	23	80
75	22	23	24	25	28	29	30	15	16	17	20	20	21	21	75
70	21	21	23	24	28	29	30	14	15	15	18	19	20	20	70
65	20	20	22	23	27	28	29	13	14	14	17	17	19	19	65
60	18	19	21	22	25	27	27	12	13	13	15	16	18	18	60
55	17	18	20	21	24	25	26	11	12	12	14	15	17	17	55
50	16	16	19	20	22	23	24	10	11	11	13	14	16	16	50
45	15	15	18	19	21	22	22	9	10	10	11	13	15	15	45
40	14	14	17	18	20	21	21	8	9	9	10	12	14	14	40
35	13	13	16	17	19	19	20	7	8	8	9	11	13	14	35
30	12	12	15	16	18	19	19	6	6	7	8	10	13	13	30
25	11	11	13	15	16	17	17	5	5	5	7	9	11	11	25
20	9	10	12	14	15	15	16	4	4	4	6	8	10	10	20
15	8	9	10	12	12	13	14	2	3	3	5	6	8	9	15
10	7	8	8	10	11	12	12	1	1	1	3	4	7	7	10
5	4	5	5	8	9	10	11	0	0	0	1	2	4	4	5
0	0	3	3	5	6	6	7	0	0	0	0	0	0	0	0

Note: From "AAHPER skills test manual—Volleyball for boys and girls," by AAHPER, 1969, Washington DC. Copyright 1969 by AAHPER. Reprinted by permission.

Table 6.21 Percentile Scores for the AAHPER Volleyball Setting Test

	Boys							Girls							
Percentile	10-11	12	13	14	15	16	17-18	10-11	12	13	14	15	16	17-18	Percentile
100	16	18	20	20	20	20	20	19	20	20	20	20	20	20	100
95	10	14	16	16	16	17	17	11	13	14	14	14	15	15	95
90	9	12	14	15	15	15	15	9	11	11	12	12	12	14	90
85	8	11	13	13	13	14	15	7	9	10	10	11	11	12	85
80	7	10	12	12	12	13	14	6	8	9	10	10	10	11	80
75	6	9	11	11	11	12	13	5	7	8	9	9	9	10	75
70	6	8	10	10	10	10	11	5	6	7	8	8	8	8	70
65	5	8	9	9	9	9	11	4	6	7	7	7	7	7	65
60	5	7	8	8	8	9	10	4	5	6	6	6	7	7	60
55	4	7	7	8	8	8	10	3	5	5	6	6	6	6	55
50	4	6	7	7	7	7	9	3	4	5	5	5	6	6	50
45	3	6	6	6	6	6	9	2	4	4	4	4	5	5	45
40	3	5	6	6	6	6	8	2	3	4	4	4	5	5	40
35	3	5	5	5	5	5	7	2	3	3	3	3	4	4	35
30	2	4	4	5	5	5	7	1	2	3	3	3	3	4	30
25	2	4	4	4	4	4	6	1	2	2	2	2	3	3	25
20	2	3	3	4	4	4	6	1	2	2	2	2	2	3	20

Percentile	Boys							Girls							Percentile
	10-11	12	13	14	15	16	17-18	10-11	12	13	14	15	16	17-18	
15	1	3	3	3	3	3	5	0	1	1	1	1	2	2	15
10	0	1	1	2	2	2	2	0	0	1	1	1	1	1	10
5	0	1	1	1	1	1	2	0	0	0	0	0	1	1	5
0	0	0	0	0	0	0	1	0	0	0	0	0	0	0	0

Note: From "AAHPER skills test manual—Volleyball for boys and girls," by AAHPER, 1969, Washington DC. Copyright 1969 by AAHPER. Reprinted by permission.

Table 6.22 Percentile Scores for the AAHPER Volleyball Volley Test

Percentile	Boys							Girls							Percentile
	10-11	12	13	14	15	16	17-18	10-11	12	13	14	15	16	17-18	
100	40	42	44	50	50	50	50	47	49	49	50	50	50	50	100
95	24	31	35	39	42	44	45	21	29	31	32	37	40	40	95
90	19	28	30	36	40	41	42	13	24	25	26	31	36	38	90
85	17	24	28	33	36	38	42	10	19	20	21	24	28	31	85
80	15	22	26	31	34	36	41	8	16	17	19	21	25	27	80
75	13	19	24	29	32	34	40	6	13	15	17	18	22	23	75
70	12	18	22	27	30	33	39	5	11	13	14	16	20	20	70
65	11	17	21	26	29	32	37	4	10	11	13	15	18	18	65
60	9	16	19	24	28	30	36	3	8	10	12	13	16	16	60
55	8	15	18	23	27	28	34	3	7	9	11	12	14	14	55
50	7	13	17	21	25	26	32	2	6	8	10	11	12	12	50
45	6	12	15	19	24	25	29	2	5	7	9	10	11	11	45
40	5	11	14	18	22	23	27	1	4	6	8	9	9	9	40
35	4	9	12	17	20	21	24	1	3	5	7	8	8	8	35
30	3	8	11	15	18	19	23	1	2	4	6	7	7	7	30
25	3	7	9	13	17	18	20	0	2	3	5	6	6	6	25
20	2	6	8	11	15	16	19	0	1	1	4	5	5	5	20
15	1	4	7	9	13	15	17	0	1	1	3	4	4	4	15
10	0	3	5	7	10	12	14	0	0	0	1	2	3	3	10
5	0	2	3	5	6	11	11	0	0	0	0	1	2	2	5
0	0	0	0	0	0	0	0	0	0	0	0	0	0	0	0

Note: From "AAHPER skills test manual—Volleyball for boys and girls," by AAHPER, 1969, Washington DC. Copyright 1969 by AAHPER. Reprinted by permission.

Kautz Volleyball Passing Test (Kautz, 1976)

Purpose. To evaluate passing ability in volleyball.

Validity and Reliability. A validity coefficient of .82 was computed by using the criterion measure of judges' ratings. The odd-even approach followed by the Spearman-Brown Prophecy Formula resulted in a reliability coefficient of .90.

Age Level and Sex. Originally conducted with high school girls. Appropriate for junior high school and senior high school students.

Personnel. One timer, one scorer, and one ball retriever at each testing station.

Equipment. Volleyballs, a measuring tape, marking tape, stop watches, score cards or recording sheets, and pencils.

Space. An unobstructed wall space at least 15 feet high and 10 feet wide.

Test Item. A repeated passing test.

Preparation. Testing stations for the passing test are prepared as shown in Figure 6.30. A restraining line is marked on the floor 10 feet from and parallel to the wall, and a scoring target with its base 10 feet above and parallel to the floor is marked on the wall. Lines 5 feet long are extended above and perpendicular to the 10-foot horizontal wall line. The target area is composed of circumscribed rectangles of 5 feet by 10 feet, 5 feet by 8 feet, and 5 feet by 6 feet with point values for the rectangles of 1, 2, and 3, respectively.

Directions. The student waits behind the 10-foot restraining line. On the "ready, go" signal, the student tosses a volleyball to himself or herself to initiate the wall volley. As the ball returns, the student repeatedly volleys it against the wall using only the forearm pass. If ball control is lost,

a test assistant gives the student another ball and the volley continues. If the series of passes is interrupted, the student starts a new series of volleys by tossing the ball to himself or herself and hitting it back to the wall. A toss-bump, toss-bump sequence is not allowed. Balls must be clearly and consecutively passed to the target area, and balls must be received and passed from behind the 10-foot restraining line. Only balls hitting in the target area count. Balls that touch the wall outside of the target area, illegal hits, hits that are not forearm passes, and hits that are executed on or over the restraining line are not counted. The timer calls out point values for the scorer. Four 30-second timed trials are allowed with a 1-minute rest period between trials.

Scoring. The score for each individual trial is the total point value of legal passes hit from behind the restraining line and landing in the marked target on the wall. Balls landing on a target line are awarded the higher point value. The final score is the average for four timed trials.

Norms. Not available.

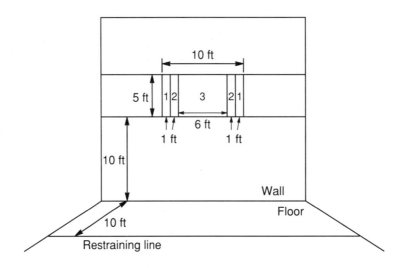

Figure 6.30 Wall markings for the Kautz Volleyball Passing Test.
Note: From "The construction of a volleyball skill test for the forearm pass," by E.M. Kautz, 1976, unpublished master's thesis, University of North Carolina, Greensboro, NC. Copyright 1976 by the author. Reprinted by permission.

NCSU Volleyball Skills Test Battery (Bartlett, Smith, Davis, & Peel, 1991)

Purpose. To evaluate serving, passing, and setting ability in volleyball.

Validity and Reliability. Content validity was claimed because all three tests are basic volleyball skills. Through intraclass correlation, reliability coefficients of .65, .73, and .88 were reported for the serve, forearm pass, and set, respectively.

Age Level and Sex. Originally conducted with college students. Appropriate for junior high school and senior high school students.

Personnel. Each station requires a recorder/scorer. The forearm pass and set tests also require set-up tossers. Students can retrieve balls.

Equipment. Volleyballs, a measuring tape, marking tape, rope, 10-foot poles, score cards or recording sheets, and pencils.

Space. Regulation-sized volleyball courts.

Test Items. Serve, forearm pass, and set.

Preparation. Testing stations for the serve test are prepared as shown in Figure 6.31. Point values are marked on the floor.

Testing stations for the forearm pass test are prepared as shown in Figure 6.32. A rope is placed 8 feet above the attack line. Marks are placed on the floor to indicate point values and where tosses and passes should be made from.

Testing stations for the set test are prepared as shown in Figure 6.33. A rope 10 feet above the floor is placed parallel to and 11 feet from the sideline. Marks are placed on the floor to indicate point values and where tosses and sets should be made from.

Directions.

Serve Test: The student stands in the serving area and serves 10 times either underhand or overhand. Balls that contact the net, antennae, or land out of bounds are scored zero. Balls landing on a line score the higher point value.

Forearm Pass Test: The student stands in one of two passing positions, 10 feet from the sidelines and 5 feet from the baseline. A tosser across the net makes two-handed tosses to the test subject. The student being tested passes the ball back over the 8-foot rope and into the target area.

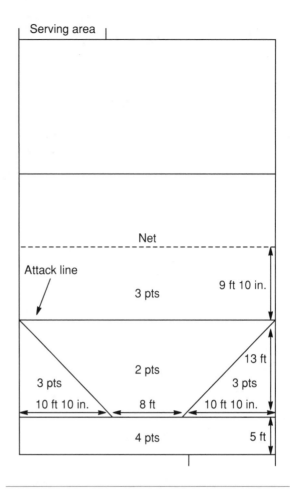

Figure 6.31 Floor plan for NCSU Volleyball Serve Test. *Note.* This figure is reprinted with permission from the *Journal of Physical Education, Recreation & Dance*, February, 1991, p. 19-21. The *Journal* is a publication of the American Alliance for Health, Physical Education, Recreation, and Dance, 1900 Association Drive, Reston, VA 22091.

Poor tosses may be repeated. No points are awarded for illegal contacts and balls that go under the rope, contact the rope, contact or go over the net, or that cross the rope but land beyond the centerline. Balls landing on the line between point values earn the higher value. Ten trials are allowed, five from the right back position and five from the left back position.

Set Test: The student waits on a starting mark 6 feet from the sideline and 5 feet from the net for a tosser to perform 10 underhand tosses. The student being tested sets the tossed balls over the 10-foot rope and into the target area. Poor tosses may be repeated. No points are awarded for illegal contact, double contacts, and balls that go under the rope, contact the rope, contact or go over the net, or balls that cross the rope but

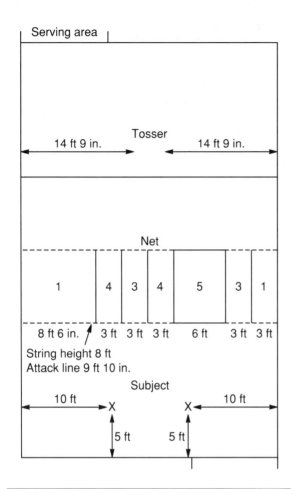

Figure 6.32 Floor plan for NCSU Volleyball Forearm Pass Test.
Note. This figure is reprinted with permission from the *Journal of Physical Education, Recreation & Dance*, February, 1991, p. 19-21. The *Journal* is a publication of the American Alliance for Health, Physical Education, Recreation, and Dance, 1900 Association Drive, Reston, VA 22091.

land beyond the centerline. Ten trials are allowed.

Scoring.

Serve Test: The score is the total points earned from 10 serves. A perfect score is 40 points.

Forearm Pass Test: The score is the total points from 10 passes. A perfect score is 50 points.

Set Test: The score is the total points from 10 sets. A perfect score is 50 points.

Norms. Not available.

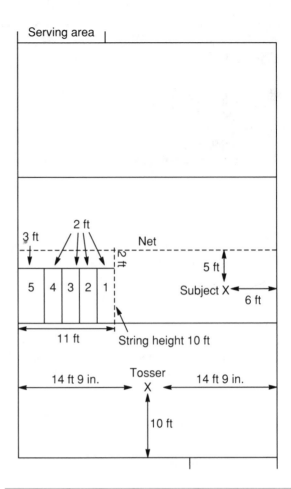

Figure 6.33 Floor plan for NCSU Volleyball Set Test.
Note. This figure is reprinted with permission from the *Journal of Physical Education, Recreation & Dance*, February, 1991, p. 19-21. The *Journal* is a publication of the American Alliance for Health, Physical Education, Recreation, and Dance, 1900 Association Drive, Reston, VA 22091.

Chamberlain Forehand Bounce Pass (Chamberlain, 1969)

Purpose. To evaluate passing ability in volleyball.

Validity and Reliability. Using Fisher's test of significance, a validity rating of 12.4 was reported. The reliability coefficient was .78 with the use of the odd-even method.

Age Level and Sex. Originally conducted with college females. Appropriate for junior high school and senior high school students.

Personnel. Each testing station requires one scorer/recorder and one tosser.

Equipment. Volleyballs, three ropes the length of a volleyball court, standards, a measuring tape, marking tape, score cards or recording sheets, and pencils.

Space. Regulation-sized volleyball court.

Test Item. The forearm bounce pass.

Preparation. Testing stations are prepared as shown in Figures 6.34 and 6.35.

Directions. The set-up person is on the same side of the court as the scoring target while the test performer is on the opposite side of the court behind the toss line. To begin, the set-up person tosses a ball between the 5- and 7-foot-high ropes and the test performer returns the ball with a forearm bounce pass that should go over the

10-foot rope and land within the scoring target. The test performer may cross the toss line to return set-up balls. Fourteen trials are allowed. If a ball hits a rope, it is replayed.

Scoring. Two points are awarded for each ball that clears the 10-foot rope. Balls landing in the concentric scoring target yield 4, 3, or 2 points depending on where they land. Balls landing on lines are awarded the higher point value. Balls that fail to go over the 10-foot rope earn no points. Six points can be earned for each bounce pass trial.

Norms. Not available.

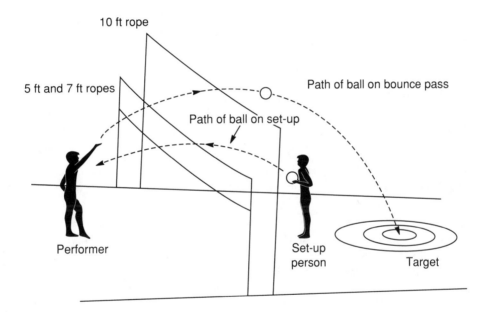

Figure 6.34 Floor plan for the Chamberlain Volleyball Test (side view).
Note. From ''Determination of validity and reliability of a skill test for the bounce pass in volleyball,'' by Diane Chamberlain, 1969, unpublished master's thesis, Brigham Young University, Provo, UT. Copyright 1969 by the author. Reprinted by permission.

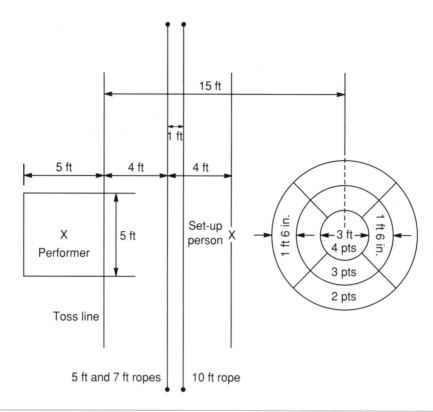

Figure 6.35 Floor plan for the Chamberlain Volleyball Test (overhead view).
Note. From ''Determination of validity and reliability of a skill test for the bounce pass in volleyball,'' by Diane Chamberlain, 1969, unpublished master's thesis, Brigham Young University, Provo, UT. Copyright 1969 by the author. Reprinted by permission.

Other Volleyball Tests

Barker, J.F. (1985). A simplified volleyball skills test for beginning level instruction. *Journal of Physical Education, Recreation and Dance,* **56**, 20-21.

Bassett, G., Glasrow, R.B., & Locke, M. (1937). Studies in testing volleyball skills. *Research Quarterly,* **8**, 60-72.

Blackman, C.J. (1968). *The development of a volleyball test for the spike.* Unpublished master's thesis, Southern Illinois University, Carbondale.

Bosben, P.A. (1971). *The development of a skill test for the volleyball bounce pass for college women beginning volleyball players.* Unpublished master's thesis, Western Illinois University, Macomb.

Brady, G.F. (1945). Preliminary investigation of volleyball playing ability. *Research Quarterly,* **16**, 14-17.

Broer, M.A. (1958). Reliability of certain skill tests for junior high school girls. *Research Quarterly,* **29**, 139-145.

Camp, B.A. (1963). *The reliability and validity of a single-hit repeated volleys test in volleyball and the relationship of height to performance on the test.* Unpublished master's thesis, University of Colorado, Boulder.

Chaney, D.S. (1966). *The development of a test of volleyball ability for college women.* Unpublished master's thesis, Texas Woman's University, Denton.

Chun, D.M. (1969). *Construction of an overhead volley-pass test for college women.* Unpublished master's thesis, Washington State University, Pullman.

Clifton, M. (1962). Single hit volley test for women volleyball players. *Research Quarterly,* **33**, 208-211.

Comeaux, B.A. (1974). *Development of a volleyball selection test battery for girls.* Unpublished master's thesis, Lamar University, Beaumont, TX.

Crogan, C. (1943). A simple volleyball classification test for high school girls. *The Physical Educator, 4,* 34-37.

Cunningham, P., & Garrison, J. (1968). High wall volley test for women's volleyball. *Research Quarterly, 39,* 486-490.

Farrow, B.E. (1970). *The development of a volleyball selection test battery for girls.* Unpublished master's thesis, Lamar University, Beaumont, TX.

French, E., & Cooper, B.I. (1937). Achievement tests in volleyball for high school girls. *Research Quarterly, 8,* 150-157.

Gorton, B. (1970). *Evaluation of the serve and pass in women's volleyball competition.* Unpublished master's thesis, George Williams College, Downers Grove, IL.

Helmen, R.M. (1971). *Development of power volleyball skill test for college women.* Paper presented at National American Alliance for Health, Physical Education and Recreation convention in Detroit.

Jackson, P. (1967). *A rating scale for discriminating relative performance of skilled female volleyball players.* Master's thesis, University of Alberta, Edmonton. (Microcard PE 931, University of Oregon, Eugene.)

Johnson, J.A. (1967). *The development of a volleyball skill test for high school girls.* Unpublished master's thesis, Illinois State University, Normal.

Jones, R.N. (1968). *The development of a volleyball skill test for adult males.* Unpublished master's thesis, Springfield College, Springfield, MA.

Kessler, A.A. (1968). *The validity and reliability of the Sandefur Volleyball Spiking Test.* Unpublished master's thesis, California State College, Long Beach.

Kronqvist, R.A., & Brumback, W.B. (1968). A modification of the Brady volleyball skill test for high school boys. *Research Quarterly, 39,* 116-120.

Lamp, N.A. (1954). Volleyball skills for junior high school students as a function of physical size and maturity. *Research Quarterly, 25,* 189-197.

Liba, M.R., & Stauff, M.R. (1963). A test for the volleyball pass. *Research Quarterly, 34,* 56-63.

Locke, M. (1936). *A survey of volleyball skills tests and studies on the reliability and validity of a proposed test.* Unpublished master's thesis, University of Wisconsin, Madison.

Londeree, B.R., & Eicholtz, E.C. (1970). *Reliabilities of selected volleyball skill tests.* Paper presented at the American Association for Health, Physical Education and Recreation convention in Seattle.

Lopez, D. (1957). Serve test. In *Volleyball Guide—1957-1958,* Washington, DC: AAHPER.

Michalski, R.A. (1963). *Construction of an objective skill test for the underhand volleyball serve.* Unpublished master's thesis, University of Iowa, Iowa City.

Mohr, D.R., & Haverstick, M.J. (1955). Repeated volleys tests for women's volleyball. *Research Quarterly, 26,* 179-184.

Petry, K. (1967). *Evaluation of a volleyball serve test.* Unpublished master's thesis, Los Angeles State College, Los Angeles.

Reynolds, H.J. (1930). Volleyball tests. *Journal of Health and Physical Education, 42,* 44.

Russell, N., & Lange, E. (1940). Achievement tests in volleyball for junior high school girls. *Research Quarterly, 11,* 33-41.

Ryan, M.F. (1969). *A study of tests for the volleyball serve.* Master's thesis, University of Wisconsin, Madison. (Microcard PE 1040, University of Oregon, Eugene.)

Shaw, J.H. (1967). *A preliminary investigation of a volleyball skill test.* Unpublished master's thesis, University of Tennessee, Knoxville.

Shavely, M. (1960). Volleyball skill tests for girls. In A. Lockhart (Ed.), *Selected volleyball articles,* Washington, DC: AAHPER.

Watkins, A. (1960). Skill testing for large groups. In A. Lockhart (Ed.), *Selected volleyball articles,* Washington, DC: AAHPER.

West, C. (1957). *A comparative study between height and wall volley test scores as related to volleyball playing ability of girls and women.* Unpublished master's thesis, University of North Carolina, Greensboro.

Wallyball

Wallyball developed in the 1980s as an alternative to racquetball. It has become a rapidly growing team sport. Most fitness clubs with racquetball courts now have male, female, and coed wallyball leagues.

Wallyball skills are similar to those of volleyball: serving, setting, passing, and spiking. No objective wallyball tests are available.

Water Polo

Water polo was developed during the 1860s when athletes became bored with swimming races. Al-though popular in Europe, the sport has had difficulty gaining acceptance in the United States. However, rules changes that brought the ball to the water's surface have enabled water polo to become the third fastest growing sport in the United States.

Water polo skills typically taught in physical education classes include shooting, passing, swimming, and goaltending. No objective water polo skills tests are available.

Chapter 7

Additional Considerations

As you know, the objectives of evaluation are many and varied. But too often the results of sport skills tests are used simply for final grade assignment. This chapter discusses formative, summative, and subjective evaluation and suggests when and how each evaluation method should be used. Special testing situations involving large groups, special populations, and coed classes are also addressed, along with tests for evaluation of skill- and health-related physical fitness.

Formative and Summative Evaluation

Evaluation is important to find out what students have learned but also as a tool to enhance learning during instruction (Baumgartner & Jackson, 1982). However, the typical practice in many physical education classes is to evaluate students only at the end of an instructional or activity unit and to provide little formal evaluation during training. For students to achieve mastery levels of learning, evaluation must be ongoing. Good evaluation systems combine two types of evaluation during an activity unit—summative and formative. Summative evaluation is done at the conclusion of the unit; formative evaluation is ongoing during activity training (Safrit, 1990).

Summative evaluation, such as a unit skills or knowledge test, determines if broad objectives have been achieved and measures the degree of achievement through grading. For example, sum-

mative evaluation is used to determine final grades, to promote from one skill level to another, and to select varsity teams. Because summative evaluation is the basis for such crucial decisions, the testing instruments used must be valid and reliable (Kirkendall et al., 1987), such as the skills tests included in this text.

Formative evaluation, on the other hand, gives daily or weekly feedback to students. This type of evaluation involves dividing an instructional or activity unit into smaller units of learning and evaluating student mastery of subunits of instruction (Baumgartner & Jackson, 1982). Although few physical educators do formal formative evaluation, it can be a vital tool in analyzing skill development by pinpointing skill strengths and weaknesses and determining for both teacher and student what must still be learned. After teachers identify strengths and weaknesses, they can prescribe activities for students to practice to improve their skills. Most students appreciate feedback about their performance while there is still time to improve (Barrow et al., 1989). Because formative evaluation tends to be highly subjective, a teacher should have expert knowledge of fundamental skills to ensure content validity.

Subjective Evaluation

Whenever feasible, evaluation should be objective, but not every instructional goal can be measured objectively. For example, how does one validly measure total playing ability when any given sport has so many skill components interacting at once? Some sports, including gymnastics, diving, and figure skating, must rely on subjective evaluations to determine final scores.

Major complaints about subjective evaluation are that it lacks objectivity, reliability, and validity. Without a clearly defined scoring system, data reflect primarily a scorer's opinion about what has been observed (Darst, Zakrajsek, & Mancini, 1989). Too often a scorer's opinions are based on bias and history of experience and tend to lack specificity.

Despite these objections, subjective evaluation may, in certain instances, be more efficient than objective testing (Baumgartner & Jackson, 1982). No special test days need be set aside because subjective evaluation can be conducted while students are practicing or competing. Also, the many test trials required for objective evaluation make it difficult to conduct testing efficiently with large classes.

If you choose subjective evaluation as a means of formative evaluation, make sure the evaluation is as objective, reliable, valid, and efficient as possible. Baumgartner and Jackson (1982) have suggested four important steps in developing a tool for subjective evaluation.

1. Determine which skills are to be evaluated.
2. Determine how much each skill will affect the final grade.
3. Formulate performance standards.
4. Develop a system for recording scores immediately. With subjective evaluation, you must ensure that you observe the same skills for each student and evaluate them with identical criteria.

Subjective evaluation is commonly conducted through eyeballing and anecdotal recording, rating scales, and/or checklists. In anecdotal recording, a tester watches activities and writes down what he or she observes. Though highly subjective, the number of observations involved may produce meaningful insight. Anecdotal recording is best used to better understand students with special problems rather than an entire class.

When anecdotal recording is used, follow Hastad and Lacy's (1989) suggestions. First, record the anecdote immediately after the incident. Second, describe the incident accurately. Third, include background to give the incident meaning. Place anecdotal recordings in student files for later reference.

Checklists and rating scales, similar in function, are popular forms of evaluation. With checklists,

as shown in Figure 7.1, an observer marks (usually "yes" or "no") whether certain things were performed. With rating scales, as shown in Figure 7.2, an observer gives his or her opinion on performance, using a Likert-type scale of 1 to 5 or from poor to excellent (Darst et al., 1989). Although checklists and rating scales appear scientific, they are still subjective. Why did one rater score a performance a 3 and another rater, viewing the same performance, score it as a 4? Or what is the difference between 3 and 4 and is that difference the same as the difference between 4 and 5? Although they are not totally objective, valid, or reliable, rating scales are often used to measure skills hard to gauge with traditional methods (Safrit, 1990).

Some believe teachers can use rating scales to objectify subjective evaluations by providing a systematic procedure for reporting the expert observers' judgments (Phillips & Hornak, 1979). Rating scales generally consist of traits for an expert to observe and a scale the expert uses to judge the extent to which each trait is present. Rating scales serve two functions. First, they direct the teacher's observation toward specific and clearly defined aspects. Second, they provide a common frame of reference for comparing all pupils on the same traits.

Although rating scales need not be complex or elaborate, they are best if they follow these guidelines:

1. They determine the scale's purpose. Rating scales are effective when there are no objective means of measurement (such as in gymnastics and diving) and as formative evaluation during an instructional or activity unit.
2. They determine and select the activity's fundamental skills. Every sport or activity has many skills that could be included on a rating scale. Selecting which skills to include is based on instructional objectives and skills taught during the unit. Whichever traits are selected must be observable.
3. They identify the number of categories. In large classes it may be wise to limit categories and subcategories to a manageable number.
4. They select rating positions on the scale. Most experts agree typical classroom evaluations need no more than seven rating points. Fewer rating points may be used where differences in performance are difficult to judge.

Skill components	Yes	No
Passing		
Accurate		
Deceptive		
Fingertip control		
Proper footwork		
Proper release		
Shooting		
Proper extension		
Proper elbow location		
Fingertip control		
Full extension		
Proper follow through		

Figure 7.1 Sample basketball skill checklist.

5. They write definitions for each rating point on the scale. These definitions must contain sufficient detail so the rater can discriminate accurately between skill levels.
6. They weigh the components to be rated. All components may not be equal. A teacher may want to award more points for components a class has spent more time developing. For example, lay-ups may be weighted more heavily than the 3-point shot in a seventh-grade physical education class.
7. They develop a rating sheet in a simple-to-understand format with items logically placed and easy to locate. List definitions of the items on the rating sheet.
8. They prepare raters. A single teacher usually will assign the ratings, but even then the teacher should make sure every evaluation is done similarly by practicing a couple of times before doing an actual evaluation. Using two trained raters increases the rating scale's reliability.

Skill components	1	2	3	4	5
Forehand stroke					
Proper ready position					
Proper grip					
Pivot and step to ball					
Proper contact point					
Bent knees during stroke					
Proper wrist action					
Proper follow-through					
Fluid stroking motion					
Serve					
Proper stance					
Effective toss					
Proper weight transfer					
Fluid stroke					
Full extension					
Proper follow-through					
Foot movement					

Scoring: 5 = exceptional; 4 = above average; 3 = average; 2 = below average; 1 = poor

Figure 7.2 Sample badminton skill rating scale.

Special Testing Situations

Testing large groups, special populations, and coed classes requires special advance consideration and additional thought.

Testing Large Groups

Many physical education teachers avoid skills testing because they have such large classes. Although large classes make testing harder, that should not be accepted as an excuse for failing to conduct skills evaluations. When testing large groups teachers must simply do a better job of test selection, site preparation, and planning. Too many teachers just won't put in the time required for proper test administration.

Assessing Sport Skills includes skills tests selected for ease of preparation and administration among other things. If teachers find these tests still too time consuming, they should shorten them. For example, a test that includes four items can be cut to two items. But cut carefully to ensure test items represent course objectives.

In large classes, teachers must use student assistants. But be sure to select students who are reliable. Select assistants who are leaders and who are respected by their peers. The teacher needs to make sure assistants understand what they are supposed to do and how. For instance, assistants can be responsible for setting up and taking down equipment, but the teacher is still responsible for bringing out the equipment, placing it in its proper testing location, and putting it away.

With large groups it also helps to have nontesting students engaged in an alternate activity during a test. For example, while two baskets are being used for a basketball skills test, nontesting students could scrimmage on other baskets. As a student finishes the test, he or she simply takes the place of a student in the scrimmage. If alternate activity is used in association with testing, give it structure so it doesn't end up in a free for all.

Testing Special Populations

Physical education plays an important role in disabled students' curriculum. Federal mandates and state and local legislation have reinforced this role. The Education for All Handicapped Children Act of 1975 focuses on the importance of evaluation in the education of disabled students. The law's major points are as follows:

I. Every state must develop a plan for identifying, locating, and evaluating all handicapped students.

II. All disabled students and their parents are guaranteed procedural safeguards.

III. Standards for evaluation must be followed. This hierarchy of physical functioning should be considered when evaluating participants (Kirkendall et al., 1987). The physical functioning areas are these:

1. Basic areas
   A. Strength
   B. Muscular and cardiovascular endurance
   C. Range of motion
   D. Balance
2. Intermediate areas
   A. Body awareness
   B. Body side awareness
   C. Space awareness
   D. Timing awareness
3. Advanced areas
   A. Coordination
   B. Agility

Perceptual-Motor Performance Tests. Perceptual-motor performance tests evaluate students' ability to integrate sensory information with past experience and movement decisions. Components of perceptual-motor efficiency include balance; postural and locomotor awareness; visual, auditory, kinesthetic and tactile perception; body awareness; directionality; and laterality.

Clifton (1970) identified five abilities perceptual-motor programs seek to provide:

1. Development and use of locomotor movement skills such as walking, running, jumping, hopping, sliding, skipping, and climbing.
2. Development and use of eye-hand and foot-hand coordination skills in throwing, catching, striking, and kicking.
3. Development of skills that are basic to movement and gross motor performance such as balance, agility, flexibility, strength, and endurance.
4. Development of a functional concept of body size and space requirements in terms of height, depth, and breadth for the body to perform in a variety of situations.
5. Opportunities for using sense modalities such as auditory, visual, tactile, and proprioceptive in gross motor activities.

It is beyond the scope of this text to discuss in depth perceptual-motor performance tests, but here are perceptual-motor tests for the reader's further consideration:

Perceptual-Motor Tests

Andover Perceptual-Motor Test—Nichols, D.B., Arsenault, D.R., & Guiffre, D.L. (1980). *Motor activities for the underachiever.* Springfield, IL: Charles C Thomas.

Ayres Southern California Perceptual-Motor Tests—Miller, A.G., & Sullivan, J.V. (1982). *Teaching physical activities to impaired youth: An approach to mainstreaming.* New York: Wiley.

Fisher Motor Performance Test—Fisher, D.H. (1970). *Effects of two different types of physical education programs upon skills development and academic readiness of kindergarten children.* Unpublished doctoral dissertation, Louisiana State University, Baton Rouge.

Perceptual-Motor Obstacle Course—Nelson, J.K. (1972). *The construction of a perceptual-motor performance course for pre-school and primary grade children.* Unpublished study, Louisiana State University, Baton Rouge.

Purdue Perceptual Motor Survey—Roach, D.B., & Kephart, N.C. (1966). *The Purdue perceptual-motor survey.* Columbus, OH: Charles E. Merrill.

Motor Performance Tests. Motor performance tests serve as screening instruments and to help identify individuals with motor deficiencies and those who need special education. Evaluation is integral to disabled students' physical education programs. As with perceptual-motor tests, a discussion of tests for assessing the motor performance of disabled students is beyond the scope of this text. These motor performance tests are available for the reader's consideration:

Motor Performance Tests

AMP Index #1—Webb, R., Schutz, R., & McMahill, J. (1977). *Manual for AMP Index #1.*

Glenwood, IA: Glenwood State Hospital School.

Basic Motor Ability Test—Arnheim, D.D., & Sinclair, W.A. (1979). *The clumsy child: A program of motor therapy.* St. Louis: Mosby.

Basic Motor Fitness Test for Emotionally Disturbed Children—Hilsendager, D.R., Jack, H., & Mann, L. (1973). *Basic motor fitness tests for emotionally disturbed children.* Report of National Institute of Mental Health, Grant 1-T1-MT1-8543-1,5, Philadelphia: Temple University.

Broadhead Dynamic Balance Test—Broadhead, G.D. (1974). Beam walking in special education. *Rehabilitation Literature, 36,* 279-283.

Bruinicks-Oseretsky Test of Motor Proficiency—Arnheim, D.D., & Sinclair, W.A. (1985). *Physical education for special populations: A developmental, adapted, and remedial approach.* Englewood Cliffs, NJ: Prentice-Hall.

Bruinicks-Oseretsky Test of Motor Proficiency for the Hearing Impaired—Brunt, D., & Dearmond, D.A. (1981). Evaluating motor profiles of the hearing impaired. *Journal of Physical Education, Recreation and Dance, 52,* 50-52.

Buell AAHPERD Youth Fitness Test Adaptation for the Blind—Buell, C.E. (1982). *Physical education and recreation for the visually handicapped.* Reston, VA: AAHPERD.

I CAN—Wessell, J.A. (1976). *I CAN.* Northbrook, IL: Hubbard Scientific.

Motor Fitness Test for the Moderately Mentally Retarded—Johnson, L., & Londeree, B. (1976). *Motor fitness testing manual for the moderately mentally retarded.* Reston, VA: AAHPER.

Testing Coed Classes

Title IX of the Educational Amendments Act of 1972—which states that programs and activities must be of equal value to both sexes—has had a significant impact on most physical education programs. One Title IX requirement is that grading procedures and standards not adversely affect either sex. Standards and skills testing situations should be fair so you can answer "yes" to the following questions:

1. Are the skills tests fair and equal for both sexes?

2. Are the standards for the skills tests fair and equal for both sexes?
3. Is the physical environment for the skills tests fair and equal for both sexes?
4. Does one sex have a physical advantage?
5. Does the testing atmosphere encourage both sexes to succeed?

Other Types of Skill Evaluation

Most physical education teachers and athletic coaches know that performing effectively in sport means more than having specific sport skills such as shooting, passing, or kicking accuracy. The importance of agility, endurance, strength, speed, flexibility, balance, reaction time, and coordination can not be ignored if one wishes to become a top-notch performer. It is hard to say which of those traits are most important for specific activities, but experts have classified one group of components as skill related and a second as health related (AAHPERD, 1980). Complete physical education programs train and test for both skill- and health-related components in addition to specific sport skills.

Skill-Related Physical Fitness

Skill-related physical fitness components include agility, balance, coordination, power, speed, and reaction time. Most motor tasks combine these components, and some tasks involve them all. For example, hitting a baseball requires balance, coordination, power, and reaction time. Running to first base requires balance and speed. Although genetic factors limit development in skill-related components, improvement occurs through training and testing. Definitions and examples of skill-related fitness components and test batteries for assessing skill-related fitness follow.

Agility is the ability to rapidly and accurately change the position of the entire body in space. Examples: skiing and wrestling.

Balance is the maintenance of equilibrium while stationary or moving. Examples: water skiing and swinging a golf club.

Coordination is the ability to use the senses with the body parts to simultaneously perform multiple motor tasks smoothly and accurately. Examples: kicking a football and hitting a baseball.

Power is the ability to transfer energy into maximum force in the fastest possible time. Examples: the long jump and the shot put.

Reaction time is the time elapsed between stimulation and the beginning of response to that stimulation. Examples: responding to a starter's pistol and reacting to a tennis serve.

Speed is the ability to perform a movement quickly. Examples: sprinting in track and chasing a fly ball in baseball.

Test Batteries for Assessing Skill-Related Physical Fitness

Barrow Motor Ability Test—Barrow, H.M. (1954). Test of motor ability for college men. *Research Quarterly,* **25**, 253-260.

North Carolina Fitness Battery—State of North Carolina. (1977). *North Carolina motor fitness battery.* Raleigh: Department of Public Instruction.

Scott Motor Ability Test—Scott, M.G. (1939). The assessment of motor abilities of college women through objective tests. *Research Quarterly,* **10**, 63-83.

Texas Physical Motor Fitness Developmental Tests—American Heart Association in Texas and Governor's Commission on Physical Fitness. (1986). *Texas physical and motor fitness development program.* Austin, TX: American Heart Association.

The Presidential Physical Fitness Award Program—President's Council on Physical Fitness and Sports. (1987). *The Presidential Physical Fitness Award Program.* Washington, DC: The President's Council on Physical Fitness and Sports.

Health-Related Physical Fitness

Health-related physical fitness components include flexibility, body composition, muscular strength and endurance, and cardiovascular endurance. In terms of lifetime health, many believe it is more important to develop these components than either skill-related components or specific sport skills (Corbin & Lindsay, 1991). Others believe the three areas are so closely related that it is difficult to have competence in one without competence in the others. To ensure overall development, a physical education program must test and train in various forms of psychomotor and fitness development. Definitions and examples of health-related fitness components and test batteries for assessing health-related fitness follow:

Flexibility refers to the range of motion available in a given joint. Examples: swimming and punting a football.

Body composition refers to the percentage of muscle, fat, bone, and other body tissues.

Muscular strength is the ability of muscles to exert force or to lift a heavy weight.

Muscular endurance is the ability of muscles to exert force over an extended period of time without undue fatigue. Examples: tackling in football and rock climbing.

Cardiovascular endurance is the ability to exercise the entire body for extended periods of time without undue fatigue. Examples: long-distance running and playing soccer.

Test Batteries for Assessing Health-Related Physical Fitness

AAHPERD Physical Best—American Alliance for Health, Physical Education, Recreation and Dance. (1988). *Physical best: the American Alliance physical fitness education and assessment program.* Reston, VA: AAHPERD.

AAU Physical Fitness Test—American Athletic Union. (1986). *AAU physical fitness program.* Bloomington, IN: Author.

Fit Youth Today—American Health and Fitness Foundation Inc. (1986). *FYT-FIT youth today.* Austin, TX: Author.

Fitnessgram—Institute for Aerobics Research

and Campbell's Soup. (1986). *FITNESS-GRAM.* Dallas: Institute for Aerobics Research.

Manitoba Physical Fitness Performance Test—Manitoba Department of Education. (1977). *Manitoba physical fitness performance test manual and fitness objectives.* Manitoba, Canada: Author.

South Carolina Test—Pate, R.R. (1978). *South Carolina physical fitness test manual.* Columbia: Governor's Council on Physical Fitness.

YMCA Test—Golding, L.A., Meyers, C.R., & Sining, W.E. (1982). *The Y's way to physical fitness.* Chicago: National Board of YMCA.

Summary

Evaluating student progress, improvement, and achievement is an ongoing process that best benefits the student when it involves both formative and summative evaluation.

Student evaluations based on objective measures make grade determination less open to question, but at times subjective evaluation helps. For some sport skills, the only measures available are subjective rating scales and/or checklists.

The last third of this chapter presents skill- and health-related fitness testing. To be well-rounded athletes, students need health-related attributes such as cardiovascular fitness and strength and skill-related attributes such as coordination and agility in addition to specific sport skills such as throwing accurately and hitting properly.

References

American Alliance for Health, Physical Education, Recreation and Dance. (1980). *Health related physical fitness test manual.* Reston, VA: AAHPERD.

American Alliance for Health, Physical Education, Recreation and Dance. (1984). *AAHPERD skills test manual: basketball for boys and girls.* Reston, VA: AAHPERD.

American Association for Health, Physical Education and Recreation. (1966). *AAHPER skills test manual for football.* Washington, DC: AAHPER.

American Association for Health, Physical Education and Recreation. (1967). *AAHPER skills test manual for archery.* Washington, DC: AAHPER.

American Association for Health, Physical Education and Recreation. (1969). *AAHPER skills test manual—volleyball for boys and girls.* Washington, DC: AAHPER.

Annarino, A.A., Cowell, C.C., & Hazelton, H.W. (1980). *Curriculum theory and design in physical education.* St. Louis: Mosby.

Barrow, H.M., & McGee, R. (1979). *A practical approach to measurement in physical education.* (3rd ed.). Philadelphia: Lea and Febiger.

Barrow, H.M., McGee, R., & Tritschler, K.A. (1989). *Practical measurement in physical education and sport.* Philadelphia: Lea and Febiger.

Bartlett, J., Smith, L., Davis, K., & Peel, J. (1991). Development of a valid volleyball skills test battery. *Journal of Physical Education, Recreation and Dance,* **62**, 19-21.

Baumgartner, T.A., & Jackson, A.S. (1982). *Measurement for evaluation in physical education.* Dubuque, IA: Brown.

Bennett, L.M. (1942). A test of diving for use in beginning classes. *Research Quarterly,* **13**, 109-115.

Benson, D.W. (1963). *Measuring golf ability through use of a number five iron test.* Paper presented to the California Association of Health, Physical Education and Recreation, Long Beach.

Bosco, J.S., & Gustafson, W.F. (1983). *Measurement and evaluation in physical education, fitness and sports.* Englewood Cliffs, NJ: Prentice Hall.

Bower, M.G. (1961). *A test of general fencing ability.* Unpublished master's thesis, University of Southern California, Los Angeles.

Bowers, C.O. (1965). *Gymnastics skill test for beginning to low intermediate girls and women.* Unpublished master's thesis, Ohio State University, Columbus.

Buchanan, R.E. (1942). *A study of achievement tests in speedball for high school girls.* Unpublished master's thesis, University of Iowa, Iowa City.

Bucher, C.A., & Wuest, D.A. (1987). *Foundations of physical education and sport.* St. Louis: Times Mirror/Mosby.

Cahill, P.J. (1977). *The construction of a skills test for squash racquets.* Unpublished doctoral dissertation, Springfield College, Springfield, MA.

Carriere, D.L. (1969). *An objective figure skating test for use in beginning classes.* Unpublished master's thesis, University of Illinois at Urbana-Champaign.

Chamberlain, D. (1969). *Determination of validity and reliability of a skill test for the bounce pass in volleyball.* Unpublished master's thesis, Brigham Young University, Provo, UT.

Chapman, N.L. (1982). Chapman ball control test—field hockey. *Research Quarterly for Exercise and Sport,* **53**, 239-242.

Clarke, H.H., & Clarke, D. (1987). *Application of measurement to physical education.* Englewood Cliffs, NJ: Prentice Hall.

Clifton, M. (1970). A developmental approach to perceptual motor experiences. *Journal of Health, Physical Education, and Recreation,* **41**, 34-37.

Collins, D.R., & Hodges, P.B. (1978). *A comprehensive guide to sport skill tests and measurement.* Springfield, IL: Charles C Thomas.

Corbin, C.B. (1987). Physical fitness in the K-12 curriculum—some defensible solutions to perennial problems. *Journal of Physical Education, Recreation and Dance,* **58**, 49-54.

Corbin, C.B., & Lindsey, R. (1991). *Concepts of physical education with laboratories.* Dubuque, IA: Brown.

Curtis, J.M. (1989). *Pickle-ball for player and teacher.* Englewood, CO: Morton.

Darst, P.W., Zakrajsek, D.B., & Mancini, V.H. (1989). *Analyzing physical education and sport instruction.* Champaign, IL: Human Kinetics.

DeGroot, W.L. (1980a). *Individual and dual sports.* Winston-Salem, NC: Hunter Textbooks.

DeGroot, W.L. (1980b). *Team sports.* Winston-Salem, NC: Hunter Textbooks.

Edgley, B.M., & Oberle, G.H. (1986). *Physical education activities handbook.* Winston-Salem, NC: Hunter Textbooks.

Ellenbrand, D.A. (1973). *Gymnastics skills test for college women.* Unpublished master's thesis, Indiana University, Bloomington.

Ennis, C.D. (1977). *The development of a multi-skill test in lacrosse for college women.* Unpublished master's thesis, University of North Carolina, Greensboro.

Farrow, A.C. (1970). *Skill and knowledge proficiencies for selected activities in the required program at Memphis State University.* Unpublished doctoral dissertation, University of North Carolina, Greensboro.

Fronske, H. (1988). *Relationships among various objective swimming tests and expert evaluations of skill in swimming.* Unpublished doctoral dissertation, Brigham Young University, Provo, UT.

Graham, G. (1987). Motor skill acquisition—an essential goal of physical education programs. *Journal of Physical Education, Recreation and Dance,* **58**, 44-48.

Harrison, E.R. (1969). *A test to measure basketball ability for boys.* Unpublished master's thesis, University of Florida, Gainesville.

Hastad, D.H., & Lacy, A.C. (1989). *Measurement and evaluation in contemporary physical education.* Scottsdale, AZ: Gorsuch Scarisbrick.

Henry, M.E. (1970). *The validation of a test of field hockey skills.* Unpublished master's thesis, Temple University, Philadelphia.

Hensley, J.E., East, W.B., & Stillwell, J.L. (1979). A racquetball skills test. *Research Quarterly,* **50**, 114-118.

Hewitt, J.E. (1966). Hewitt's tennis achievement test. *Research Quarterly,* **37**, 231-240.

Hooks, G.E. (1959). Prediction of baseball ability through an analysis of measures of strength and structure. *Research Quarterly,* **30**, 38-43.

Jackson, A., Jackson, A.S., & Frankiewicz, R.G. (1979). The construct and concurrent validity of a 12 minute crawl stroke as a field test of swimming endurance. *Research Quarterly for Exercise and Sport,* **50**, 641-648.

Jacobson, T.V. (1960). *An evaluation of performance in certain physical ability tests administered to selected secondary school boys.* Unpublished master's thesis, University of Washington, Seattle.

Jeffreys, A. (1987). *A rating scale for rhythmic aerobics.* Unpublished paper, University of North Carolina, Greensboro.

Jenson, C.R., & Hirst, C.C. (1980). *Measurement in physical education and athletics.* New York: Mayfield.

Johnson, B.L., & Nelson, J.K. (1986). *Practical measurement for evaluation in physical education* (4th ed.). Edina, MN: Burgess International.

Johnson, J.R. (1963). *The development of a single-item test as a measure of soccer skill.* Microcarded master's thesis, University of British Columbia, Vancouver.

Jones, S.K. (1967). *A measure of tennis serving ability.* Unpublished master's thesis, University of California, Los Angeles.

Kautz, E.M. (1976). *The construction of a volleyball skill test for the forearm pass.* Unpublished master's thesis, University of North Carolina, Greensboro.

Kehtel, E.H. (1958). *The development of a test to measure the ability of a softball player to field a ground ball and successfully throw it at a target.* Unpublished master's thesis, University of Colorado, Boulder.

Kemp, J., & Vincent, M.F. (1968). Kemp-Vincent rally test of tennis skill. *Research Quarterly,* **39**, 1000-1004.

Kirkendall, E., Gruber, J., & Johnson, R. (1987). *Measurement and evaluation for physical education.* Champaign, IL: Human Kinetics.

Koski, W.A. (1950). *A basketball classification test.* Unpublished master's thesis, University of Michigan, Ann Arbor.

LaVay, B., & DePaepe, J. (1987). The harbinger helper: Why mainstreaming in physical education doesn't always work. *Journal of Physical Education, Recreation and Dance, **58**, 98-103.*

Lockhart, A., & McPherson, F.A. (1949). The development of a test of badminton playing ability. *Research Quarterly, **20**,* 402-405.

Martin, J.L. (1960). Bowling norms for college men and women. *Research Quarterly, **31**,* 113-116.

Matthews, D.K. (1968). *Measurement in physical education.* Philadelphia: W.B. Saunders.

Merrifield, H.H., & Walford, G.A. (1969). Battery of ice hockey skill tests. *Research Quarterly, **40**,* 146-152.

Miller, D.A. (1988). *Measurement by the physical educator.* Indianapolis: Benchmark Press.

Mood, D., Musker, F.F., & Rink, J.E. (1987). *Sports and recreational activities for men and women.* St. Louis: Times Mirror/Mosby.

Mor, D., & Christian, V. (1979). The development of a skill test battery to measure general soccer ability. *North Carolina Journal of Health and Physical Education, **15**,* 30-39.

Mott, J.A., & Lockhart, A. (1946). Table tennis backboard test. *Journal of Health and Physical Education, **17**,* 550-552.

Nelson, J.K. (1967). *An achievement test for golf.* Unpublished study, Louisiana State University, Baton Rouge.

Phillips, D.A., & Hornak, J.E. (1979). *Measurement and evaluation in physical education.* New York: Wiley.

Poole, J., & Nelson, J.K. (1970). *Construction of a badminton skills test battery.* Unpublished manuscript, Louisiana State University, Baton Rouge.

Reznik, J., & Byrd, R. (1987). *Badminton.* Scottsdale, AZ: Gorsuch Scarisbrick.

Rogers, M.H. (1954). *Construction of objectively scored skill tests for beginning skiers.* Unpublished master's thesis, University of Washington, Seattle.

Safrit, M.J. (1990). *Introduction to measurement in physical education and exercise science.* St. Louis: Times Mirror/Mosby.

Sattler, T. (1973). *The development of an instrument to measure handball ability of beginning level players in a physical education class.* Unpublished doctoral dissertation, Oklahoma State University, Stillwater.

Schick, J., & Berg, N.G. (1983). Indoor golf skill test for junior high school boys. *Research Quarterly for Exercise and Sport, **54**,* 75-78.

Schutz, A.J. (1940). *Construction of an achievement scale in fencing for women.* Unpublished master's thesis, University of Washington, Seattle.

Scott, M.G., Carpenter, A., French, E., & Kuhl, L. (1941). Achievement examinations in badminton. *Research Quarterly, **12**,* 242-253.

Seaton, D.C., Schmottlach, N., Clayton, I.A., Leibee, H.C., & Messersmith, L.L. (1983). *Physical Education Handbook.* Englewood Cliffs, NJ: Prentice-Hall.

Siedentop, D. (1991). *Developing teaching skills in physical education.* Mountain View, CA: Mayfield.

Smith, G. (1947). *Speedball skill tests for college women.* Unpublished study, Illinois State University, Normal.

Tyson, D.W. (1970). *A handball skill test for college men.* Unpublished master's thesis, University of Texas, Austin.

Underkofler, A. (1942). *A study of skill tests for evaluating the ability of junior high school girls in softball.* Unpublished master's thesis, University of Iowa, Iowa City.

Vanderhoof, E.R. (1956). *Beginning golf achievement test.* Unpublished master's thesis, University of Iowa, Iowa City.

Whiddon, N.S., & Reynolds, H. (1983). *Teaching basketball.* New York: Macmillan.

Yeagley, J. (1972). *Soccer skills test.* Unpublished paper, Indiana University, Bloomington.

Zinn, J.L. (1981). *Construction of a battery of team handball skills tests.* Unpublished master's thesis, University of Iowa, Iowa City.

Index